All the pages in this book were created—and are printed here—in Japanese RIGHT-to-LEFT format. No artwork has been reversed or altered, so you can read the stories the way the creators meant for them to be read.

FLIP IT!

S0-AIW-895

RIGHT TO LEFT?!

Traditional Japanese manga starts at the upper right-hand corner, and moves right-to-left as it goes down the page. Follow this guide for an easy understanding.

For more information and sneak previews, visit cmxmanga.com. Call 1-888-COMIC BOOK for the nearest comics shop or head to your local book store.

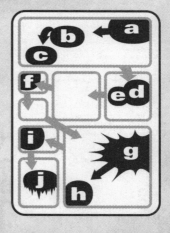

EMMA Vol. 6 © 2005 Kaoru Mori. All Rights Reserved. First
published in Japan in 2005 by ENTERBRAIN, INC.

EMMA Volume 6, published by WildStorm Productions, an
imprint of DC Comics, 888 Prospect St. #240, La Jolla, CA
92037. English Translation © 2008. All Rights Reserved.
English translation rights in U.S.A. and Canada arranged by
ENTERBRAIN, INC. through Tuttle-Mori Agency, Inc., Tokyo.
CMX is a trademark of DC Comics. The stories, characters,
and incidents mentioned in this magazine are entirely
fictional. Printed on recyclable paper. WildStorm does not
read or accept unsolicited submissions of ideas, stories or
artwork. Printed in Canada.

DC Comics, a Warner Bros. Entertainment Company.

Sheldon Drzka – Translation and Adaptation
Janice Chiang – Lettering
Larry Berry – Design
Jim Chadwick – Editor

ISBN: 1-4012-1137-2
ISBN-13: 978-1-4012-1137-0

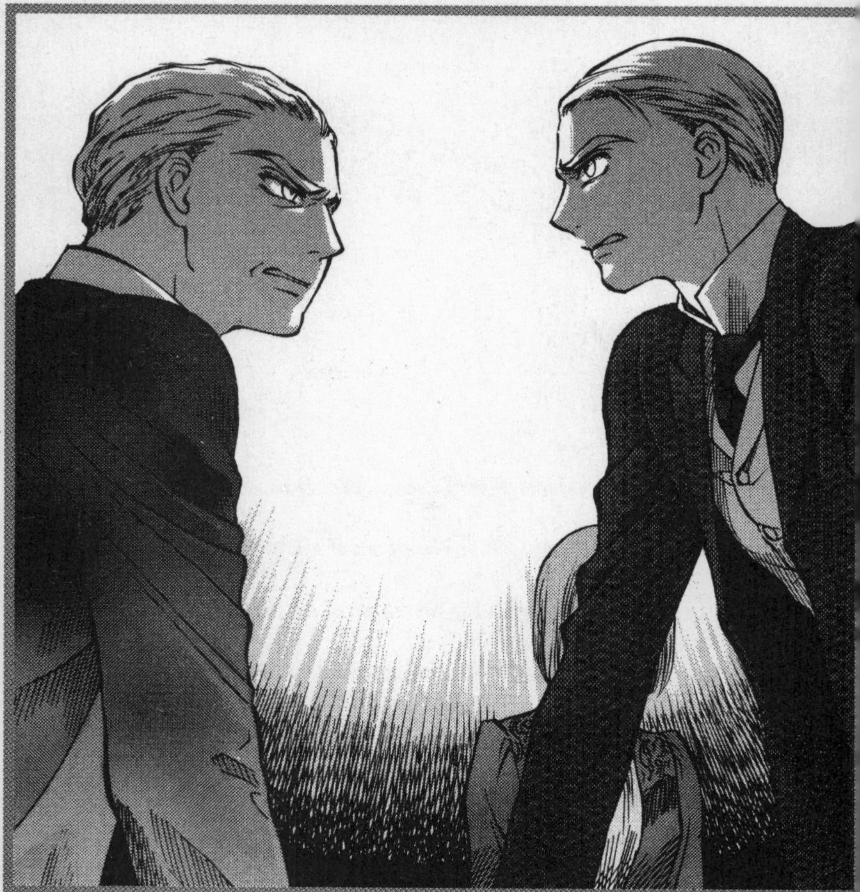

EMMA

Volume 6 **By Kaoru Mori**

-Contents-

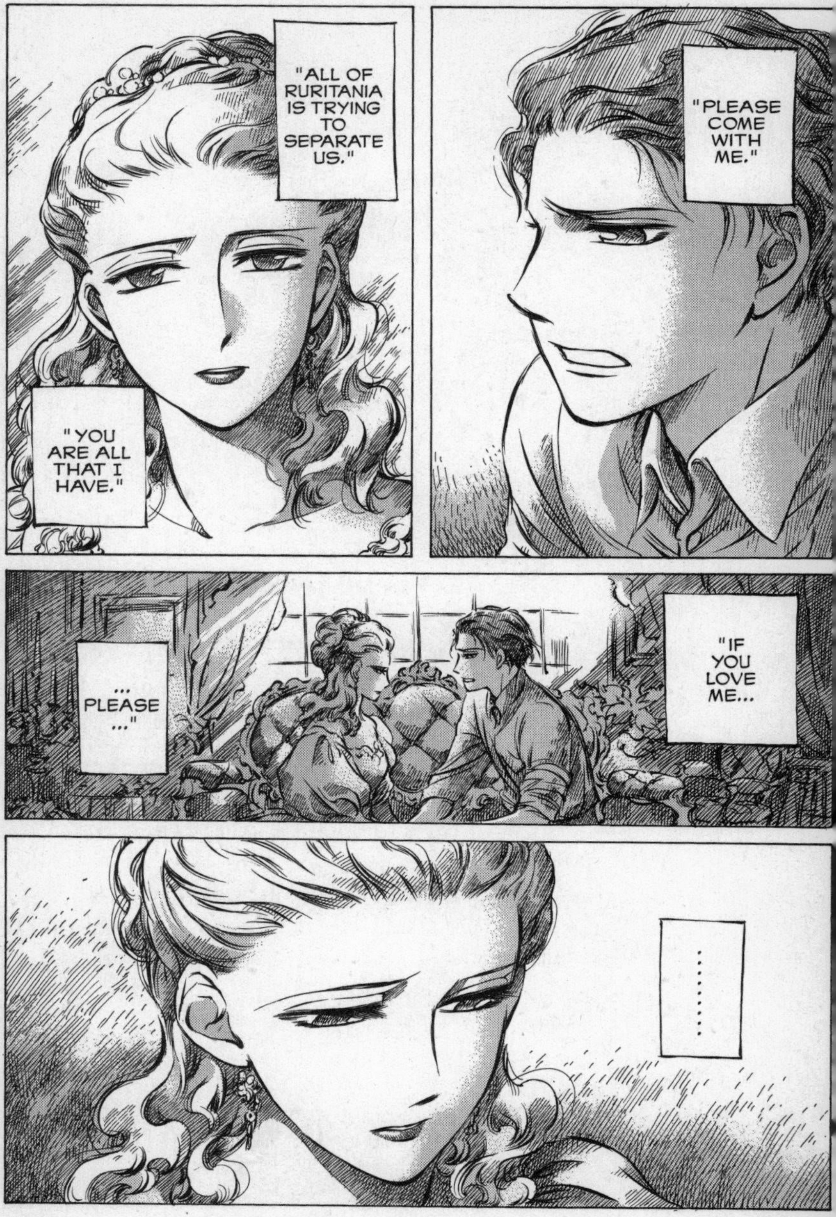
"PLEASE COME WITH ME."
"ALL OF RURITANIA IS TRYING TO SEPARATE US."
"YOU ARE ALL THAT I HAVE."
"IF YOU LOVE ME...
... PLEASE ..."
....

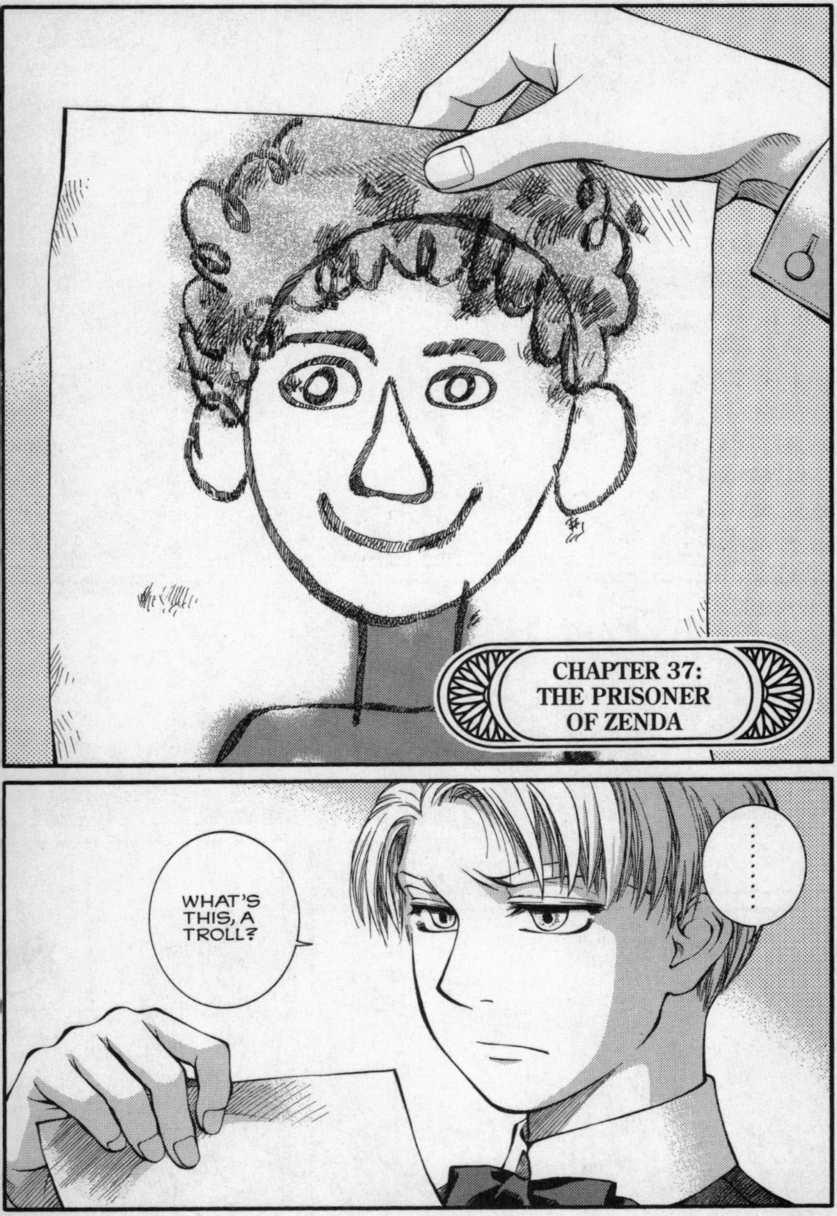
CHAPTER 37: THE PRISONER OF ZENDA
......
WHAT'S THIS, A TROLL?

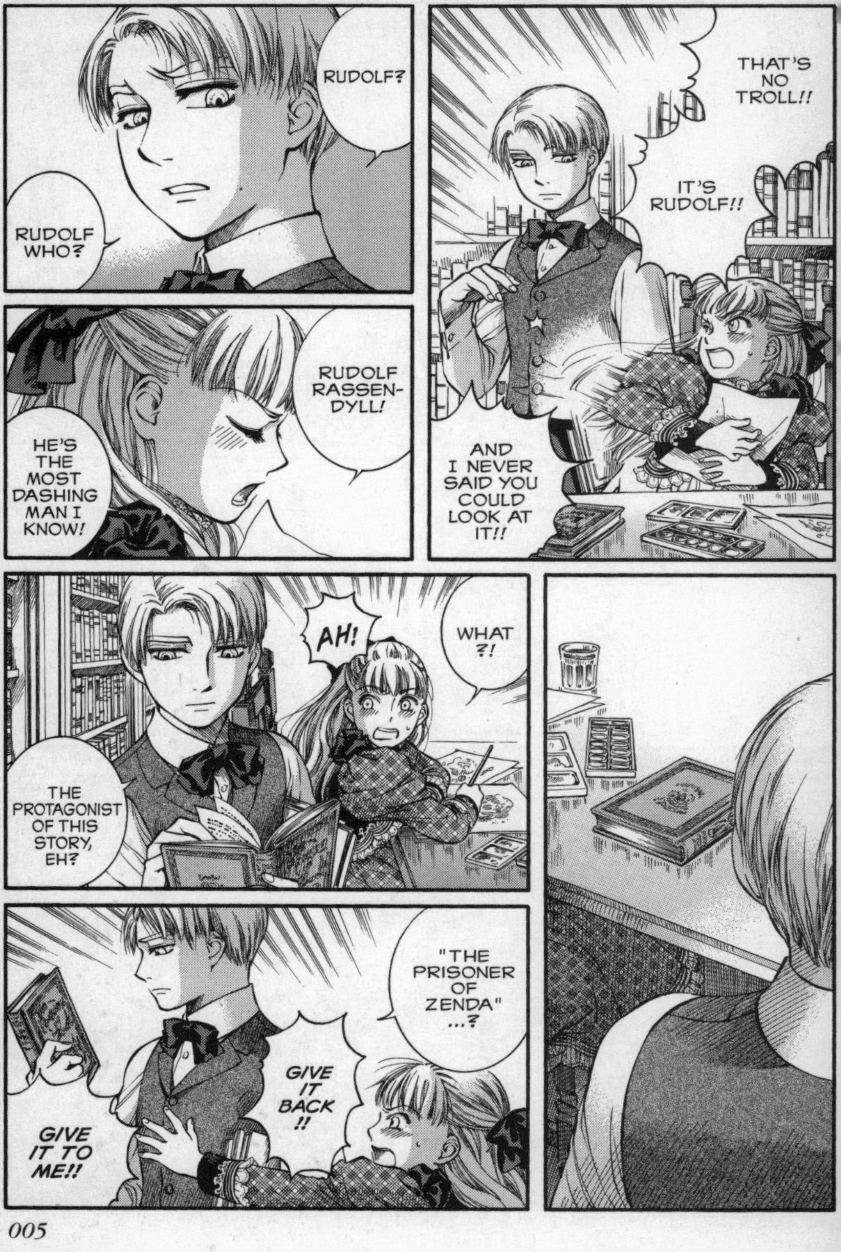
THAT'S NO TROLL!!
IT'S RUDOLF!!
AND I NEVER SAID YOU COULD LOOK AT IT!!
RUDOLF?
RUDOLF WHO?
RUDOLF RASSENDYLL!
HE'S THE MOST DASHING MAN I KNOW!
WHAT ?!
AH!
THE PROTAGONIST OF THIS STORY, EH?
"THE PRISONER OF ZENDA" ...?
GIVE IT BACK !!
GIVE IT TO ME!!

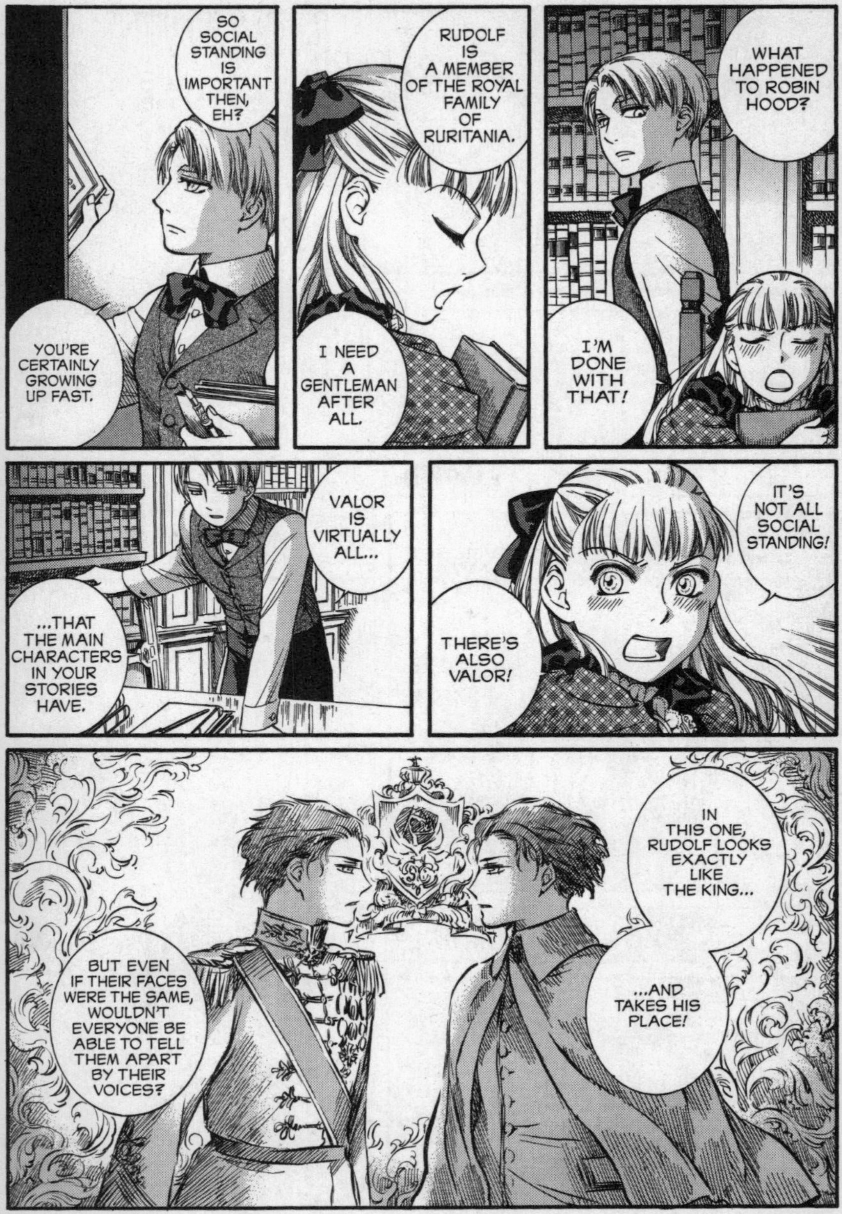
WHAT HAPPENED TO ROBIN HOOD?
I'M DONE WITH THAT!
RUDOLF IS A MEMBER OF THE ROYAL FAMILY OF RURITANIA.
I NEED A GENTLEMAN AFTER ALL.
SO SOCIAL STANDING IS IMPORTANT THEN, EH?
YOU'RE CERTAINLY GROWING UP FAST.
IT'S NOT ALL SOCIAL STANDING!
THERE'S ALSO VALOR!
VALOR IS VIRTUALLY ALL...
...THAT THE MAIN CHARACTERS IN YOUR STORIES HAVE.
IN THIS ONE, RUDOLF LOOKS EXACTLY LIKE THE KING...
...AND TAKES HIS PLACE!
BUT EVEN IF THEIR FACES WERE THE SAME, WOULDN'T EVERYONE BE ABLE TO TELL THEM APART BY THEIR VOICES?

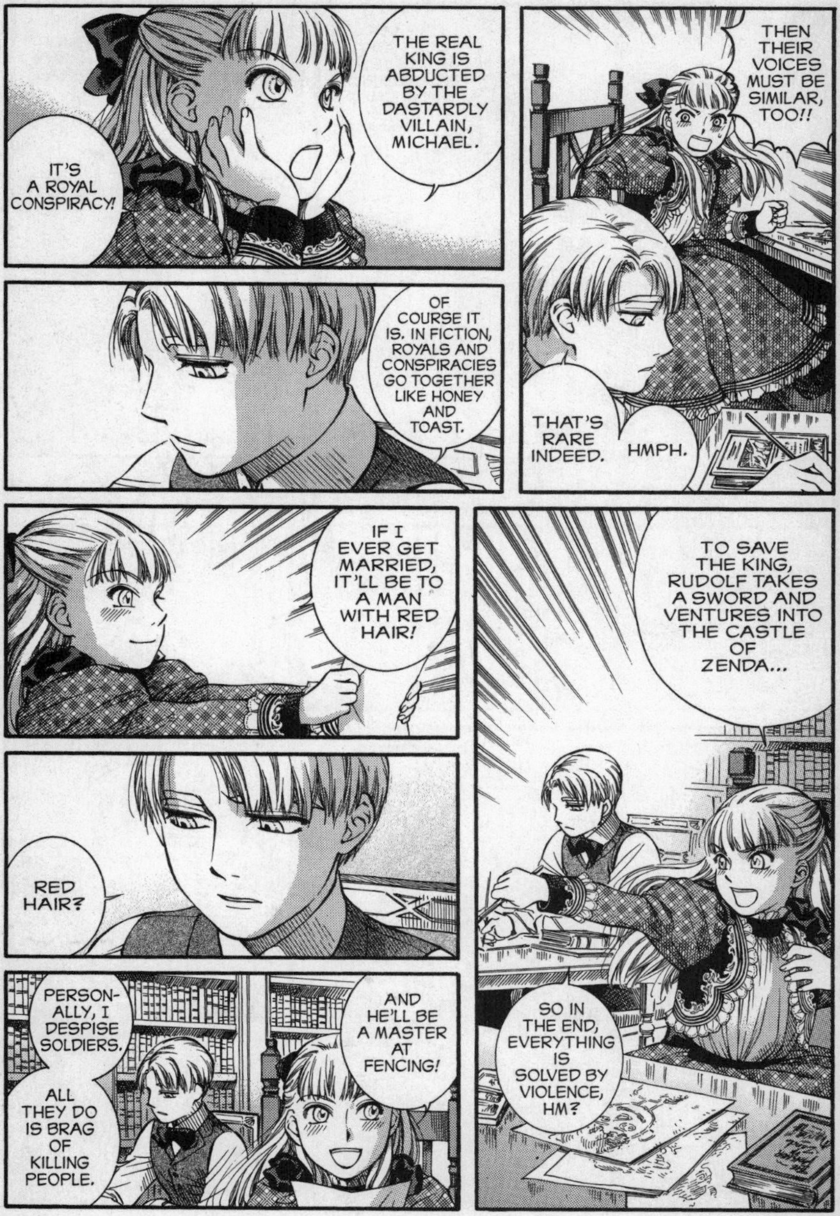
THEN THEIR VOICES MUST BE SIMILAR, TOO!!
THAT'S RARE INDEED.
HMPH.
THE REAL KING IS ABDUCTED BY THE DASTARDLY VILLAIN, MICHAEL.
IT'S A ROYAL CONSPIRACY!
OF COURSE IT IS. IN FICTION, ROYALS AND CONSPIRACIES GO TOGETHER LIKE HONEY AND TOAST.
TO SAVE THE KING, RUDOLF TAKES A SWORD AND VENTURES INTO THE CASTLE OF ZENDA...
SO IN THE END, EVERYTHING IS SOLVED BY VIOLENCE, HM?
IF I EVER GET MARRIED, IT'LL BE TO A MAN WITH RED HAIR!
RED HAIR?
AND HE'LL BE A MASTER AT FENCING!
PERSONALLY, I DESPISE SOLDIERS.
ALL THEY DO IS BRAG OF KILLING PEOPLE.

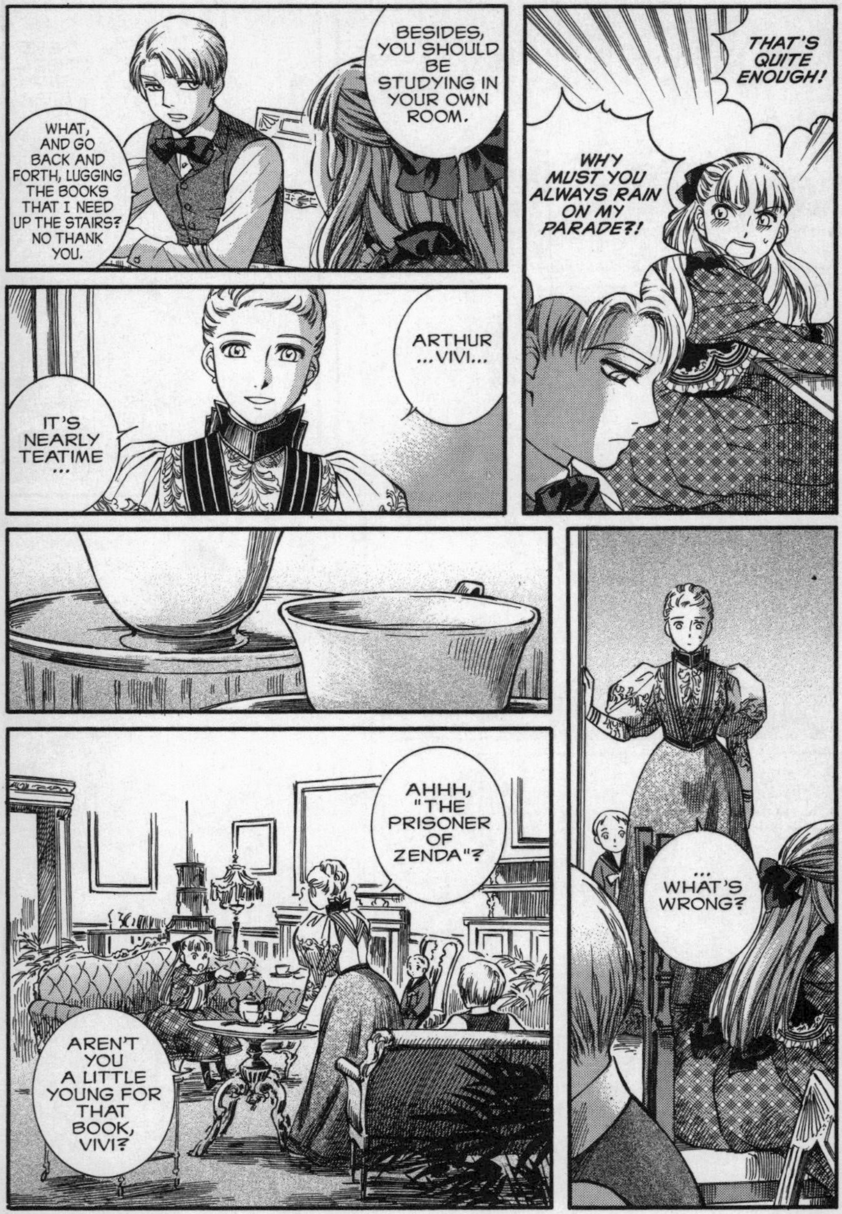
BESIDES, YOU SHOULD BE STUDYING IN YOUR OWN ROOM.
WHAT, AND GO BACK AND FORTH, LUGGING THE BOOKS THAT I NEED UP THE STAIRS? NO THANK YOU.
THAT'S QUITE ENOUGH!
WHY MUST YOU ALWAYS RAIN ON MY PARADE?!
ARTHUR ...VIVI...
IT'S NEARLY TEATIME ...
AHHH, "THE PRISONER OF ZENDA"?
AREN'T YOU A LITTLE YOUNG FOR THAT BOOK, VIVI?
... WHAT'S WRONG?

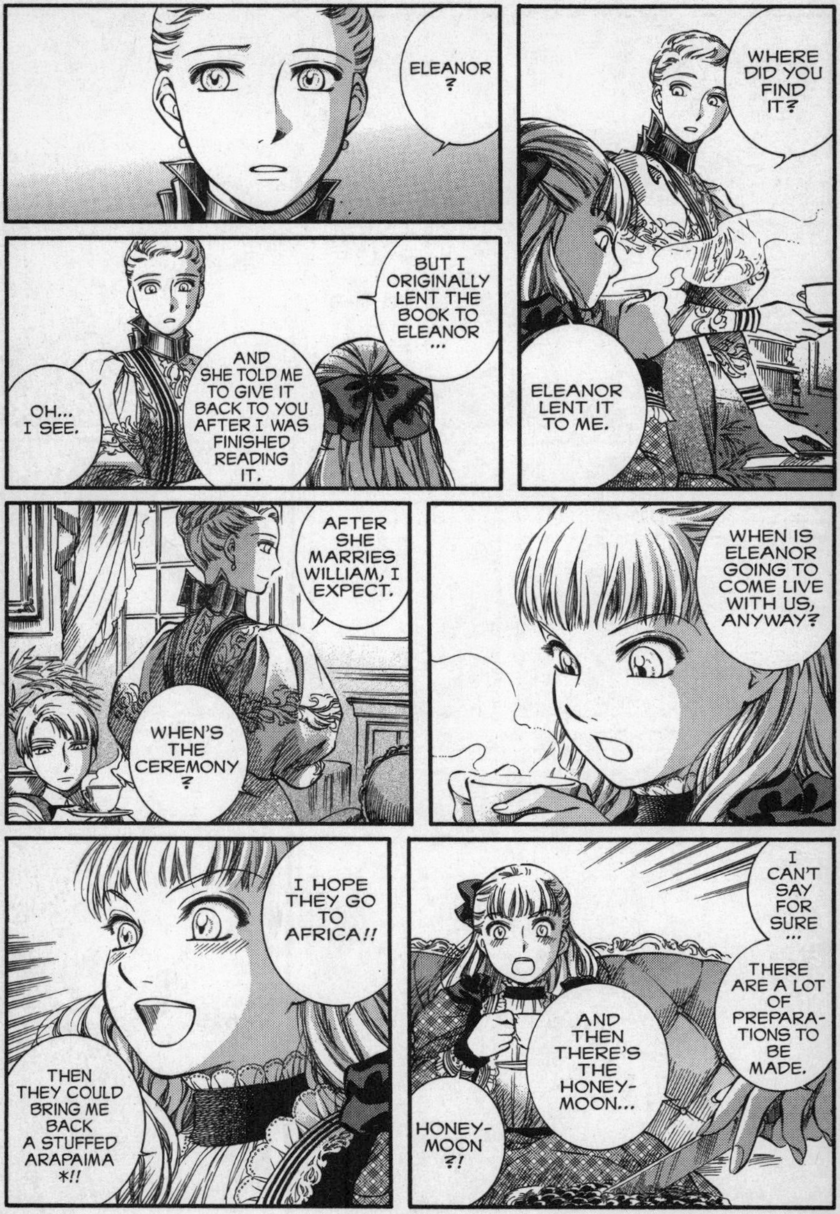
WHERE DID YOU FIND IT?
ELEANOR LENT IT TO ME.
ELEANOR?
BUT I ORIGINALLY LENT THE BOOK TO ELEANOR...
AND SHE TOLD ME TO GIVE IT BACK TO YOU AFTER I WAS FINISHED READING IT.
OH... I SEE.
WHEN IS ELEANOR GOING TO COME LIVE WITH US, ANYWAY?
AFTER SHE MARRIES WILLIAM, I EXPECT.
WHEN'S THE CEREMONY?
I CAN'T SAY FOR SURE...
THERE ARE A LOT OF PREPARATIONS TO BE MADE.
AND THEN THERE'S THE HONEY-MOON...
HONEY-MOON?!
I HOPE THEY GO TO AFRICA!!
THEN THEY COULD BRING ME BACK A STUFFED ARAPAIMA*!!

* ONE OF THE LARGEST FRESHWATER FISH IN THE WORLD

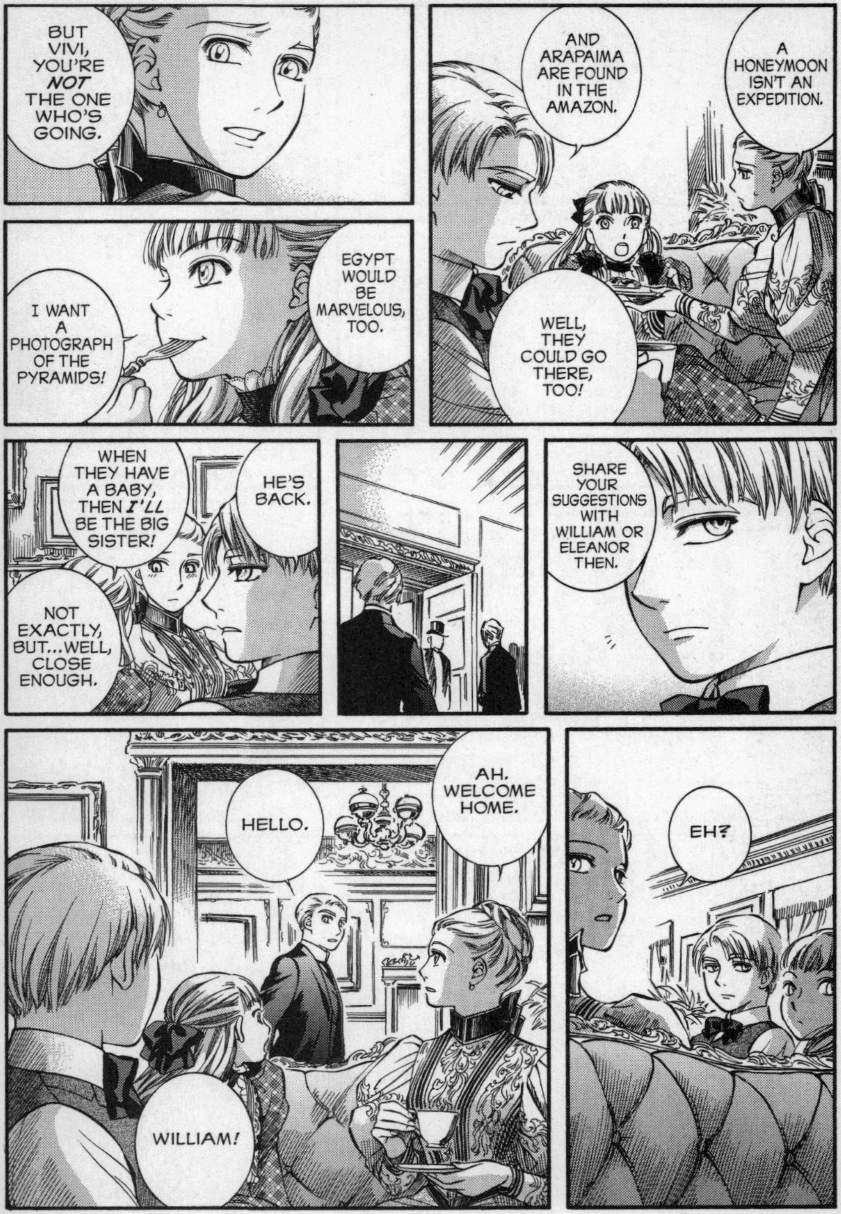
A HONEYMOON ISN'T AN EXPEDITION.
AND ARAPAIMA ARE FOUND IN THE AMAZON.
WELL, THEY COULD GO THERE, TOO!
BUT VIVI, YOU'RE *NOT* THE ONE WHO'S GOING.
EGYPT WOULD BE MARVELOUS, TOO.
I WANT A PHOTOGRAPH OF THE PYRAMIDS!
SHARE YOUR SUGGESTIONS WITH WILLIAM OR ELEANOR THEN.
HE'S BACK.
WHEN THEY HAVE A BABY, THEN *I'LL* BE THE BIG SISTER!
NOT EXACTLY, BUT...WELL, CLOSE ENOUGH.
EH?
AH. WELCOME HOME.
HELLO.
WILLIAM!

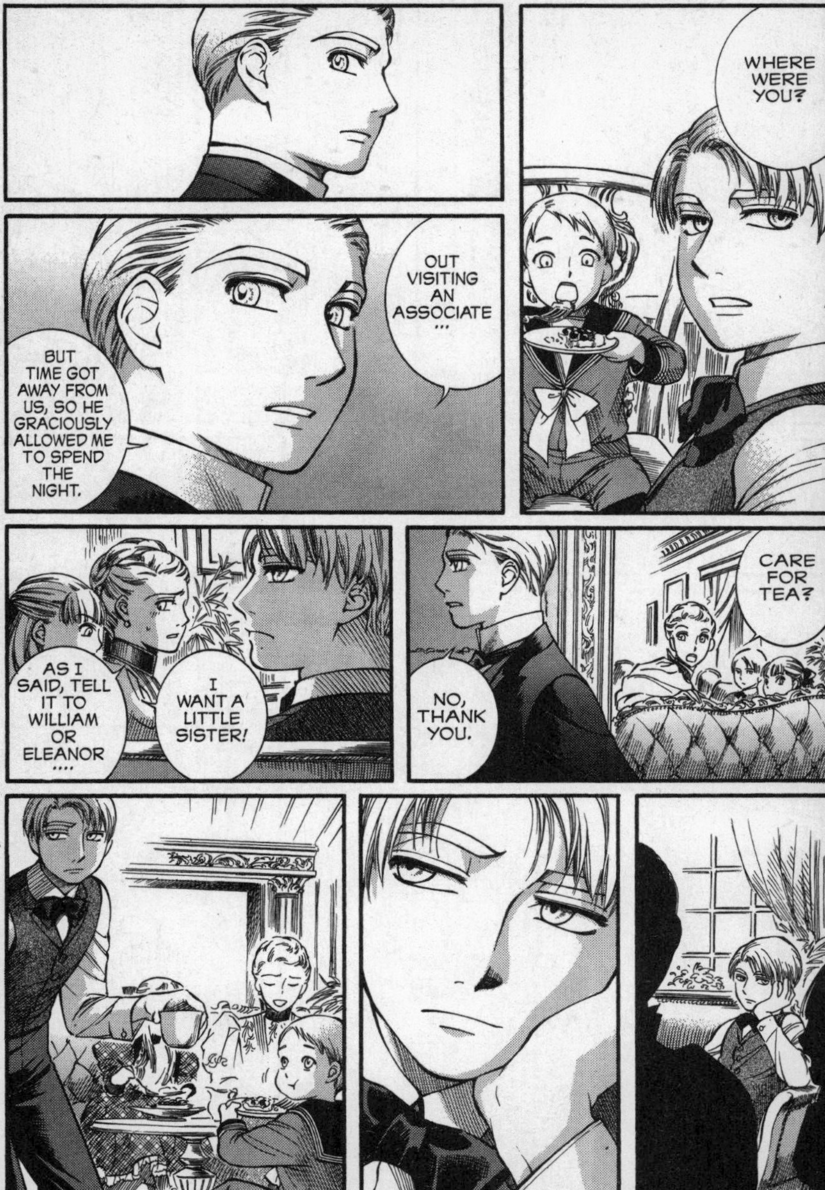
WHERE WERE YOU?
OUT VISITING AN ASSOCIATE...
BUT TIME GOT AWAY FROM US, SO HE GRACIOUSLY ALLOWED ME TO SPEND THE NIGHT.
CARE FOR TEA?
NO, THANK YOU.
I WANT A LITTLE SISTER!
AS I SAID, TELL IT TO WILLIAM OR ELEANOR....

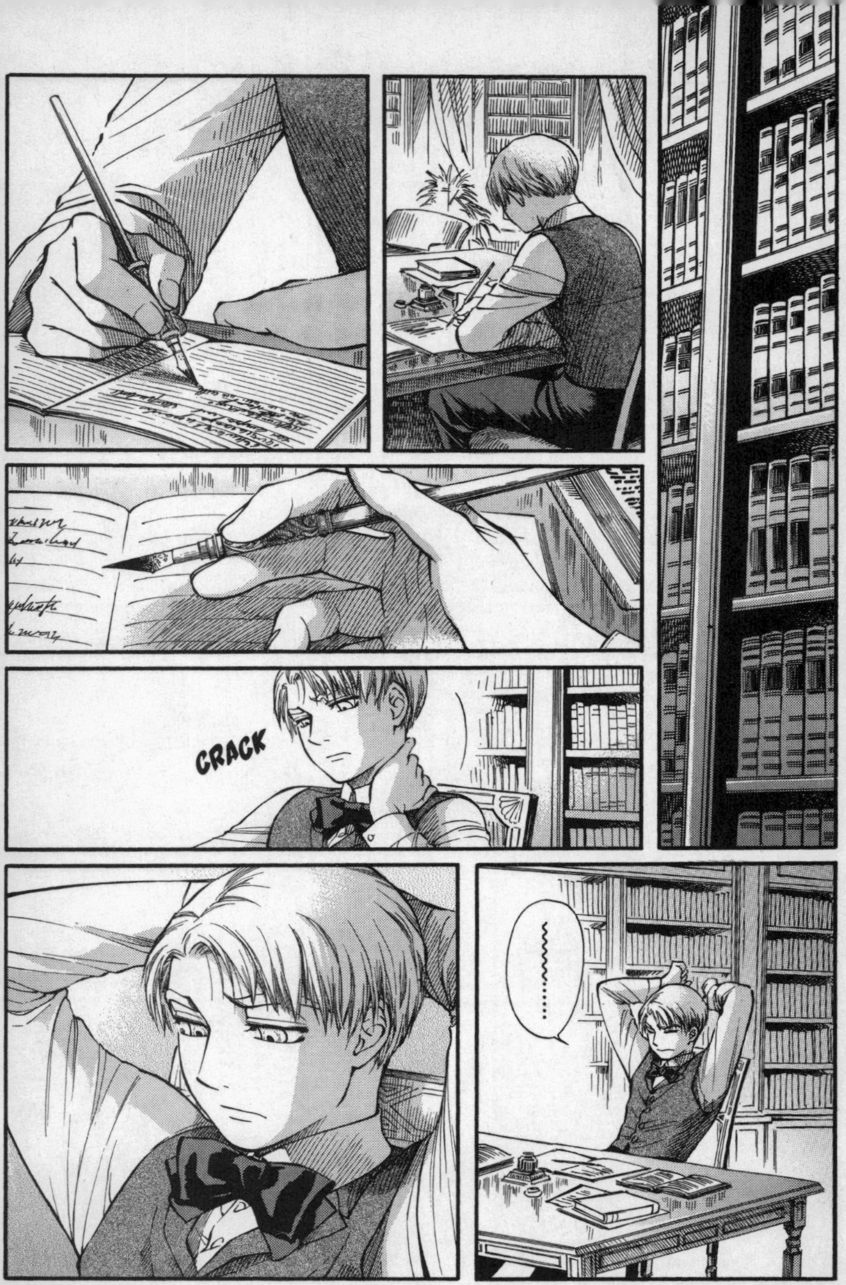
CRACK
......

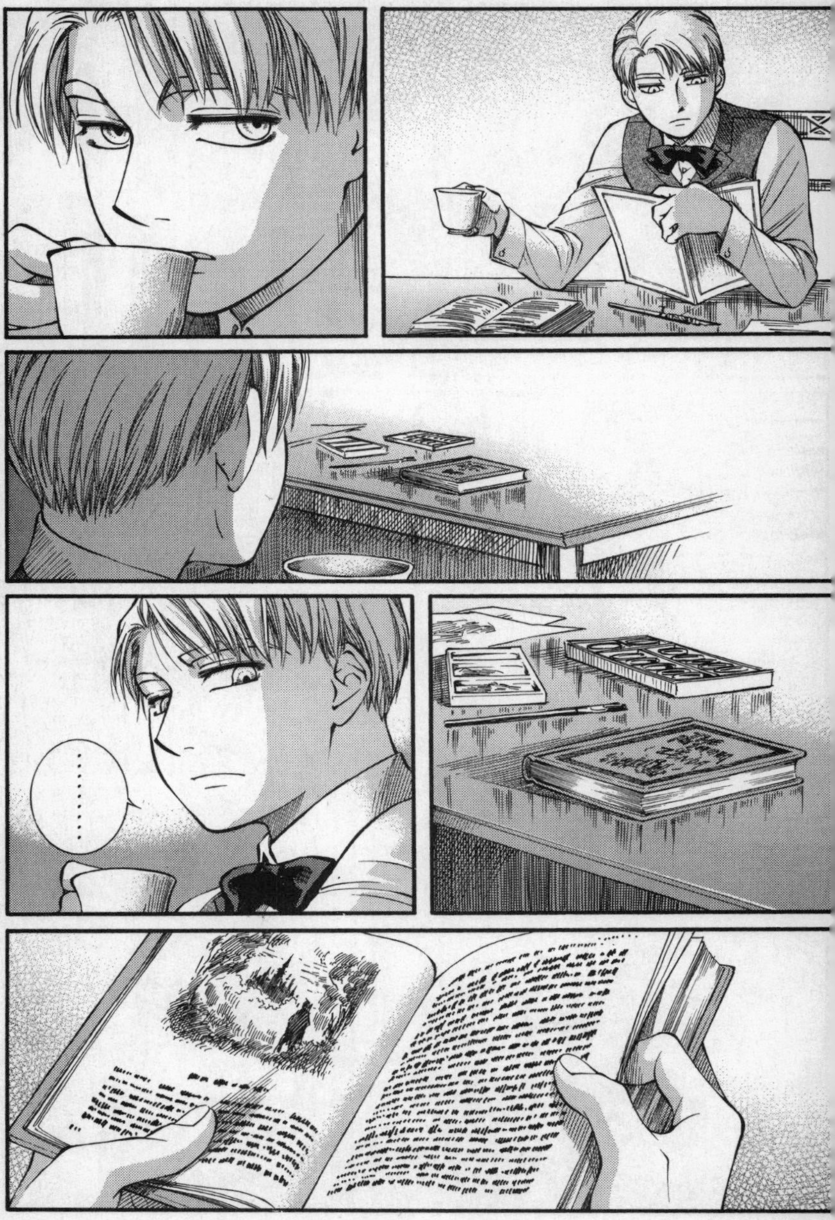
……

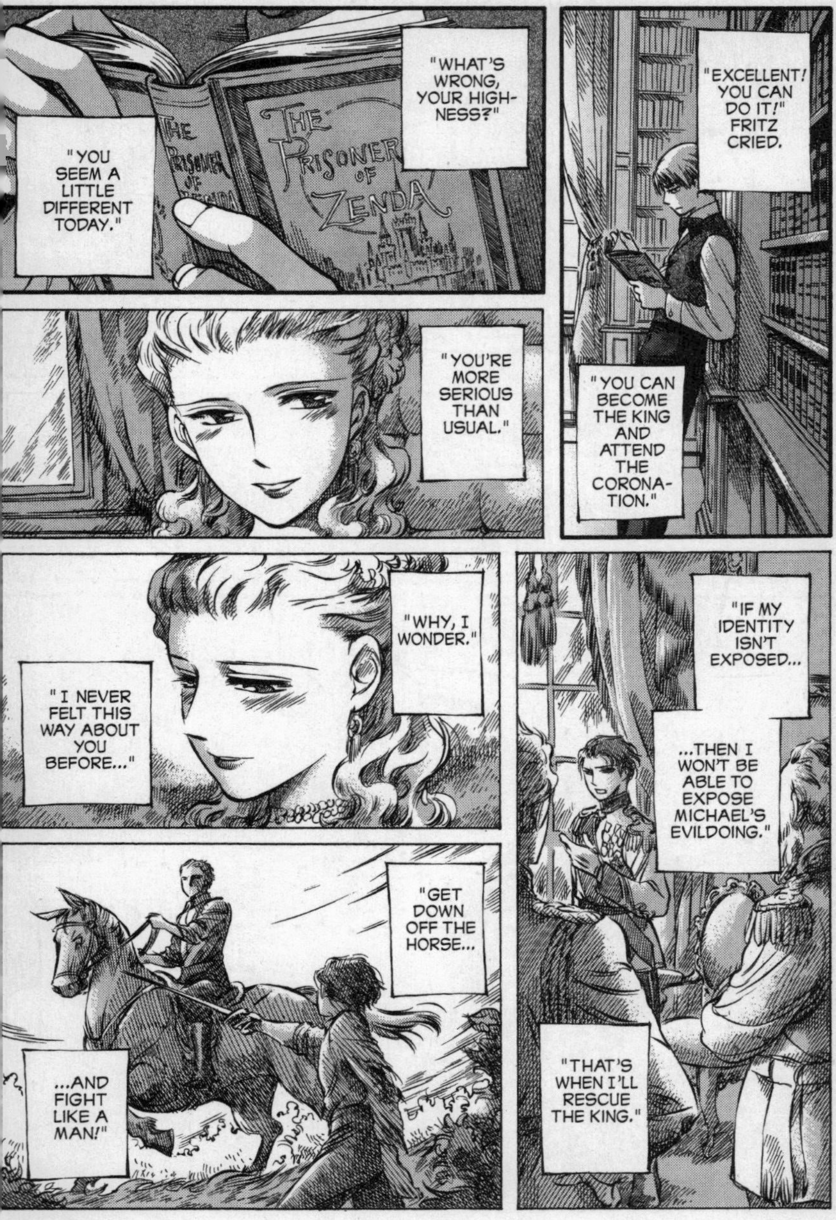
"EXCELLENT! YOU CAN DO IT!" FRITZ CRIED.
"YOU CAN BECOME THE KING AND ATTEND THE CORONATION."
"WHAT'S WRONG, YOUR HIGHNESS?"
THE PRISONER OF ZENDA
"YOU SEEM A LITTLE DIFFERENT TODAY."
"YOU'RE MORE SERIOUS THAN USUAL."
"IF MY IDENTITY ISN'T EXPOSED...
...THEN I WON'T BE ABLE TO EXPOSE MICHAEL'S EVILDOING."
"THAT'S WHEN I'LL RESCUE THE KING."
"WHY, I WONDER."
"I NEVER FELT THIS WAY ABOUT YOU BEFORE..."
"GET DOWN OFF THE HORSE...
...AND FIGHT LIKE A MAN!"

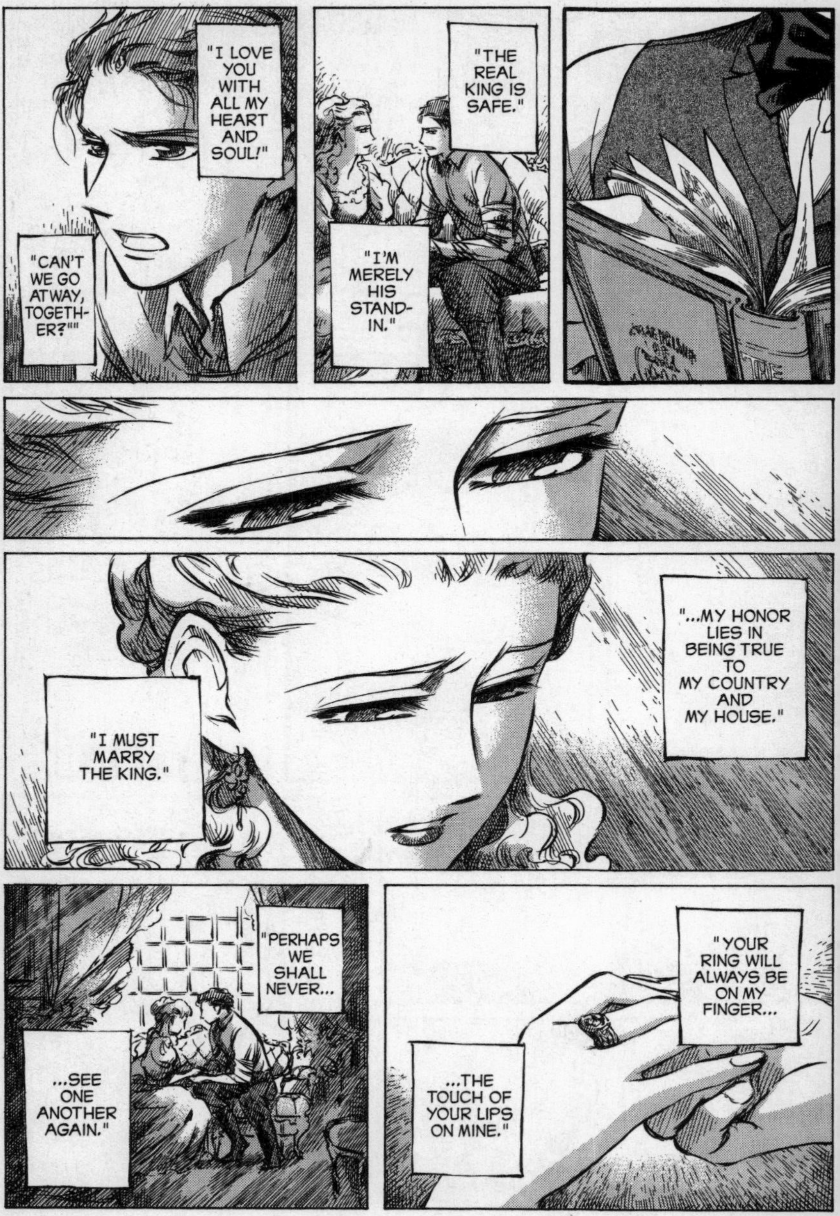
"I LOVE YOU WITH ALL MY HEART AND SOUL!"
"CAN'T WE GO ATWAY, TOGETHER?'"
"THE REAL KING IS SAFE."
"I'M MERELY HIS STAND-IN."
"I MUST MARRY THE KING."
"...MY HONOR LIES IN BEING TRUE TO MY COUNTRY AND MY HOUSE."
"PERHAPS WE SHALL NEVER...
...SEE ONE ANOTHER AGAIN."
"YOUR RING WILL ALWAYS BE ON MY FINGER...
...THE TOUCH OF YOUR LIPS ON MINE."

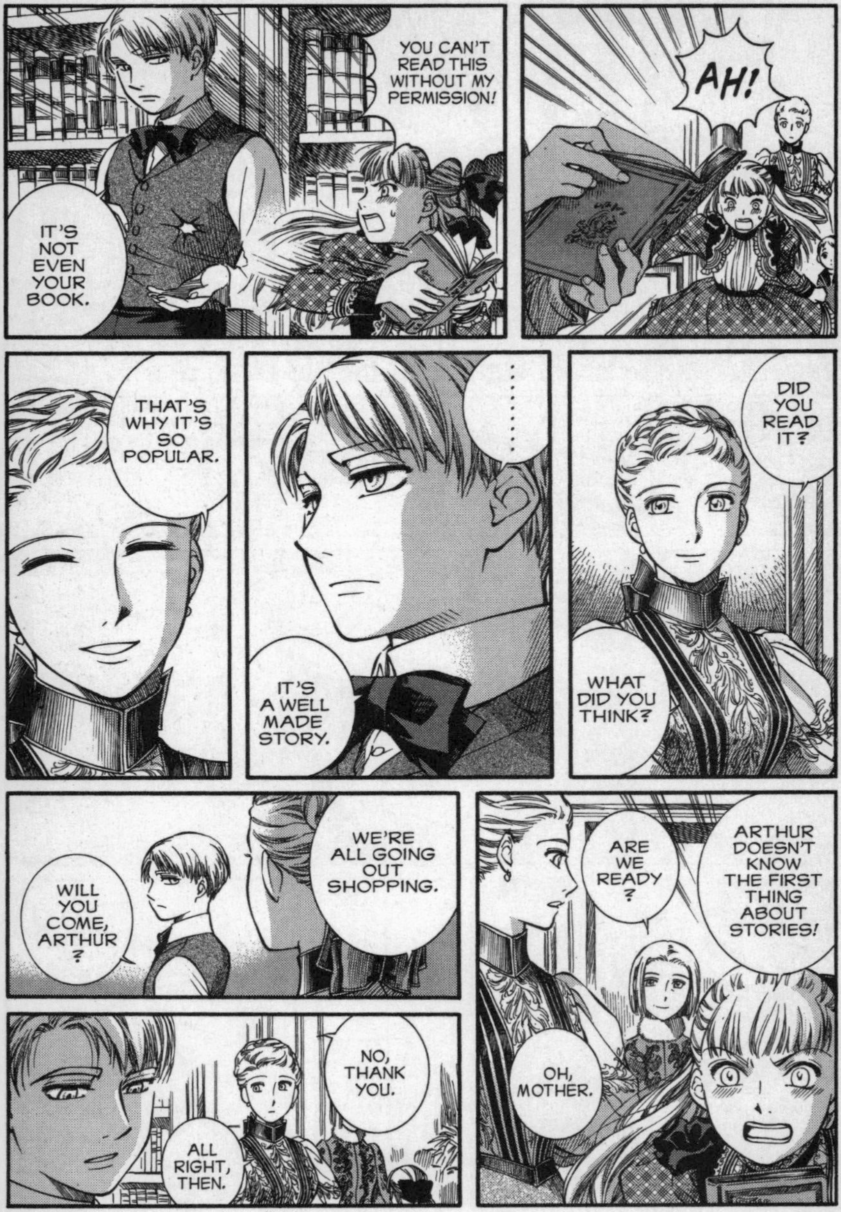
AH!
YOU CAN'T READ THIS WITHOUT MY PERMISSION!
IT'S NOT EVEN YOUR BOOK.
DID YOU READ IT?
WHAT DID YOU THINK?
......
IT'S A WELL MADE STORY.
THAT'S WHY IT'S SO POPULAR.
ARTHUR DOESN'T KNOW THE FIRST THING ABOUT STORIES!
ARE WE READY?
OH, MOTHER.
WE'RE ALL GOING OUT SHOPPING.
WILL YOU COME, ARTHUR?
NO, THANK YOU.
ALL RIGHT, THEN.

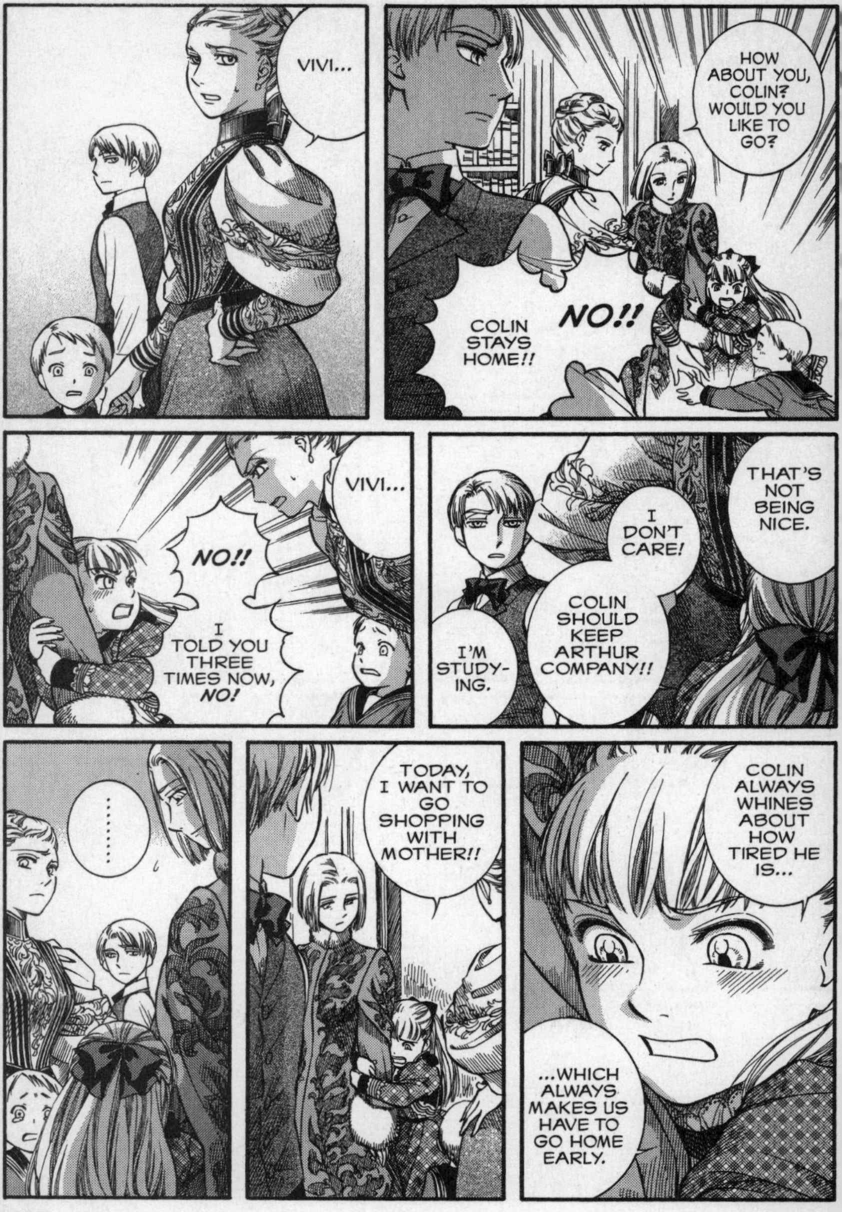
HOW ABOUT YOU, COLIN? WOULD YOU LIKE TO GO?
NO!!
COLIN STAYS HOME!!
VIVI...
THAT'S NOT BEING NICE.
I DON'T CARE!
COLIN SHOULD KEEP ARTHUR COMPANY!!
I'M STUDYING.
VIVI...
NO!!
I TOLD YOU THREE TIMES NOW, *NO!*
COLIN ALWAYS WHINES ABOUT HOW TIRED HE IS...
...WHICH ALWAYS MAKES US HAVE TO GO HOME EARLY.
TODAY, I WANT TO GO SHOPPING WITH MOTHER!!
......

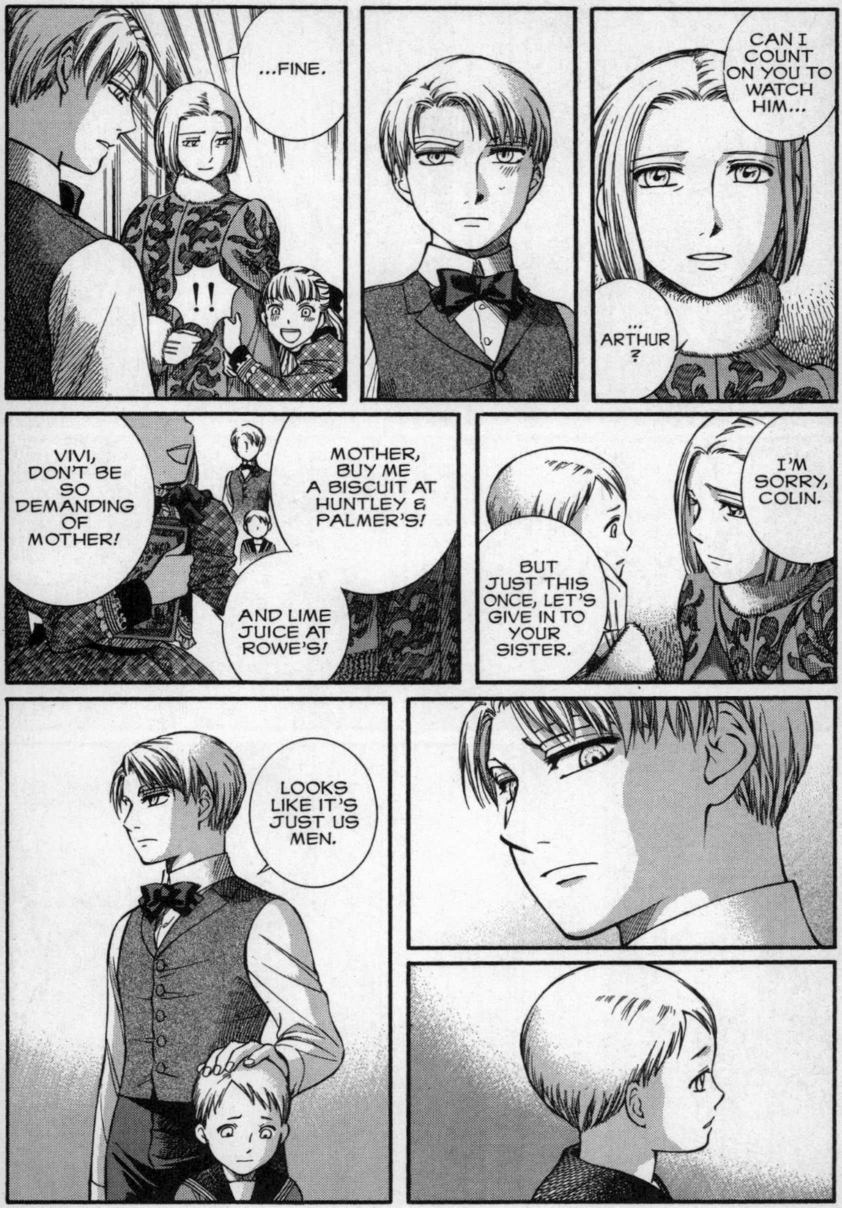
CAN I COUNT ON YOU TO WATCH HIM...
... ARTHUR?
...FINE.
!!
I'M SORRY, COLIN.
BUT JUST THIS ONCE, LET'S GIVE IN TO YOUR SISTER.
MOTHER, BUY ME A BISCUIT AT HUNTLEY & PALMER'S!
AND LIME JUICE AT ROWE'S!
VIVI, DON'T BE SO DEMANDING OF MOTHER!
LOOKS LIKE IT'S JUST US MEN.

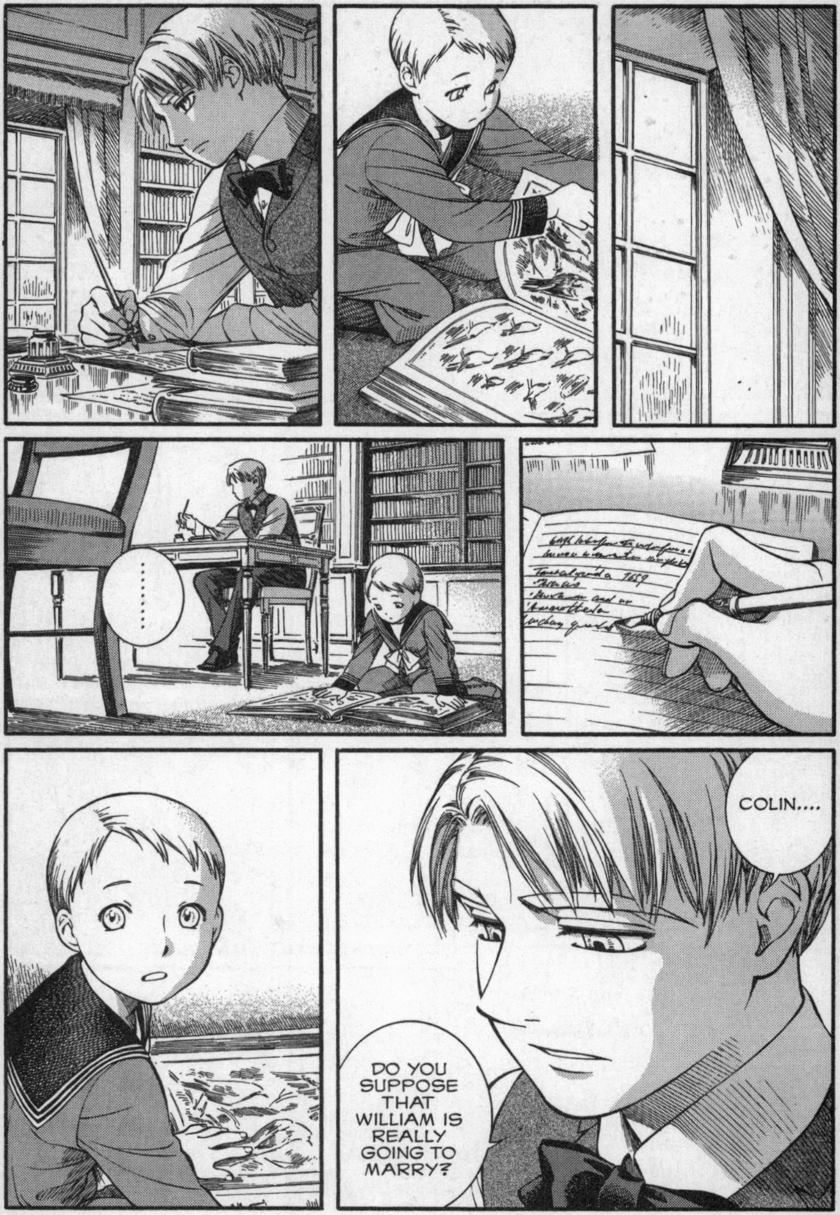
......
COLIN....
DO YOU SUPPOSE THAT WILLIAM IS REALLY GOING TO MARRY?

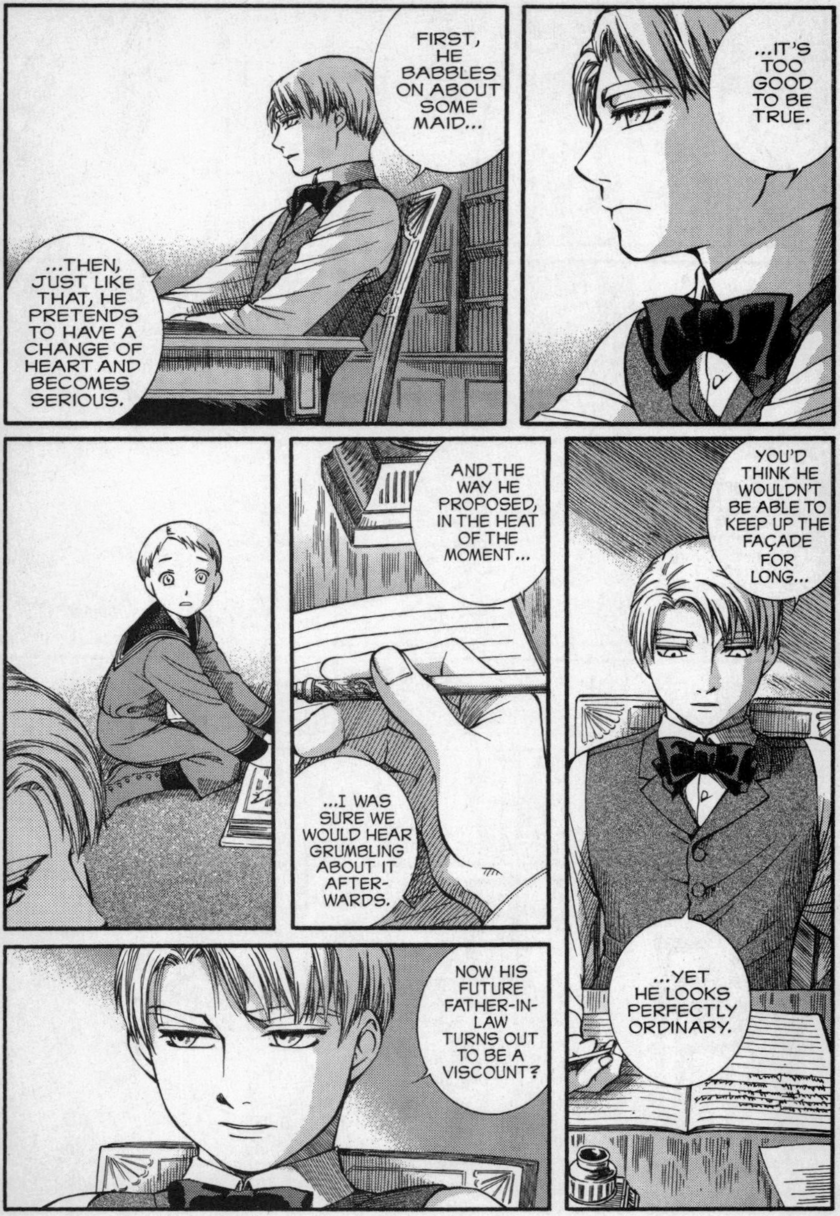
FIRST, HE BABBLES ON ABOUT SOME MAID...
...THEN, JUST LIKE THAT, HE PRETENDS TO HAVE A CHANGE OF HEART AND BECOMES SERIOUS.
...IT'S TOO GOOD TO BE TRUE.
AND THE WAY HE PROPOSED, IN THE HEAT OF THE MOMENT...
...I WAS SURE WE WOULD HEAR GRUMBLING ABOUT IT AFTER-WARDS.
YOU'D THINK HE WOULDN'T BE ABLE TO KEEP UP THE FAÇADE FOR LONG...
...YET HE LOOKS PERFECTLY ORDINARY.
NOW HIS FUTURE FATHER-IN-LAW TURNS OUT TO BE A VISCOUNT?

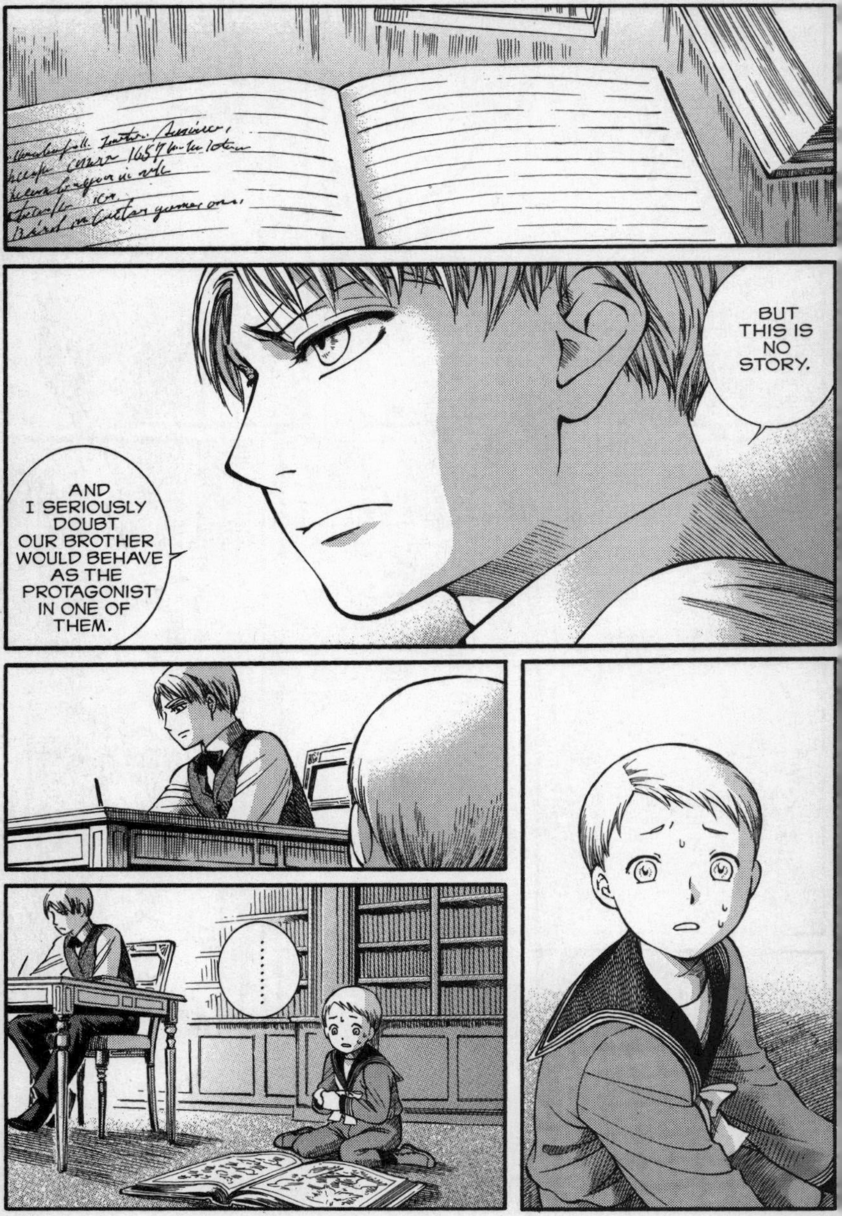
BUT THIS IS NO STORY.
AND I SERIOUSLY DOUBT OUR BROTHER WOULD BEHAVE AS THE PROTAGONIST IN ONE OF THEM.
......

TAP

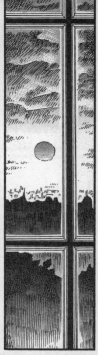

SQUEAK

KA-CHA

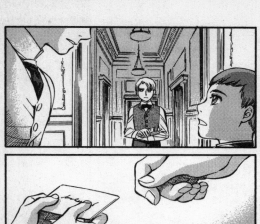

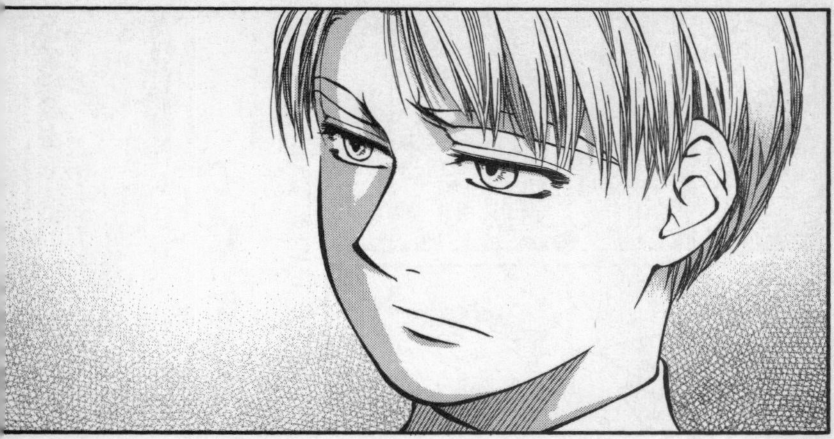
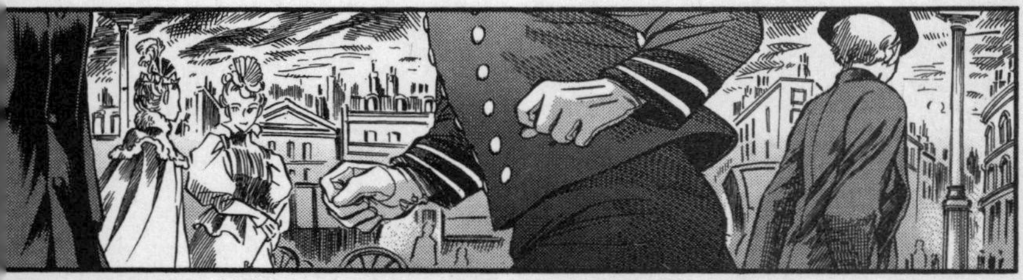
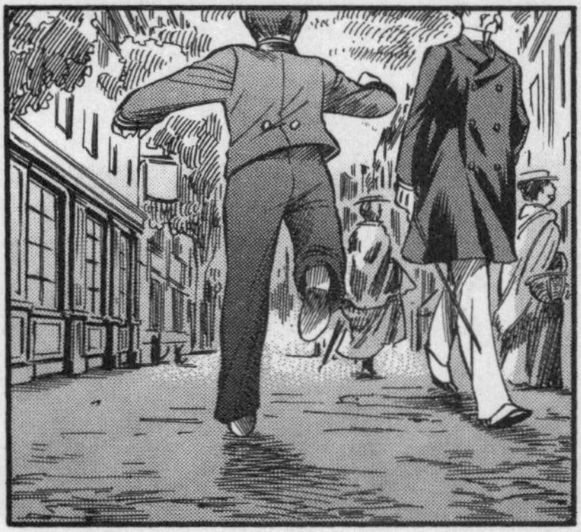
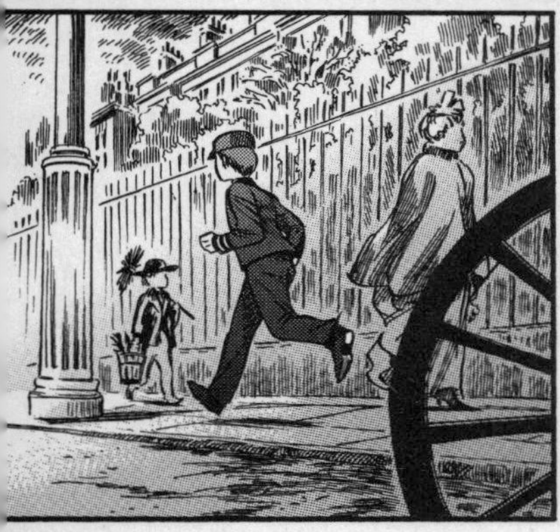

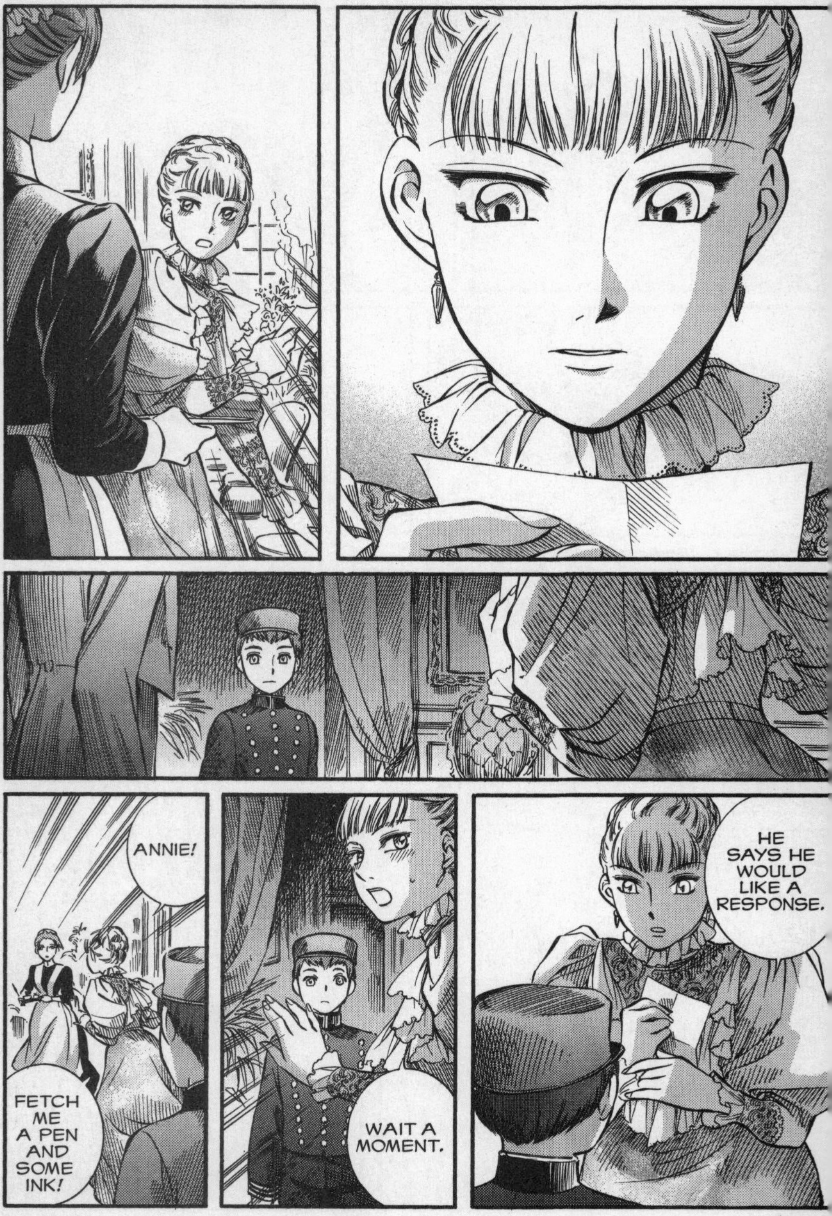
HE SAYS HE WOULD LIKE A RESPONSE.
WAIT A MOMENT.
ANNIE!
FETCH ME A PEN AND SOME INK!

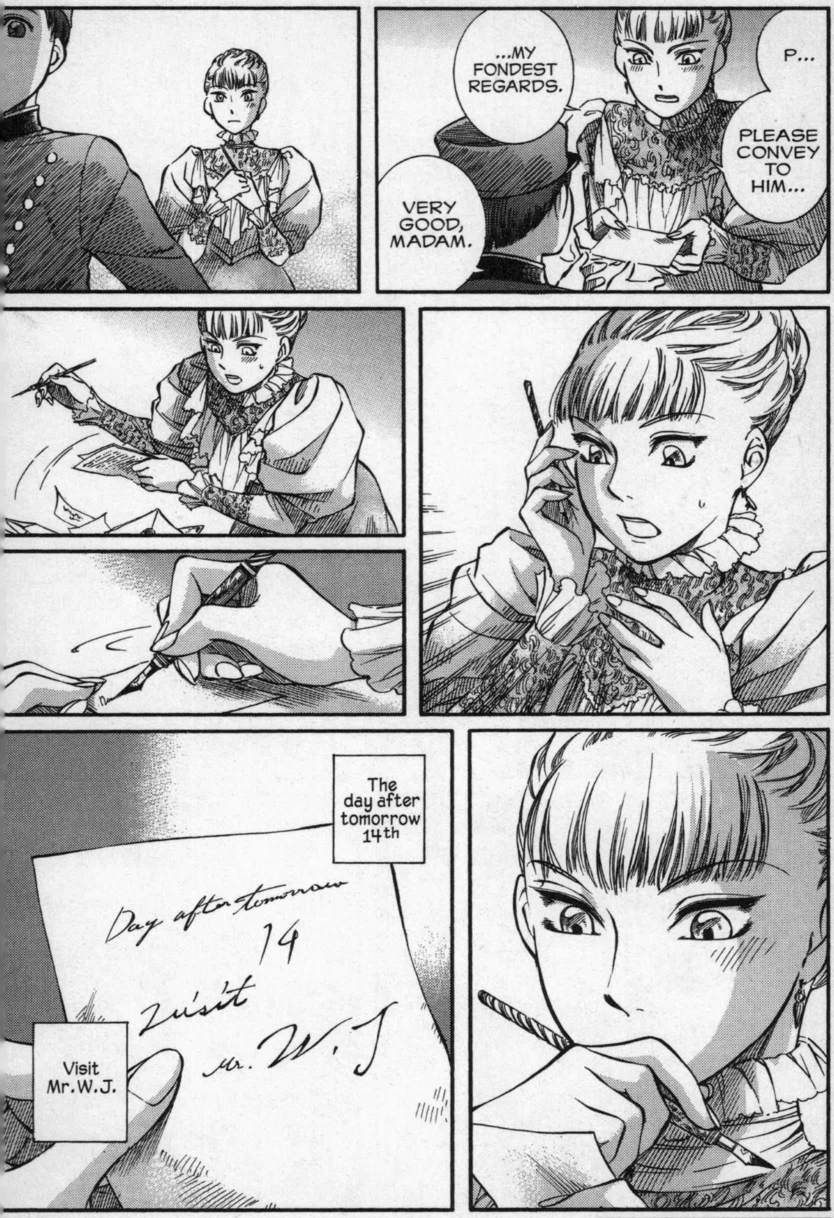
P...
PLEASE CONVEY TO HIM...
...MY FONDEST REGARDS.
VERY GOOD, MADAM.
The day after tomorrow 14th
Visit Mr.W.J.

Chapter Thirty Seven: The End

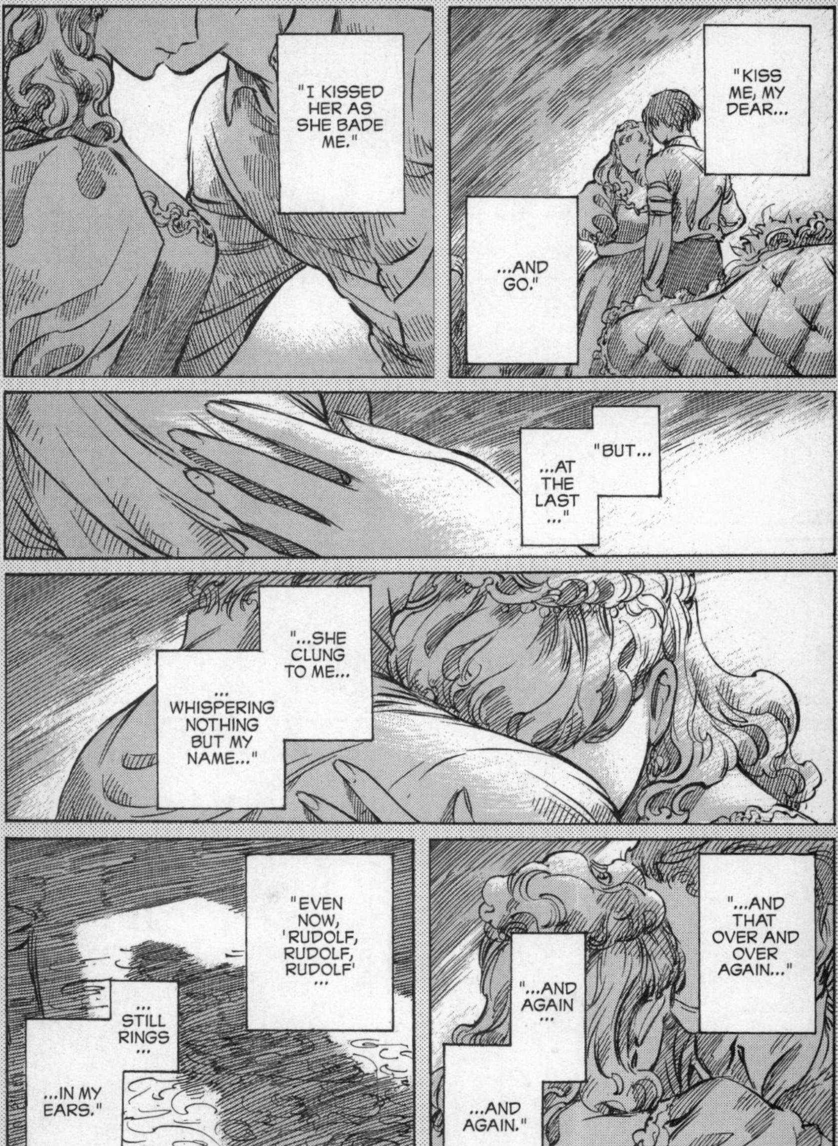
"KISS ME, MY DEAR...
...AND GO."
"I KISSED HER AS SHE BADE ME."
"BUT...
...AT THE LAST..."
"...SHE CLUNG TO ME...
...WHISPERING NOTHING BUT MY NAME..."
"...AND THAT OVER AND OVER AGAIN..."
"...AND AGAIN...
...AND AGAIN."
"EVEN NOW, 'RUDOLF, RUDOLF, RUDOLF'...
...STILL RINGS...
...IN MY EARS."

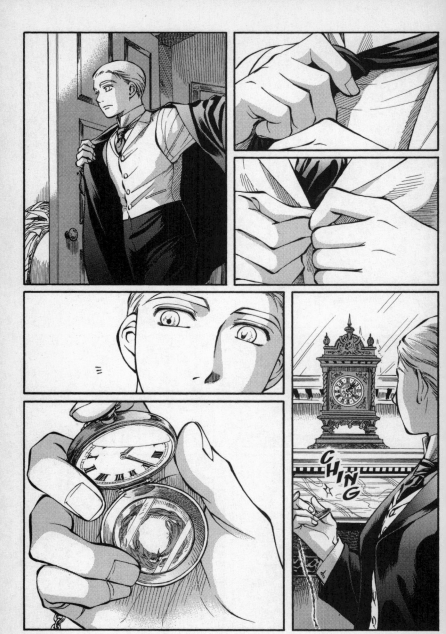

CHING

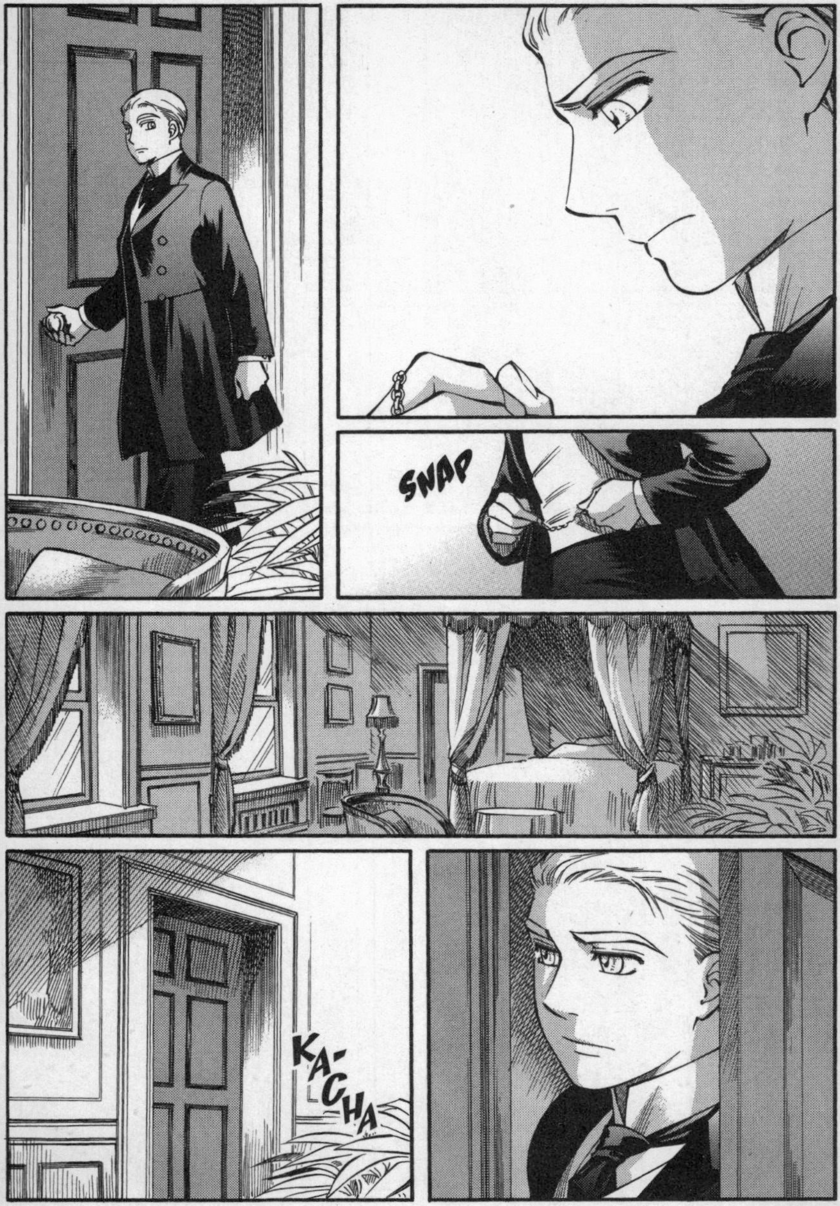
SNAP
KA-CHA

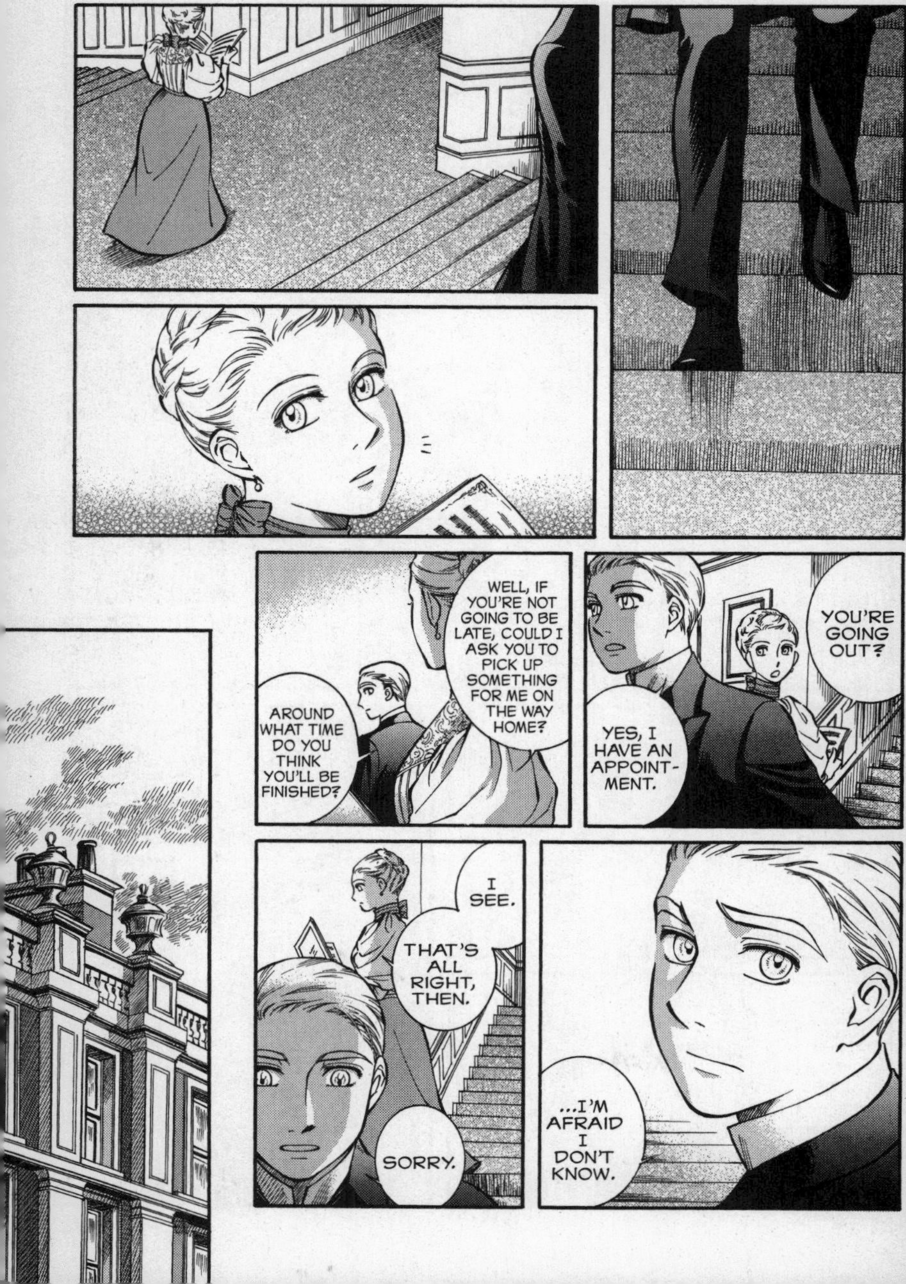
YOU'RE GOING OUT?
YES, I HAVE AN APPOINT-MENT.
WELL, IF YOU'RE NOT GOING TO BE LATE, COULD I ASK YOU TO PICK UP SOMETHING FOR ME ON THE WAY HOME?
AROUND WHAT TIME DO YOU THINK YOU'LL BE FINISHED?
...I'M AFRAID I DON'T KNOW.
I SEE.
THAT'S ALL RIGHT, THEN.
SORRY.

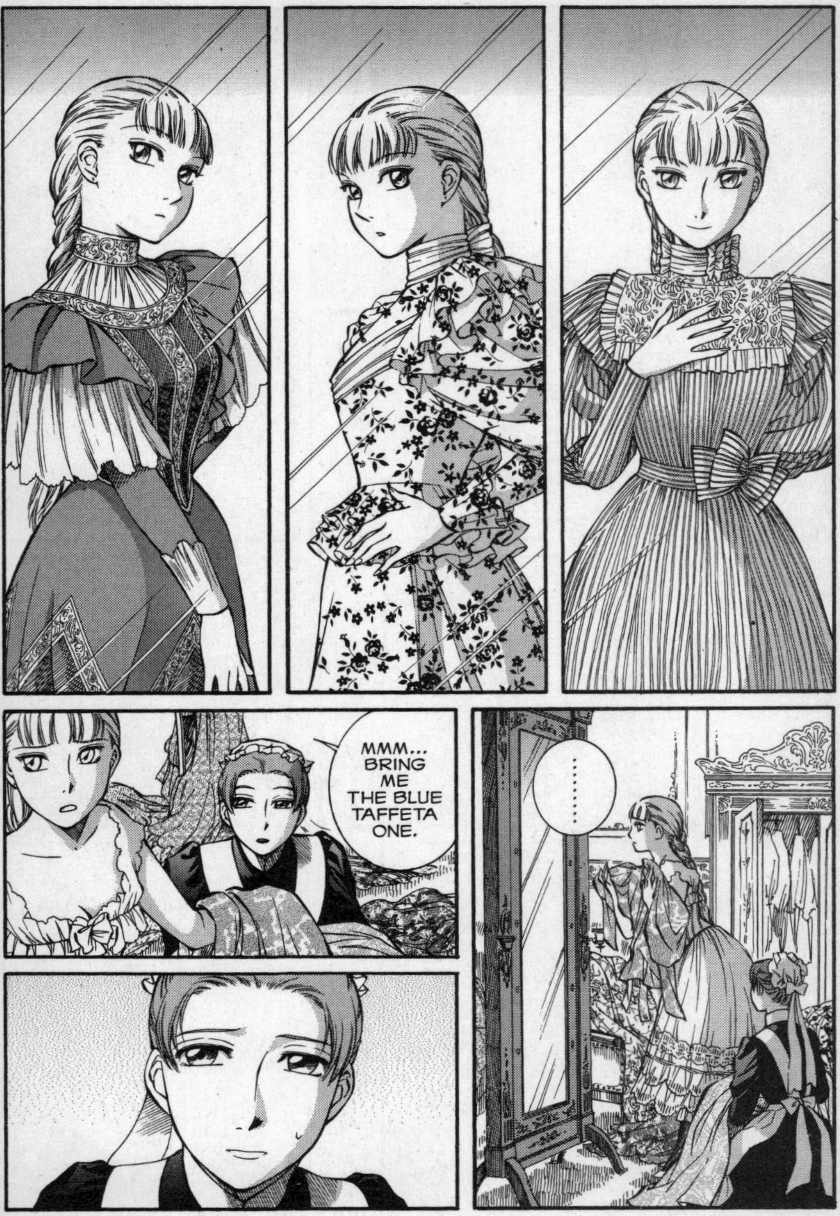
MMM... BRING ME THE BLUE TAFFETA ONE.
......

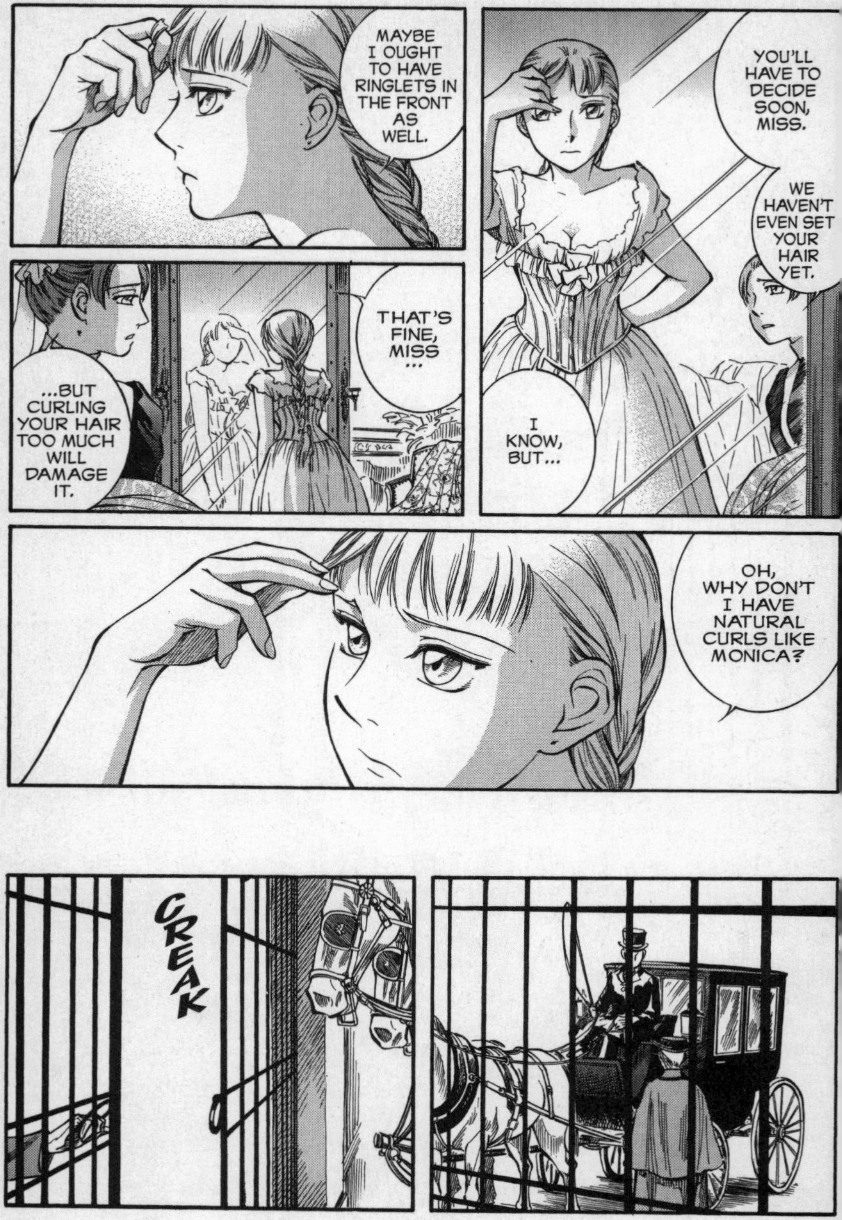
YOU'LL HAVE TO DECIDE SOON, MISS.
WE HAVEN'T EVEN SET YOUR HAIR YET.
I KNOW, BUT...
MAYBE I OUGHT TO HAVE RINGLETS IN THE FRONT AS WELL.
THAT'S FINE, MISS...
...BUT CURLING YOUR HAIR TOO MUCH WILL DAMAGE IT.
OH, WHY DON'T I HAVE NATURAL CURLS LIKE MONICA?
CREAK

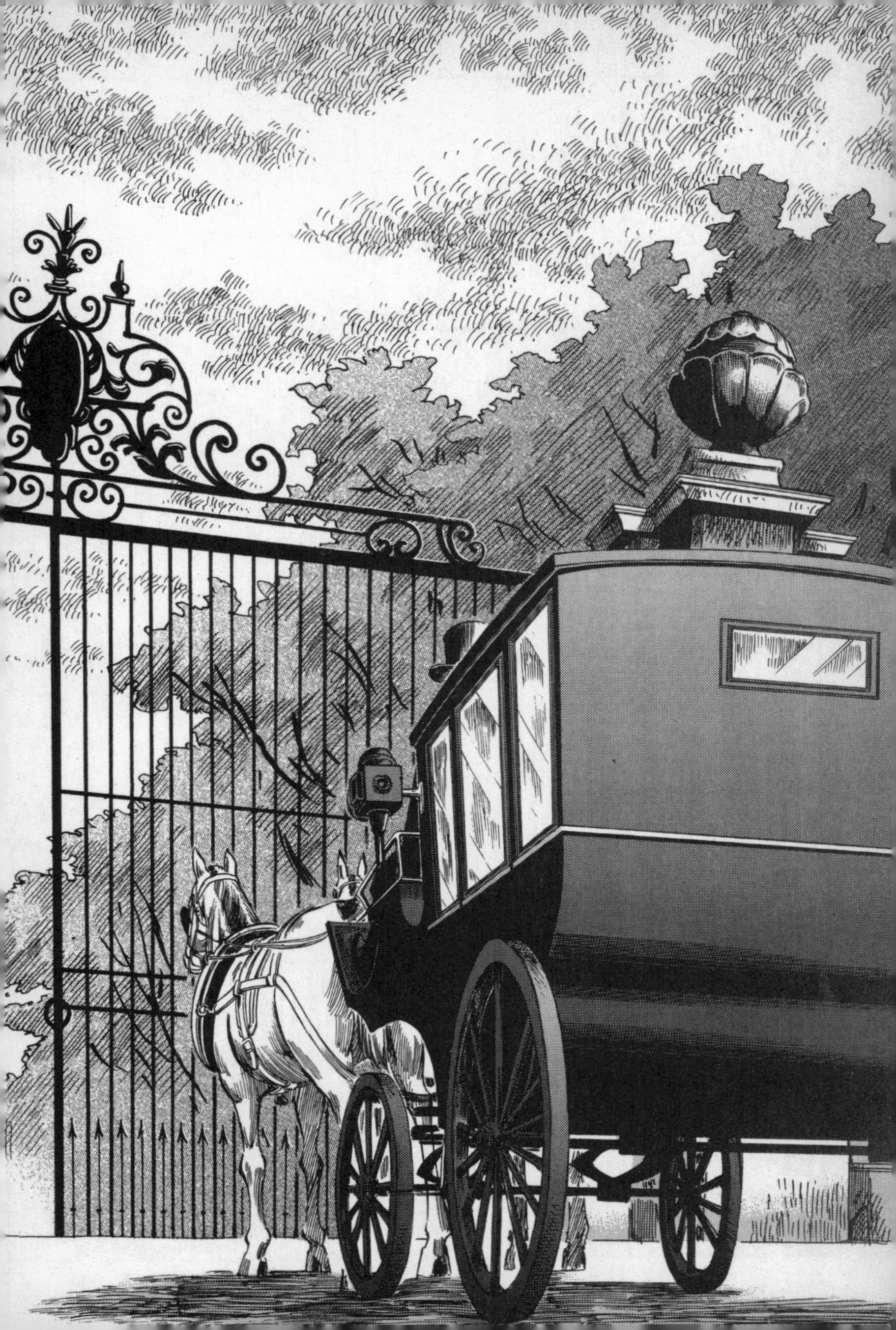

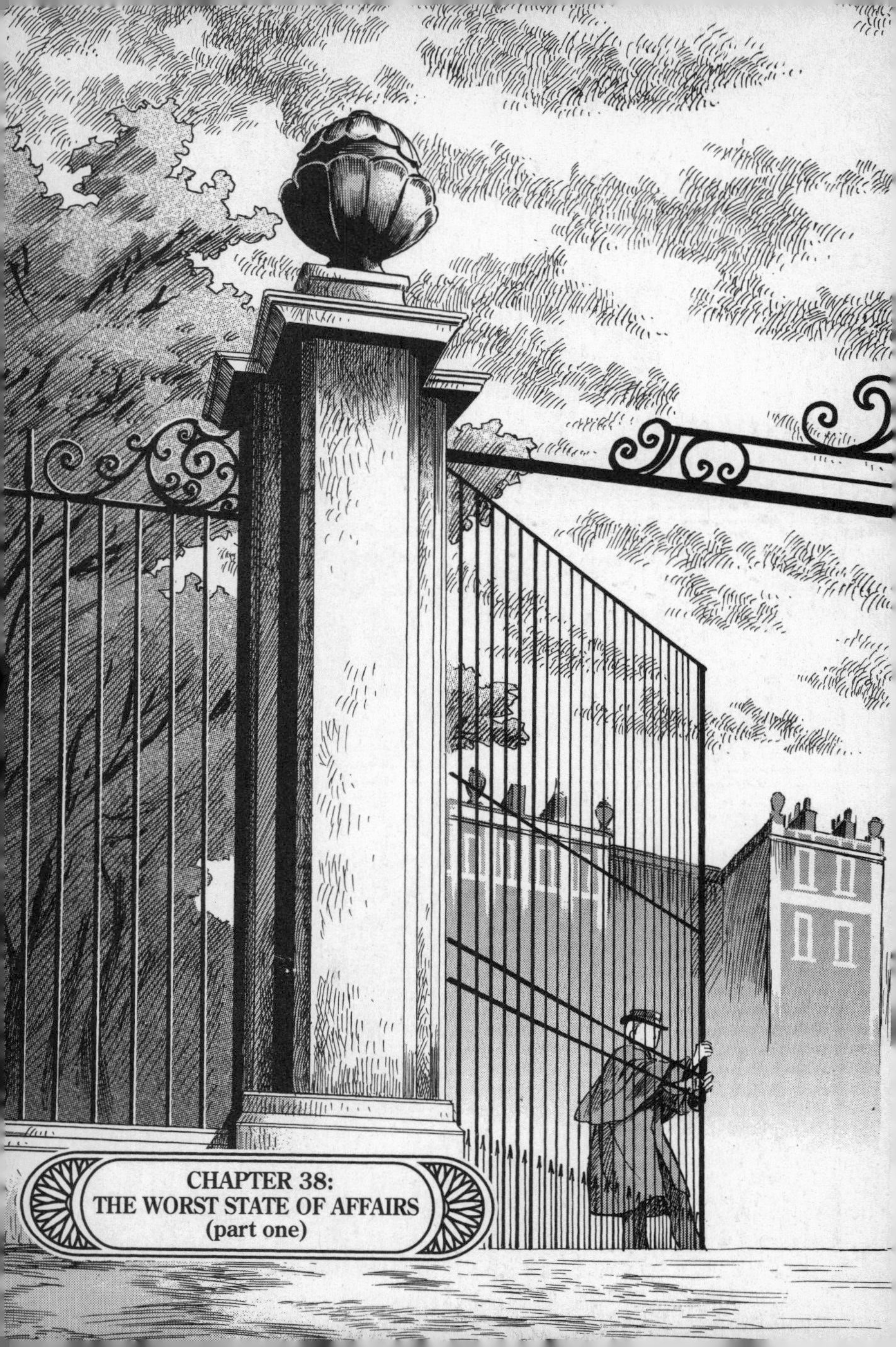
CHAPTER 38:
THE WORST STATE OF AFFAIRS
(part one)

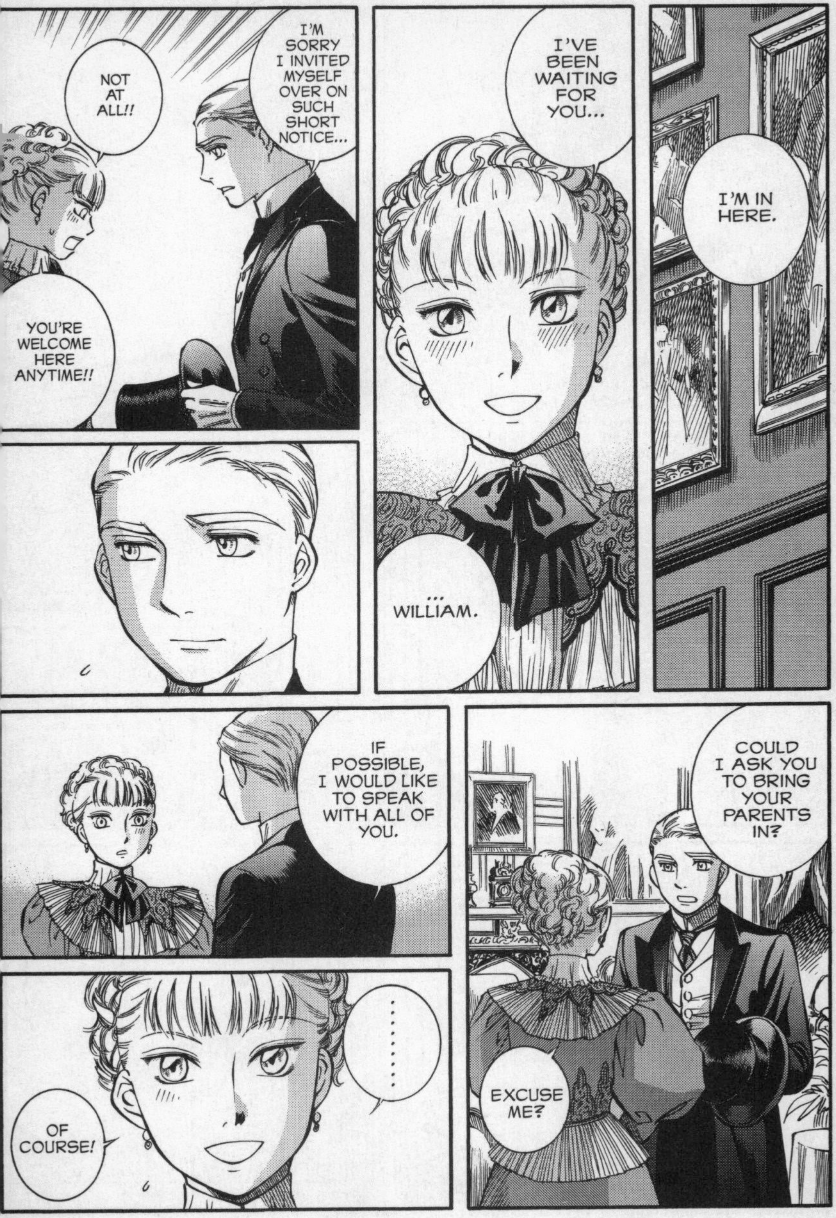
I'M IN HERE.
I'VE BEEN WAITING FOR YOU...
... WILLIAM.
I'M SORRY I INVITED MYSELF OVER ON SUCH SHORT NOTICE...
NOT AT ALL!!
YOU'RE WELCOME HERE ANYTIME!!
COULD I ASK YOU TO BRING YOUR PARENTS IN?
EXCUSE ME?
IF POSSIBLE, I WOULD LIKE TO SPEAK WITH ALL OF YOU.
......
OF COURSE!

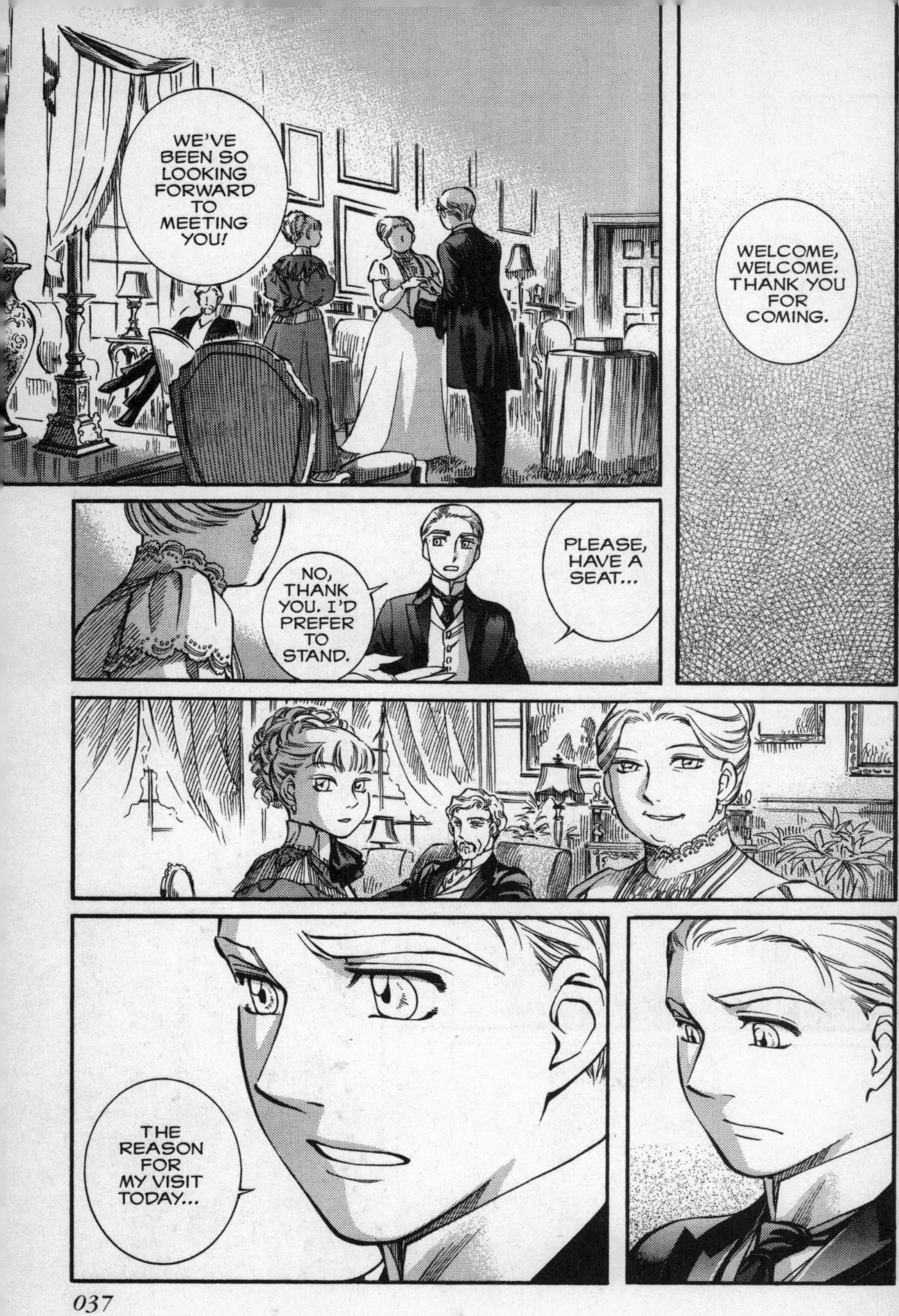
WELCOME, WELCOME. THANK YOU FOR COMING.
WE'VE BEEN SO LOOKING FORWARD TO MEETING YOU!
PLEASE, HAVE A SEAT...
NO, THANK YOU. I'D PREFER TO STAND.
THE REASON FOR MY VISIT TODAY...

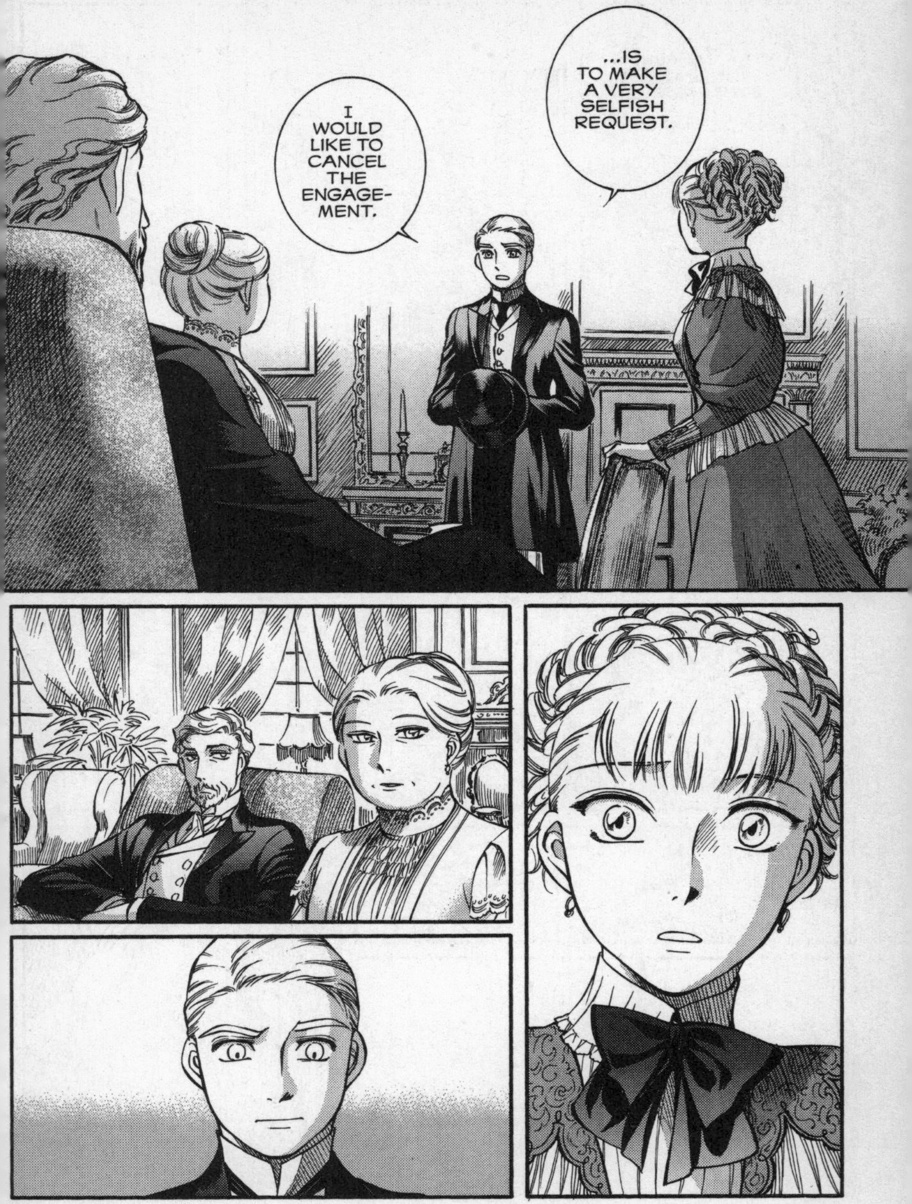
...IS TO MAKE A VERY SELFISH REQUEST.
I WOULD LIKE TO CANCEL THE ENGAGE- MENT.

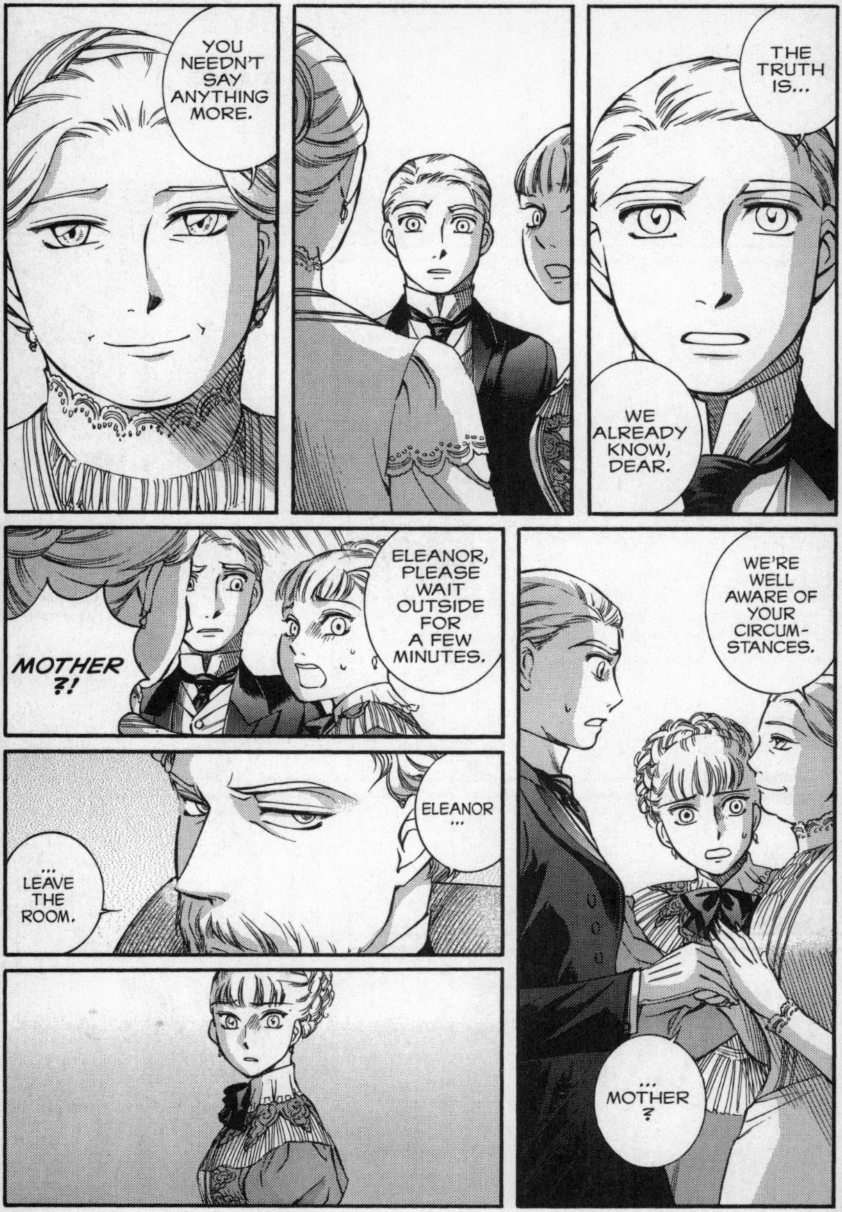
THE TRUTH IS...
WE ALREADY KNOW, DEAR.
YOU NEEDN'T SAY ANYTHING MORE.
WE'RE WELL AWARE OF YOUR CIRCUM-STANCES.
...MOTHER?
ELEANOR, PLEASE WAIT OUTSIDE FOR A FEW MINUTES.
MOTHER?!
ELEANOR...
...LEAVE THE ROOM.

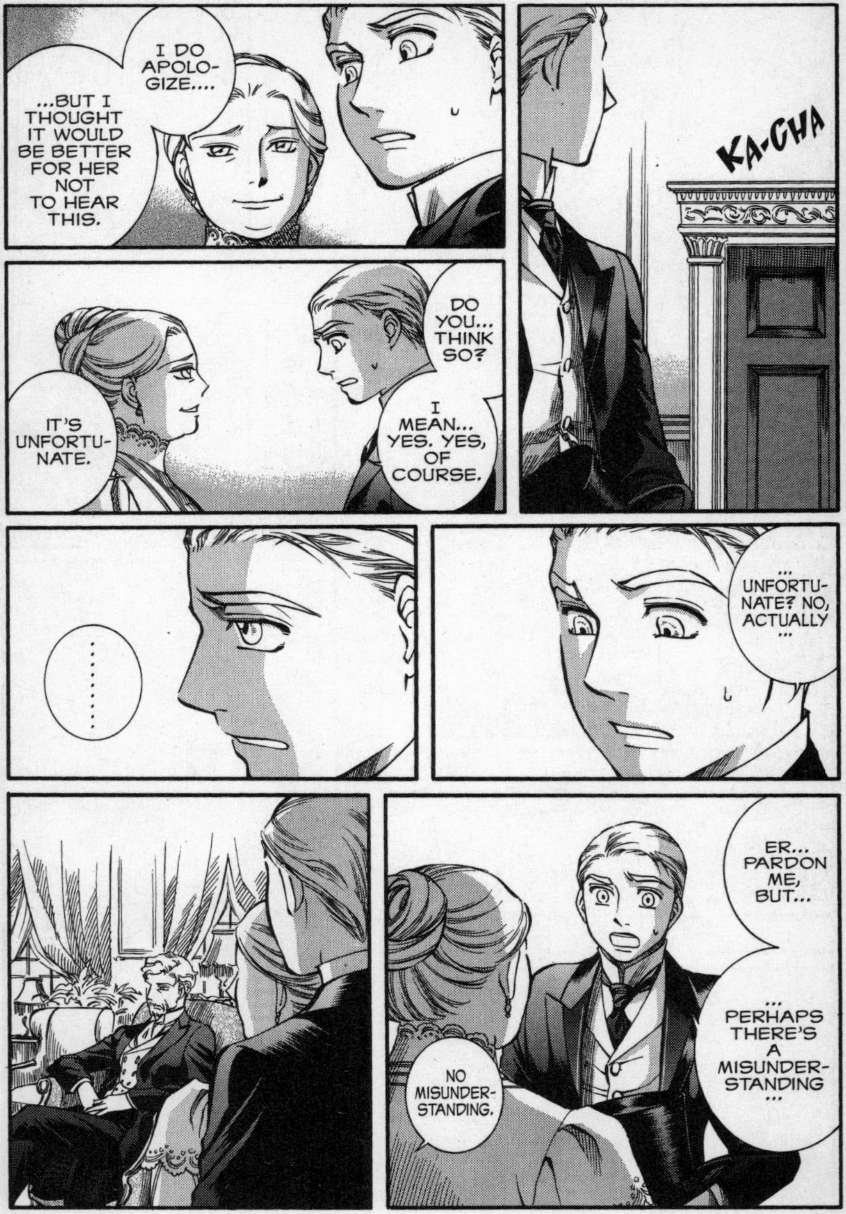
KA-CHA
I DO APOLOGIZE....
...BUT I THOUGHT IT WOULD BE BETTER FOR HER NOT TO HEAR THIS.
DO YOU... THINK SO?
I MEAN... YES. YES, OF COURSE.
IT'S UNFORTUNATE.
...UNFORTUNATE? NO, ACTUALLY...
......
ER... PARDON ME, BUT...
...PERHAPS THERE'S A MISUNDERSTANDING...
NO MISUNDERSTANDING.

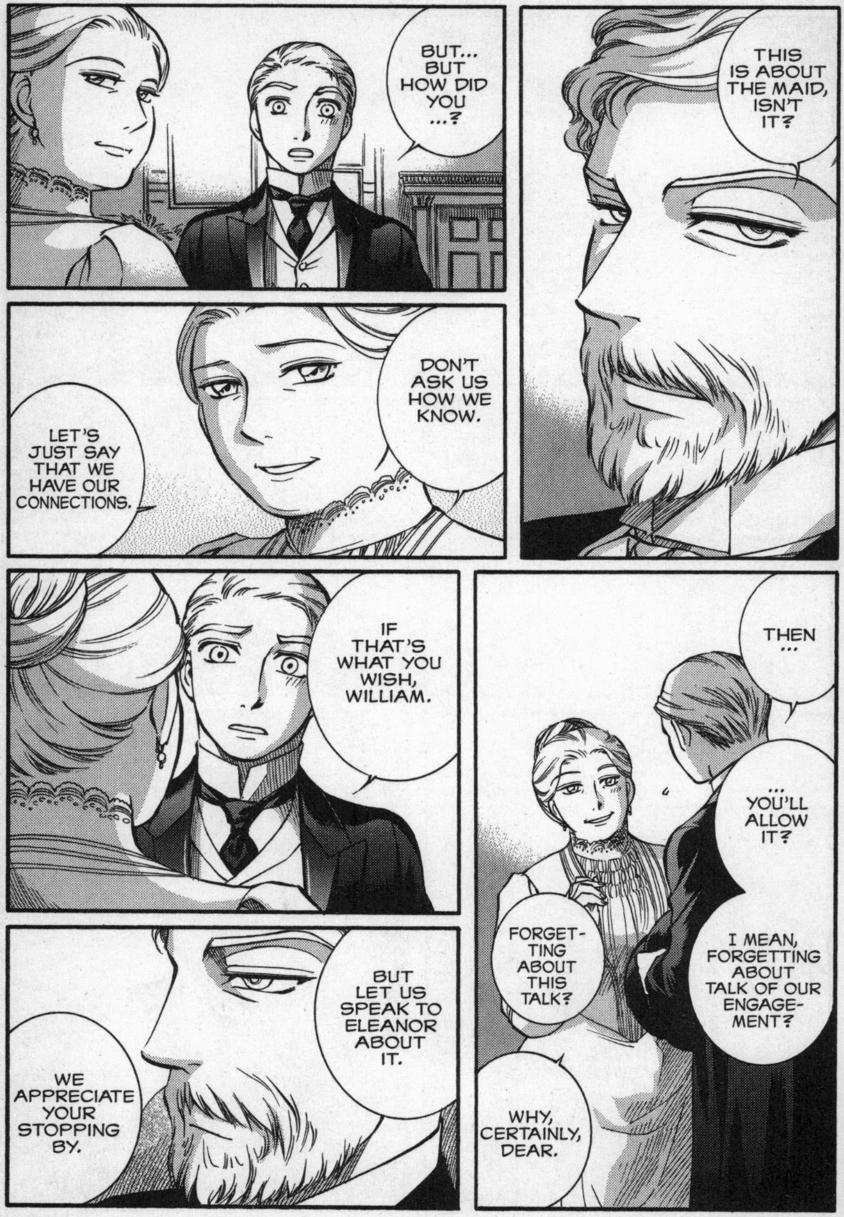
THIS IS ABOUT THE MAID, ISN'T IT?
BUT... BUT HOW DID YOU ...?
DON'T ASK US HOW WE KNOW.
LET'S JUST SAY THAT WE HAVE OUR CONNECTIONS.
THEN ...
... YOU'LL ALLOW IT?
FORGET-TING ABOUT THIS TALK?
I MEAN, FORGETTING ABOUT TALK OF OUR ENGAGE-MENT?
WHY, CERTAINLY, DEAR.
IF THAT'S WHAT YOU WISH, WILLIAM.
BUT LET US SPEAK TO ELEANOR ABOUT IT.
WE APPRECIATE YOUR STOPPING BY.

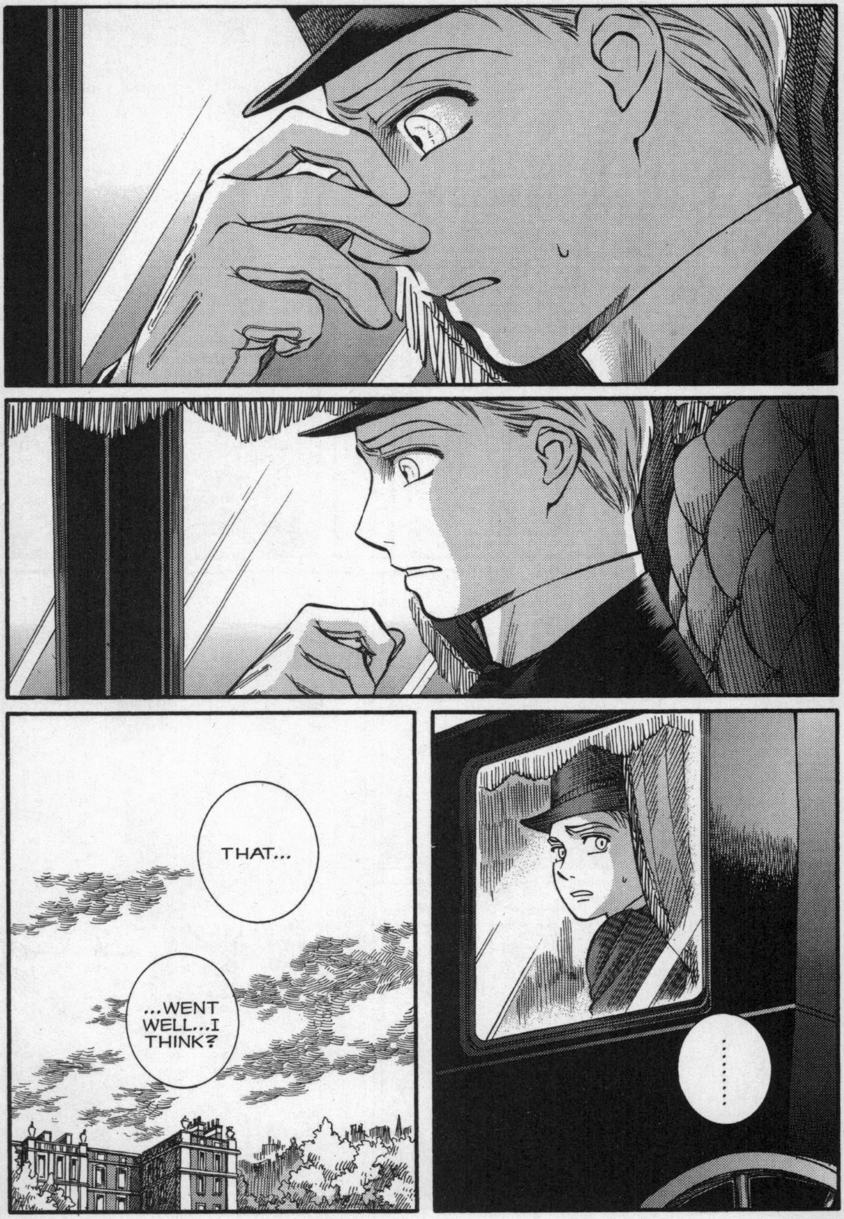
THAT...
...WENT WELL...I THINK?
....

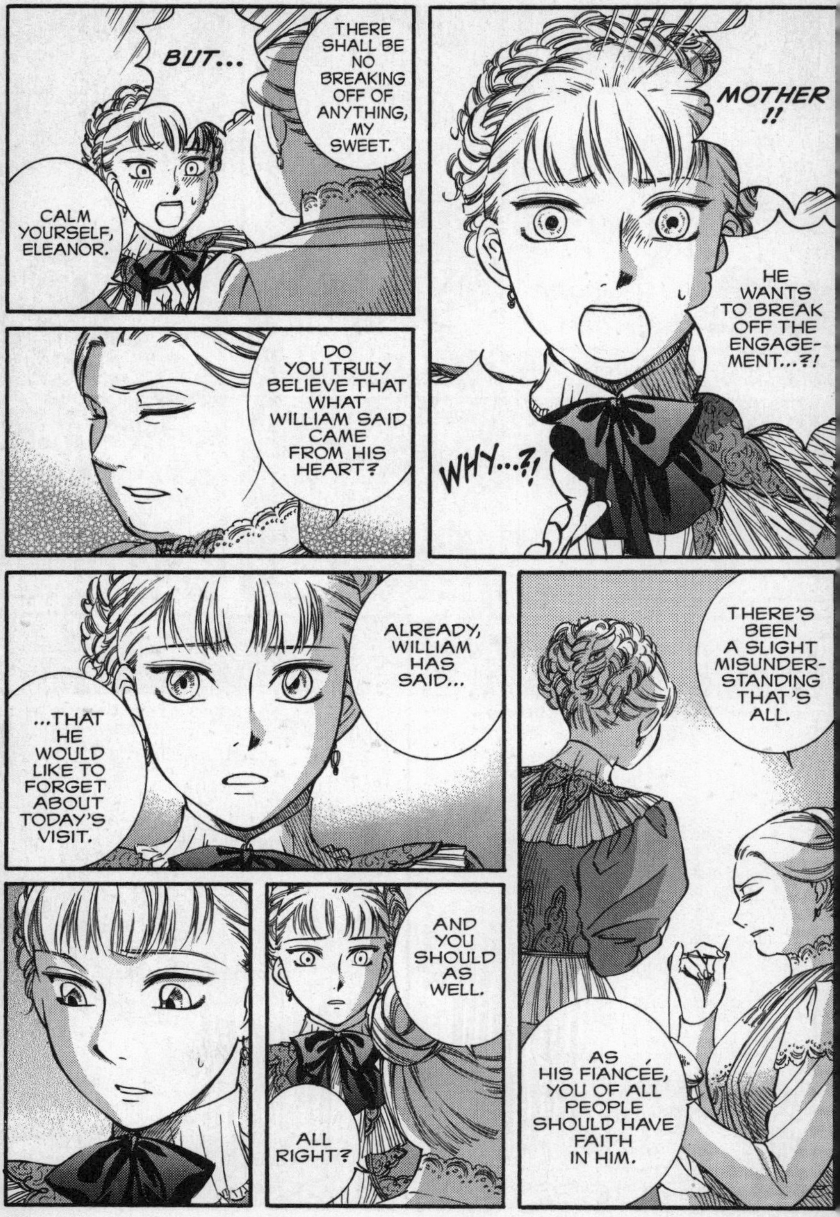
MOTHER !!
HE WANTS TO BREAK OFF THE ENGAGE- MENT...?!
WHY...?!
BUT...
CALM YOURSELF, ELEANOR.
THERE SHALL BE NO BREAKING OFF OF ANYTHING, MY SWEET.
DO YOU TRULY BELIEVE THAT WHAT WILLIAM SAID CAME FROM HIS HEART?
THERE'S BEEN A SLIGHT MISUNDER- STANDING THAT'S ALL.
AS HIS FIANCÉE, YOU OF ALL PEOPLE SHOULD HAVE FAITH IN HIM.
ALREADY, WILLIAM HAS SAID...
...THAT HE WOULD LIKE TO FORGET ABOUT TODAY'S VISIT.
AND YOU SHOULD AS WELL.
ALL RIGHT?

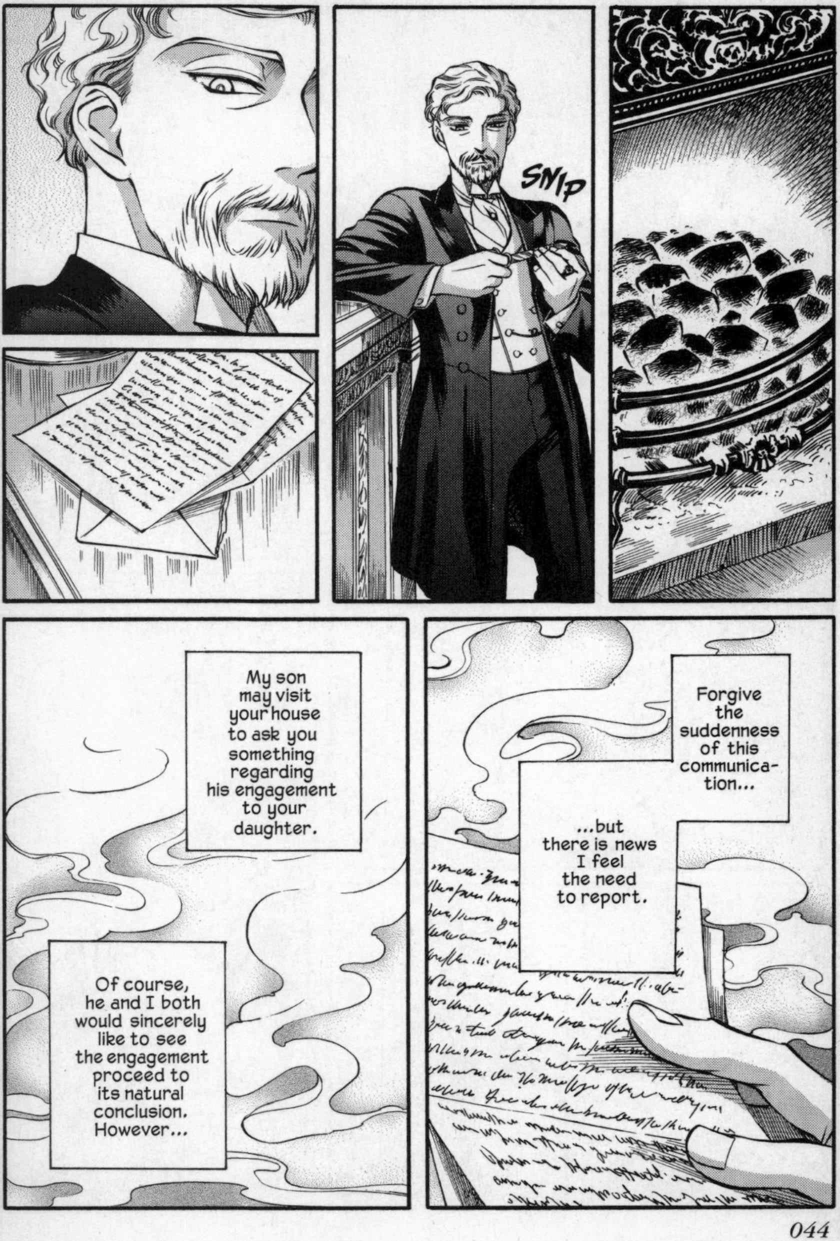
SNIP
Forgive the suddenness of this communication...
...but there is news I feel the need to report.
My son may visit your house to ask you something regarding his engagement to your daughter.
Of course, he and I both would sincerely like to see the engagement proceed to its natural conclusion. However...

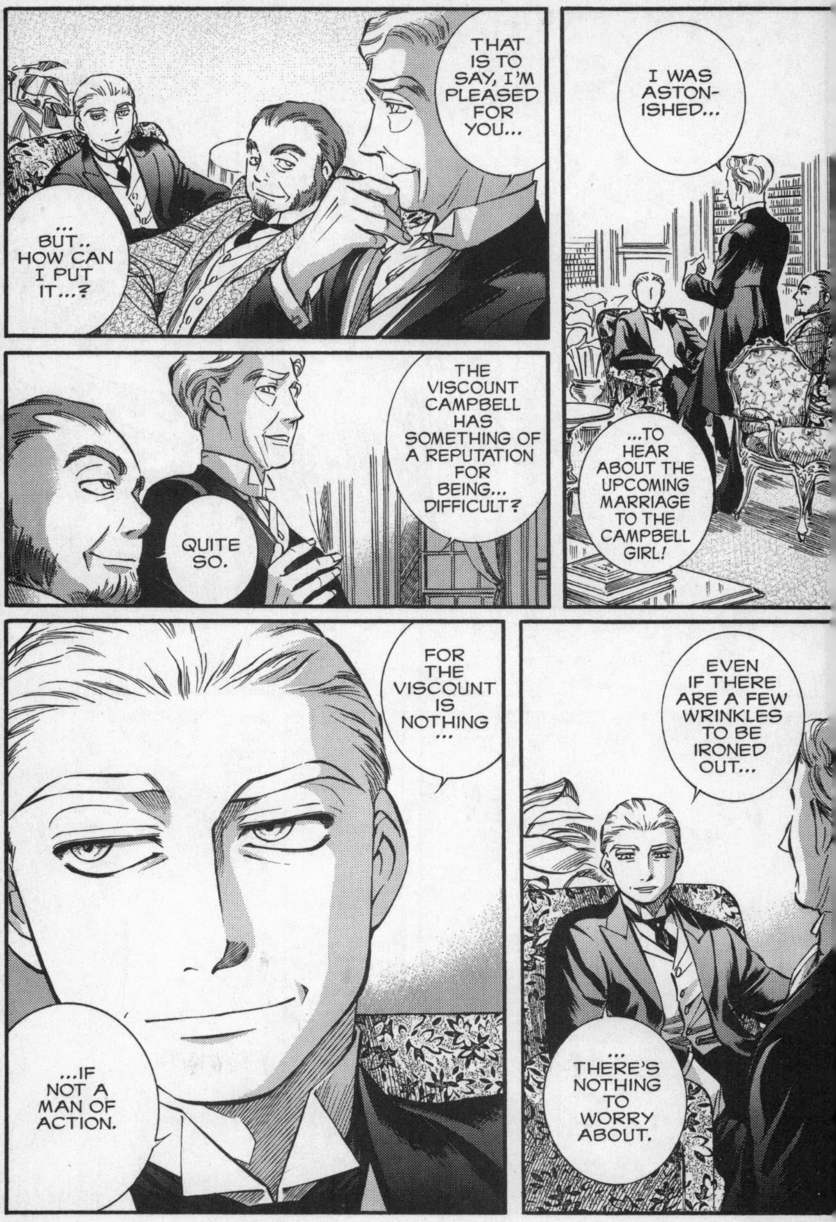
I WAS ASTON-ISHED...
...TO HEAR ABOUT THE UPCOMING MARRIAGE TO THE CAMPBELL GIRL!
THAT IS TO SAY, I'M PLEASED FOR YOU...
...BUT.. HOW CAN I PUT IT...?
THE VISCOUNT CAMPBELL HAS SOMETHING OF A REPUTATION FOR BEING... DIFFICULT?
QUITE SO.
EVEN IF THERE ARE A FEW WRINKLES TO BE IRONED OUT...
...THERE'S NOTHING TO WORRY ABOUT.
FOR THE VISCOUNT IS NOTHING...
...IF NOT A MAN OF ACTION.

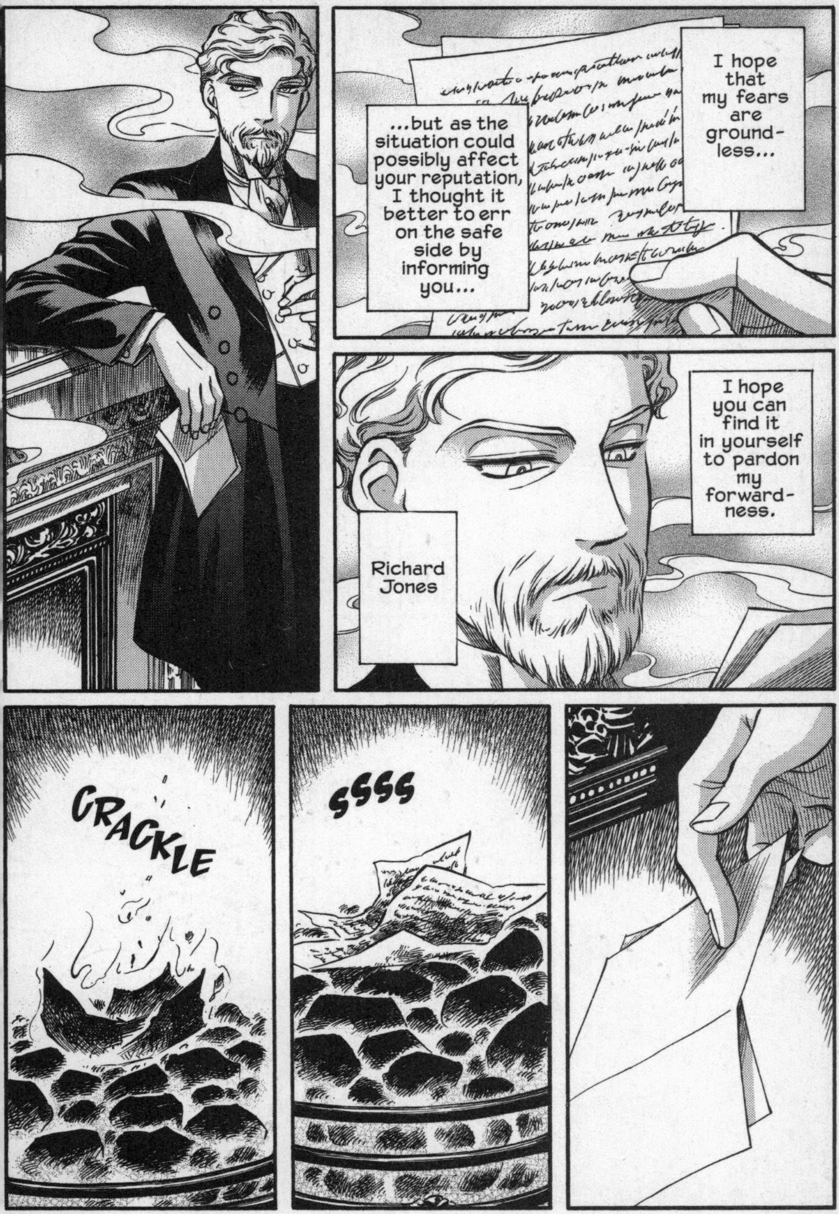
I hope that my fears are groundless...
...but as the situation could possibly affect your reputation, I thought it better to err on the safe side by informing you...
I hope you can find it in yourself to pardon my forwardness.
Richard Jones
SSSS
CRACKLE

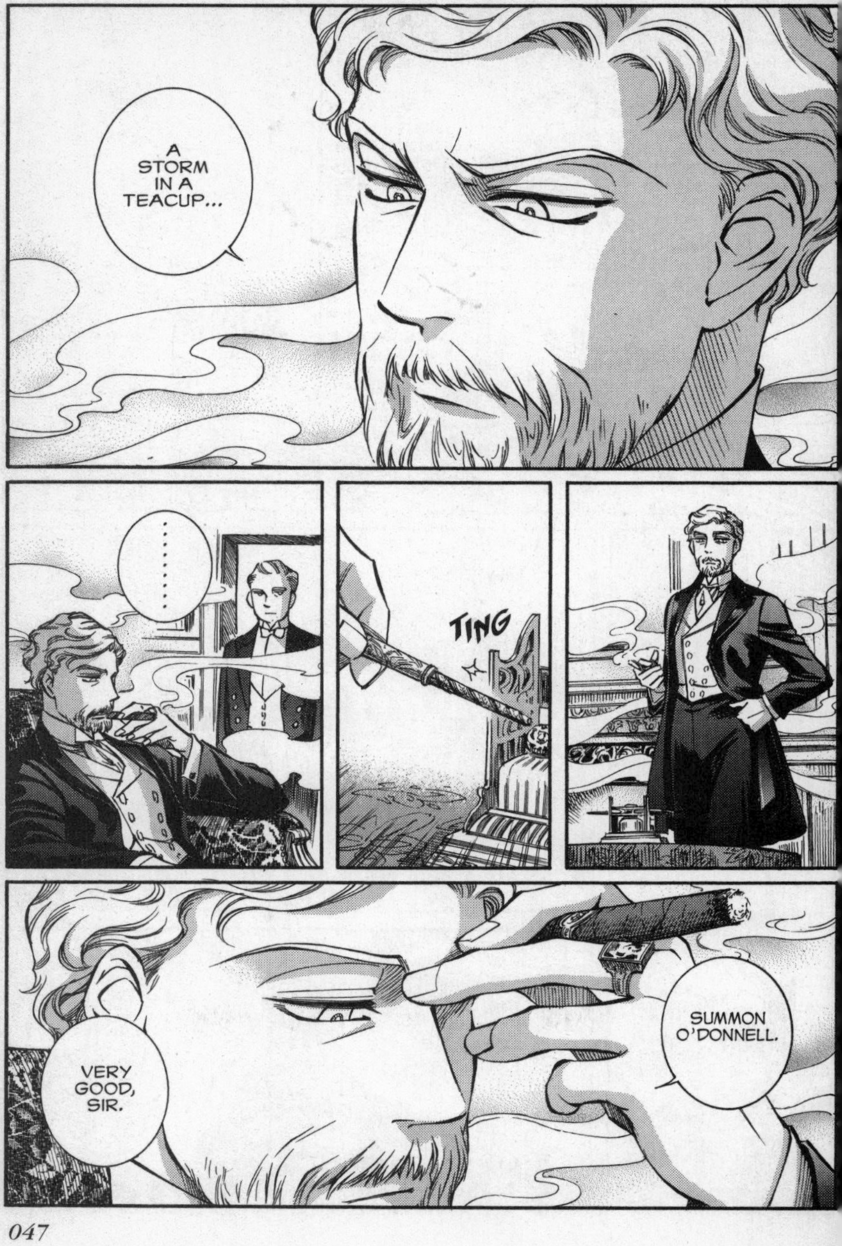
A STORM IN A TEACUP...
TING
......
SUMMON O'DONNELL.
VERY GOOD, SIR.

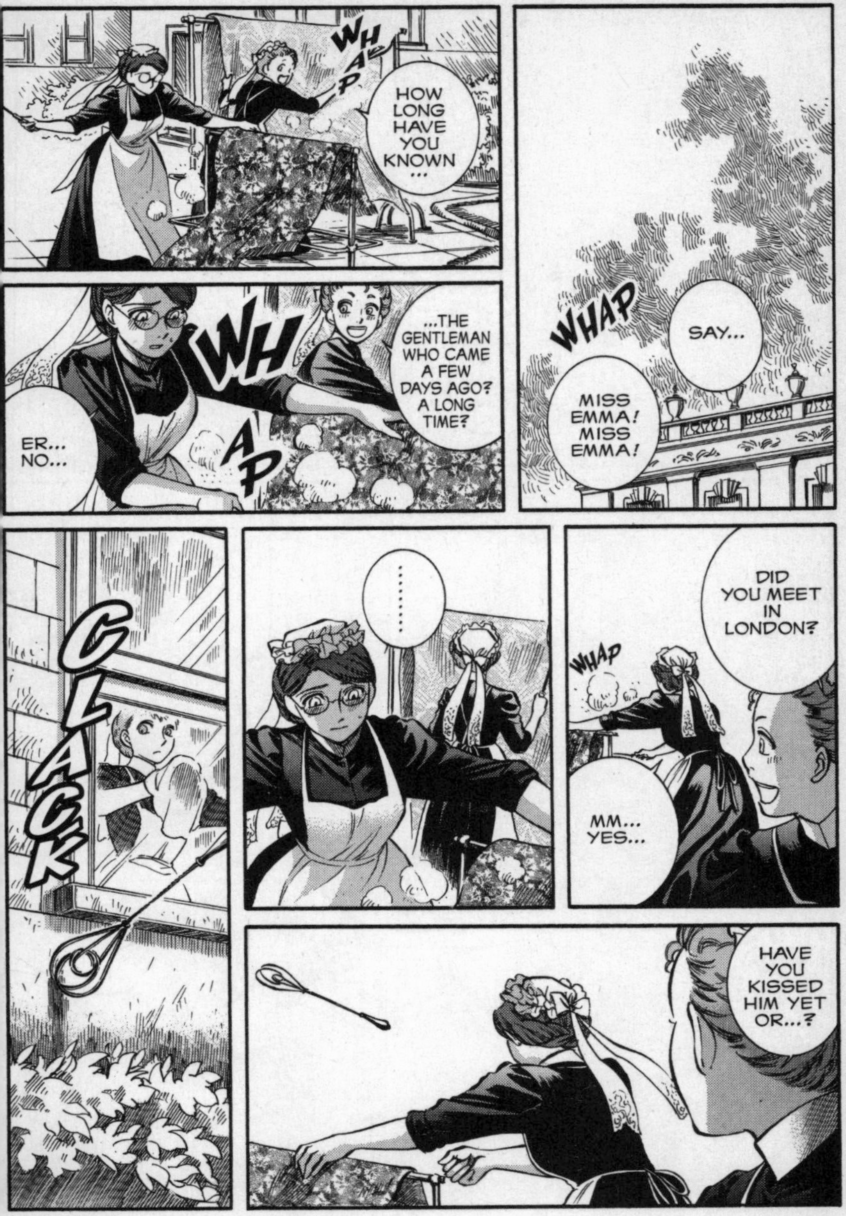
WHAP
MISS EMMA! MISS EMMA!
SAY...
WHAP
HOW LONG HAVE YOU KNOWN...
WHAP
...THE GENTLEMAN WHO CAME A FEW DAYS AGO? A LONG TIME?
ER... NO...
WHAP
DID YOU MEET IN LONDON?
MM... YES...
......
CLACK
HAVE YOU KISSED HIM YET OR...?

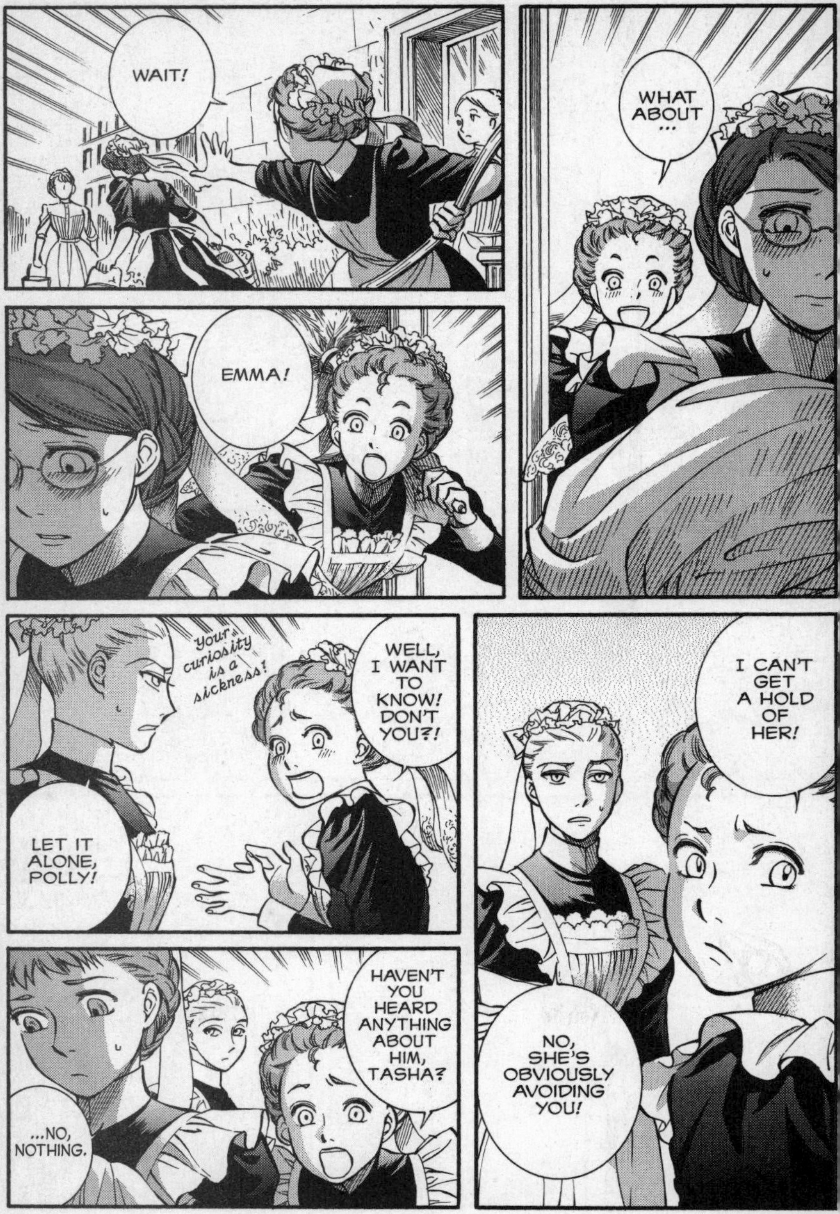
WHAT ABOUT ...
WAIT!
EMMA!
I CAN'T GET A HOLD OF HER!
NO, SHE'S OBVIOUSLY AVOIDING YOU!
WELL, I WANT TO KNOW! DON'T YOU?!
your curiosity is a sickness!
LET IT ALONE, POLLY!
HAVEN'T YOU HEARD ANYTHING ABOUT HIM, TASHA?
...NO, NOTHING.

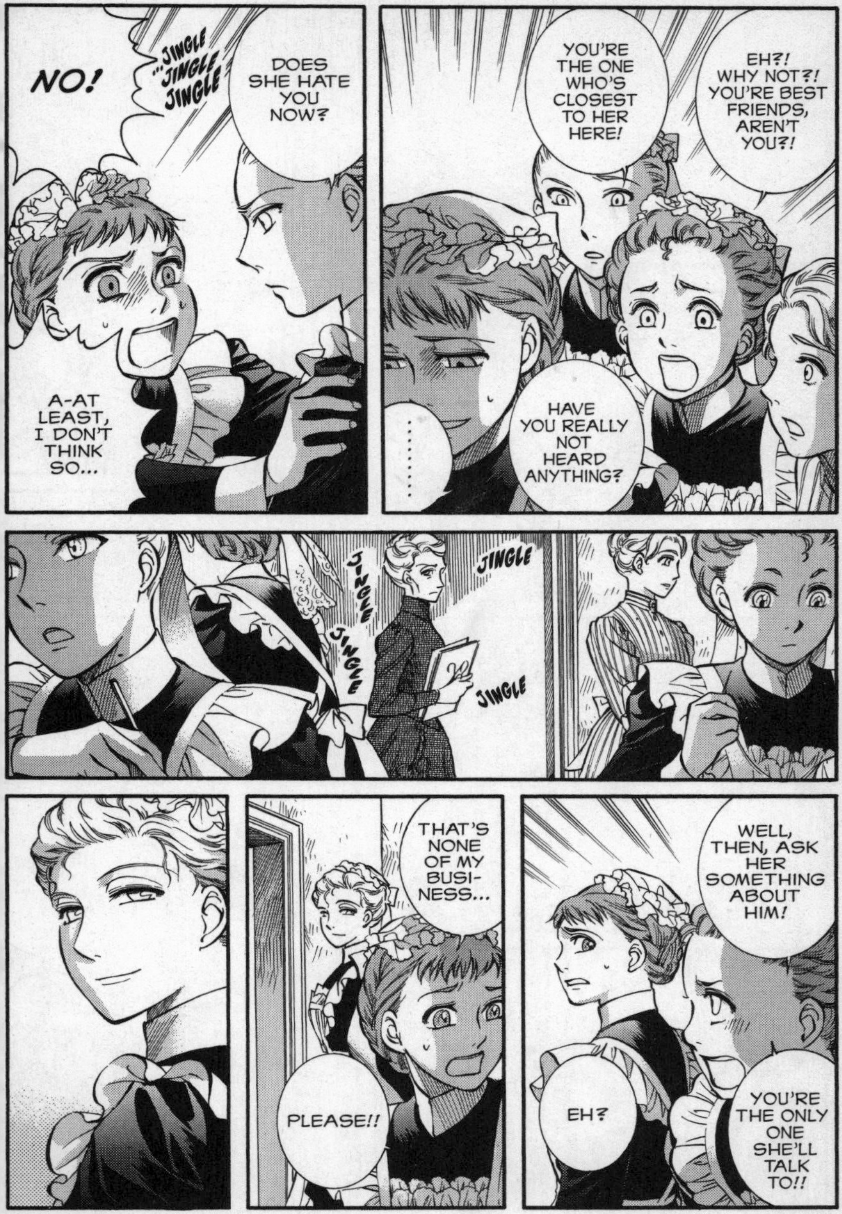

EH?! WHY NOT?! YOU'RE BEST FRIENDS, AREN'T YOU?!
YOU'RE THE ONE WHO'S CLOSEST TO HER HERE!
HAVE YOU REALLY NOT HEARD ANYTHING?
......
DOES SHE HATE YOU NOW?
...JINGLE JINGLE JINGLE
NO!
A-AT LEAST, I DON'T THINK SO...
JINGLE
JINGLE
JINGLE
JINGLE
JINGLE
WELL, THEN, ASK HER SOMETHING ABOUT HIM!
YOU'RE THE ONLY ONE SHE'LL TALK TO!!
EH?
THAT'S NONE OF MY BUSI-NESS...
PLEASE!!

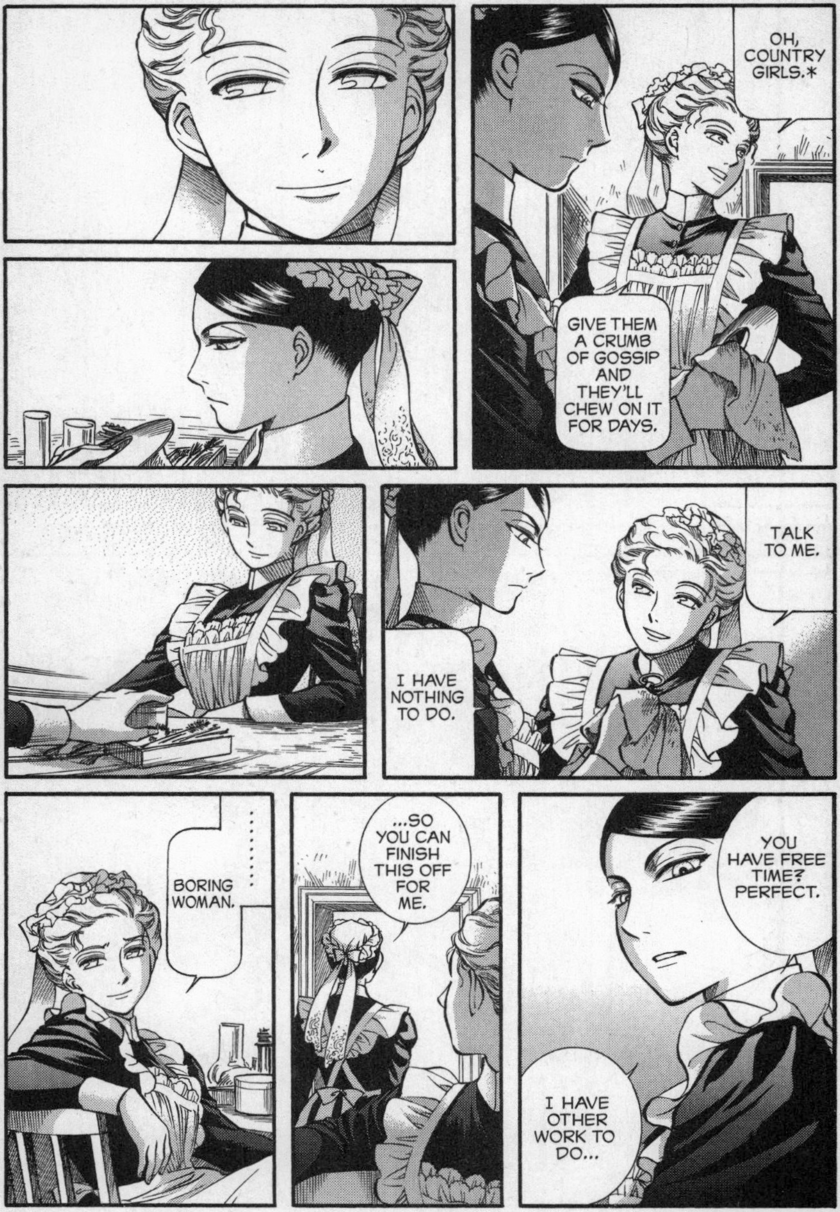

OH, COUNTRY GIRLS.*
GIVE THEM A CRUMB OF GOSSIP AND THEY'LL CHEW ON IT FOR DAYS.
TALK TO ME.
I HAVE NOTHING TO DO.
YOU HAVE FREE TIME? PERFECT.
I HAVE OTHER WORK TO DO...
...SO YOU CAN FINISH THIS OFF FOR ME.
......
BORING WOMAN.

*NOTE: SQUARED BALLOONS INDICATE THE CHARACTERS ARE SPEAKING GERMAN.

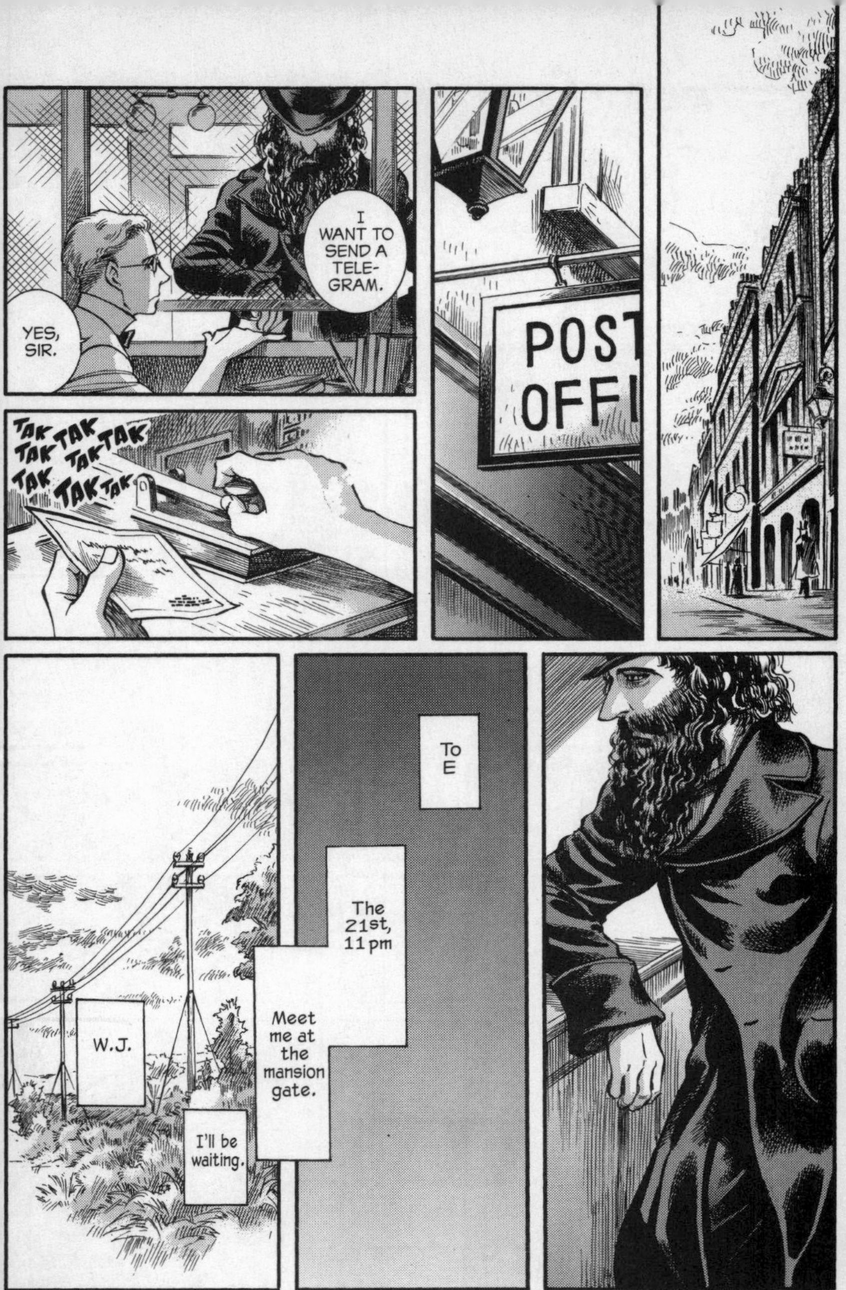
POST
OFFI
I WANT TO SEND A TELE-GRAM.
YES, SIR.
TAK TAK TAK TAK TAK TAK TAK TAK TAK
To E
The 21st, 11 pm
Meet me at the mansion gate.
I'll be waiting.
W.J.

Chapter Thirty Eight: The End

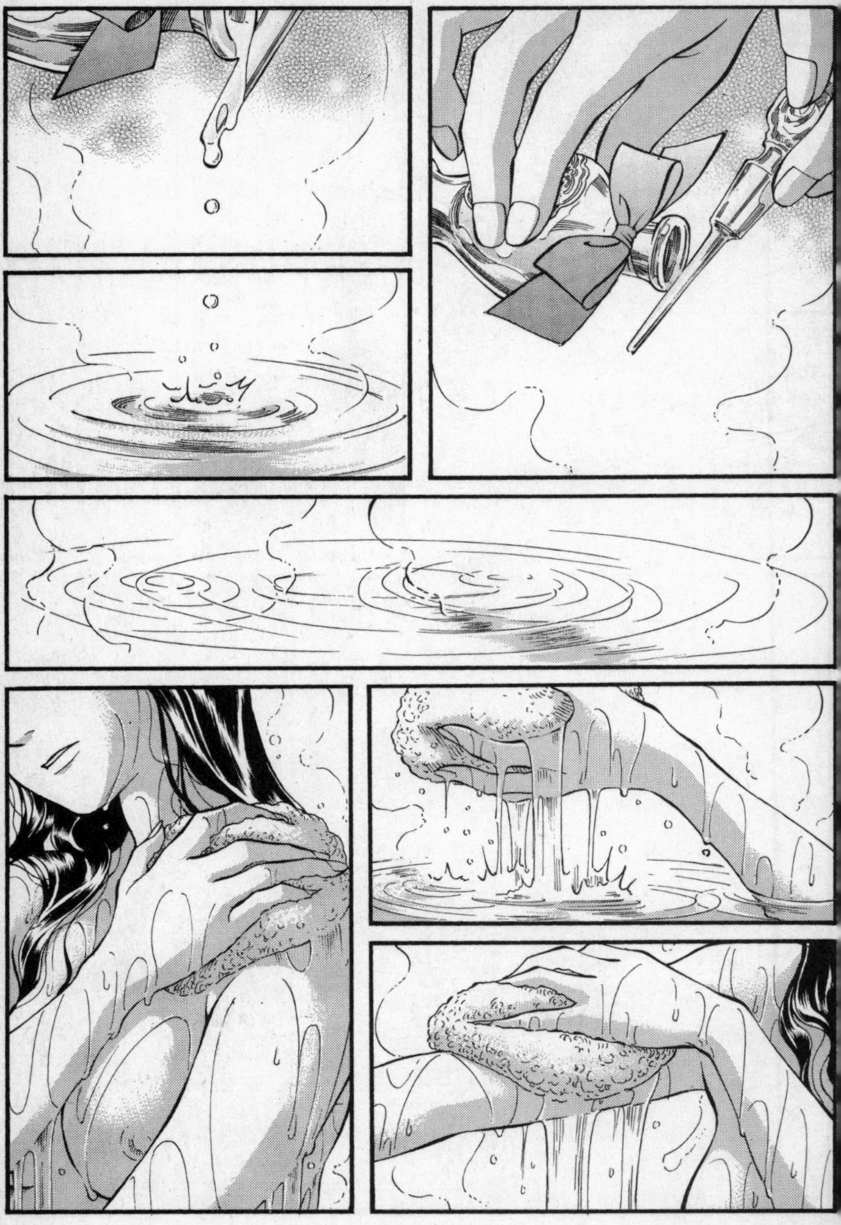

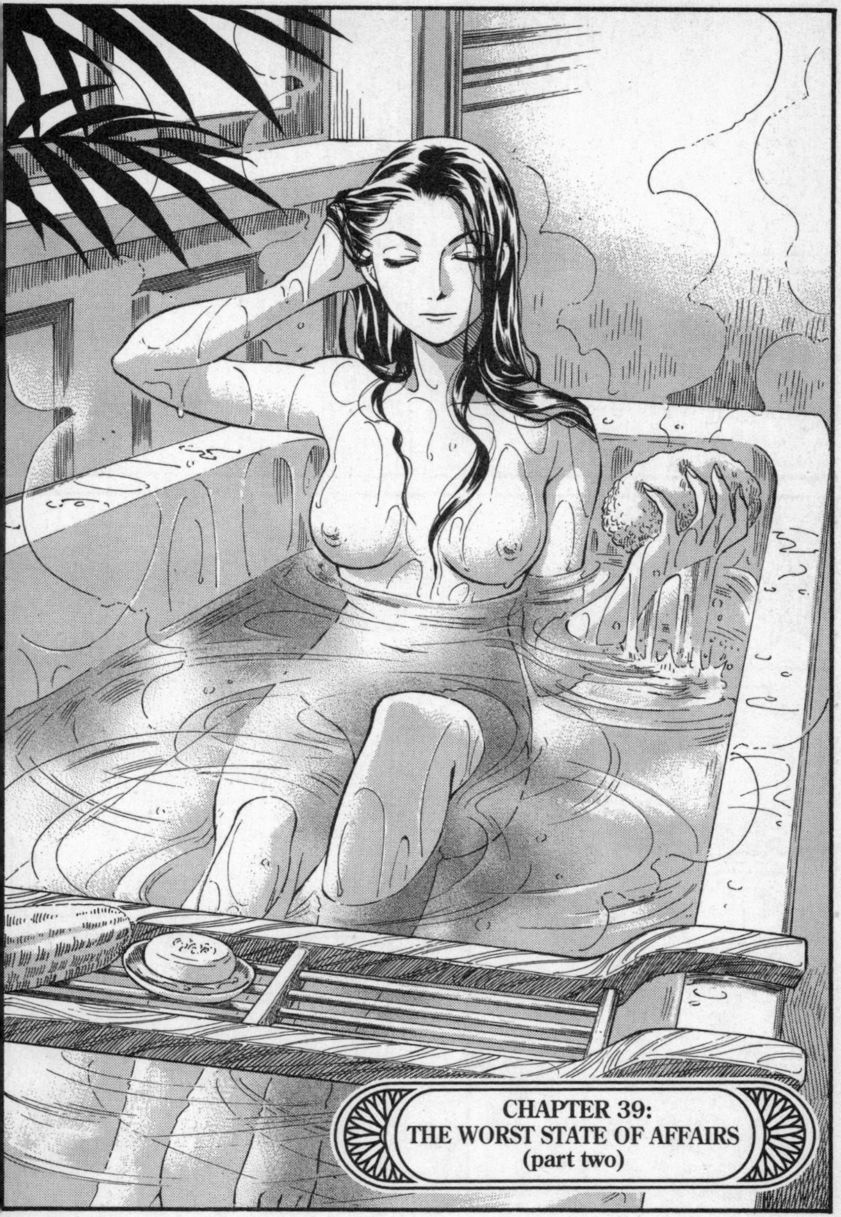
CHAPTER 39:
THE WORST STATE OF AFFAIRS
(part two)

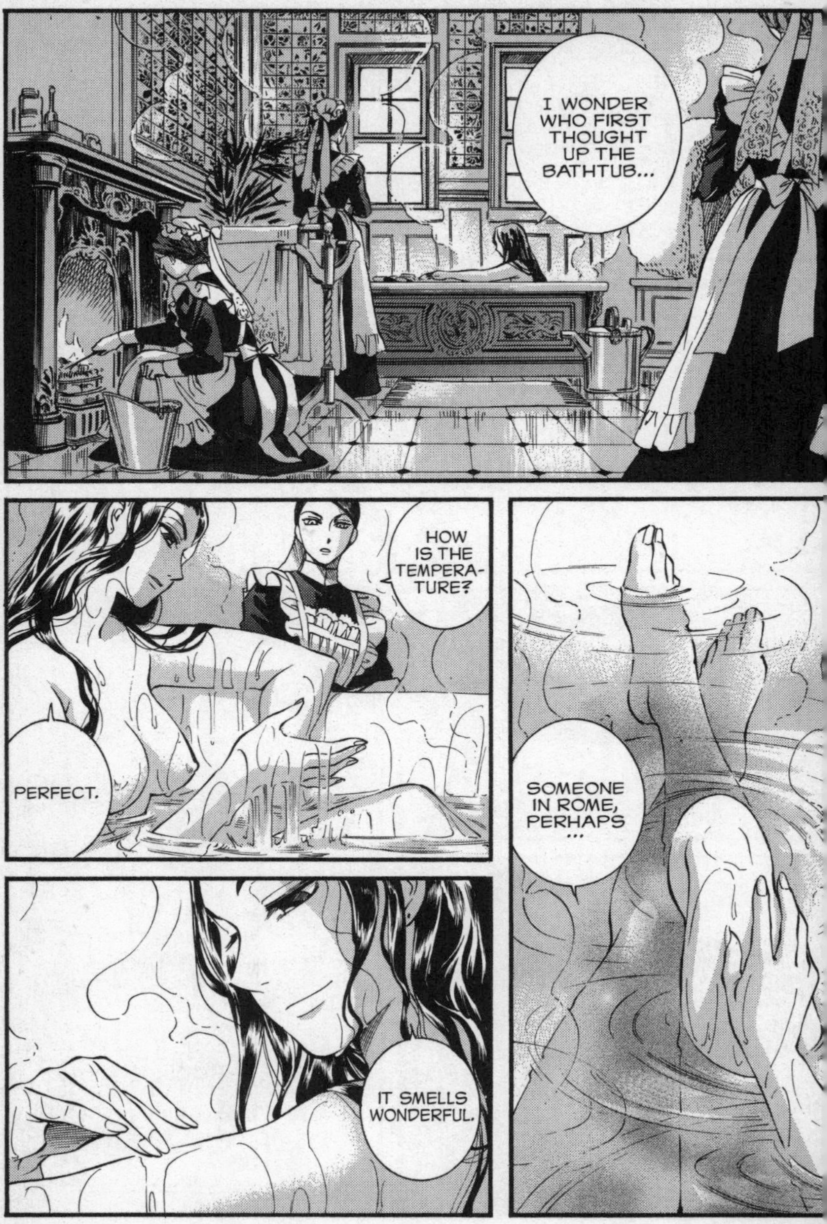
I WONDER WHO FIRST THOUGHT UP THE BATHTUB...
SOMEONE IN ROME, PERHAPS ...
HOW IS THE TEMPERA-TURE?
PERFECT.
IT SMELLS WONDERFUL.

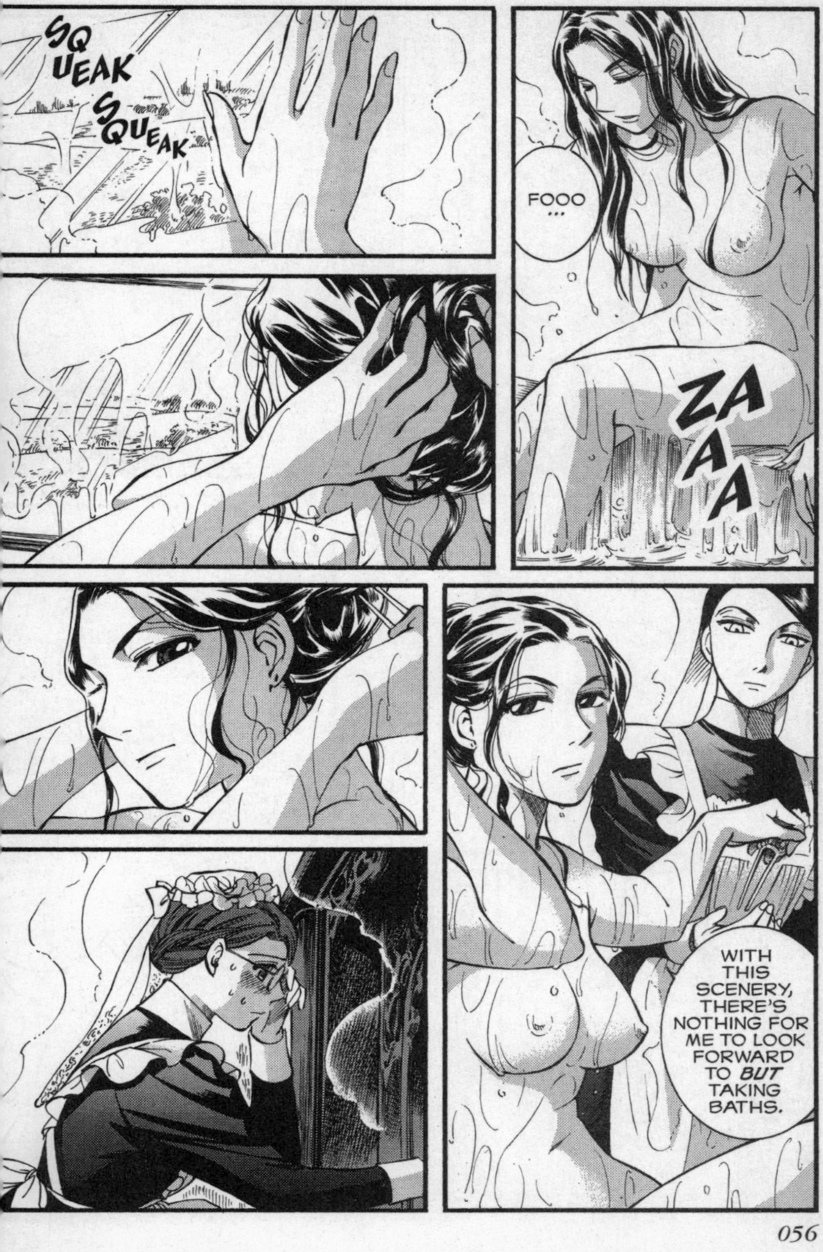
FOOO...
ZAAA
SQUEAK SQUEAK
WITH THIS SCENERY, THERE'S NOTHING FOR ME TO LOOK FORWARD TO *BUT* TAKING BATHS.

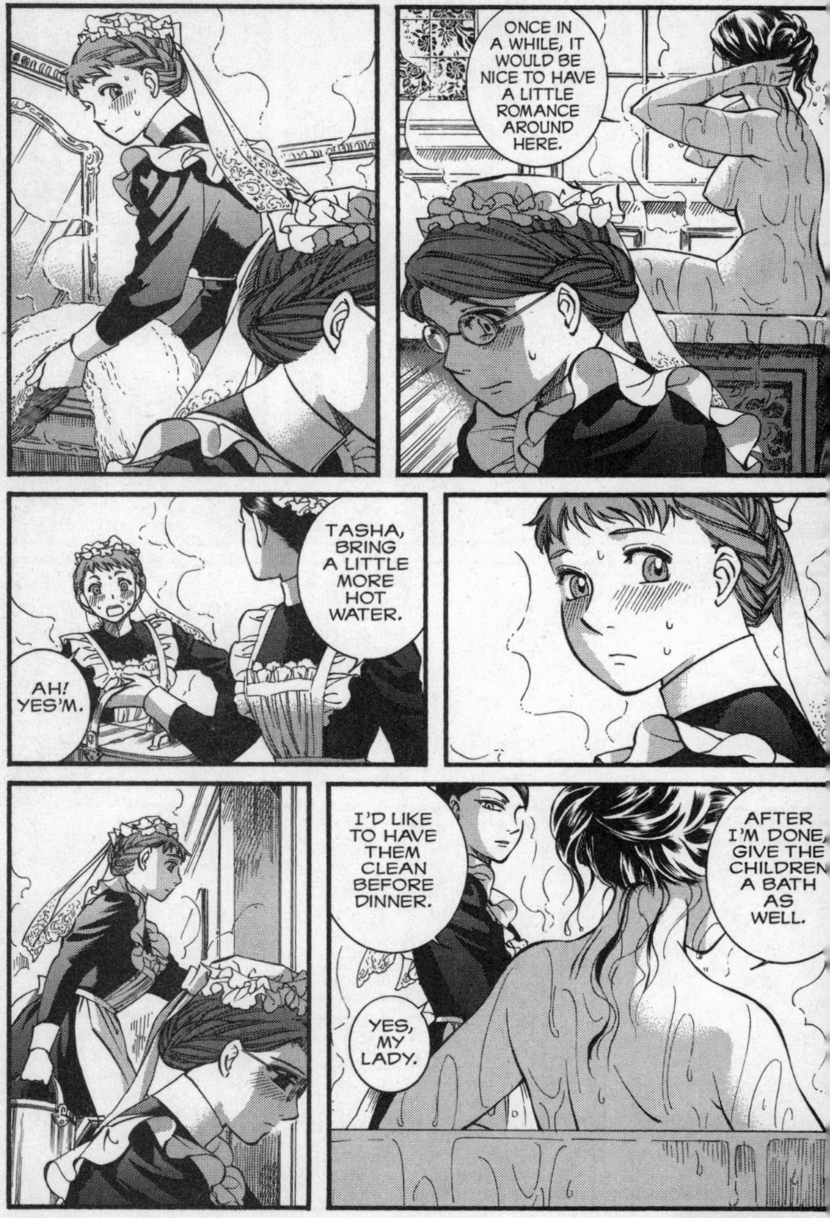
ONCE IN A WHILE, IT WOULD BE NICE TO HAVE A LITTLE ROMANCE AROUND HERE.
TASHA, BRING A LITTLE MORE HOT WATER.
AH! YES'M.
AFTER I'M DONE, GIVE THE CHILDREN A BATH AS WELL.
I'D LIKE TO HAVE THEM CLEAN BEFORE DINNER.
YES, MY LADY.

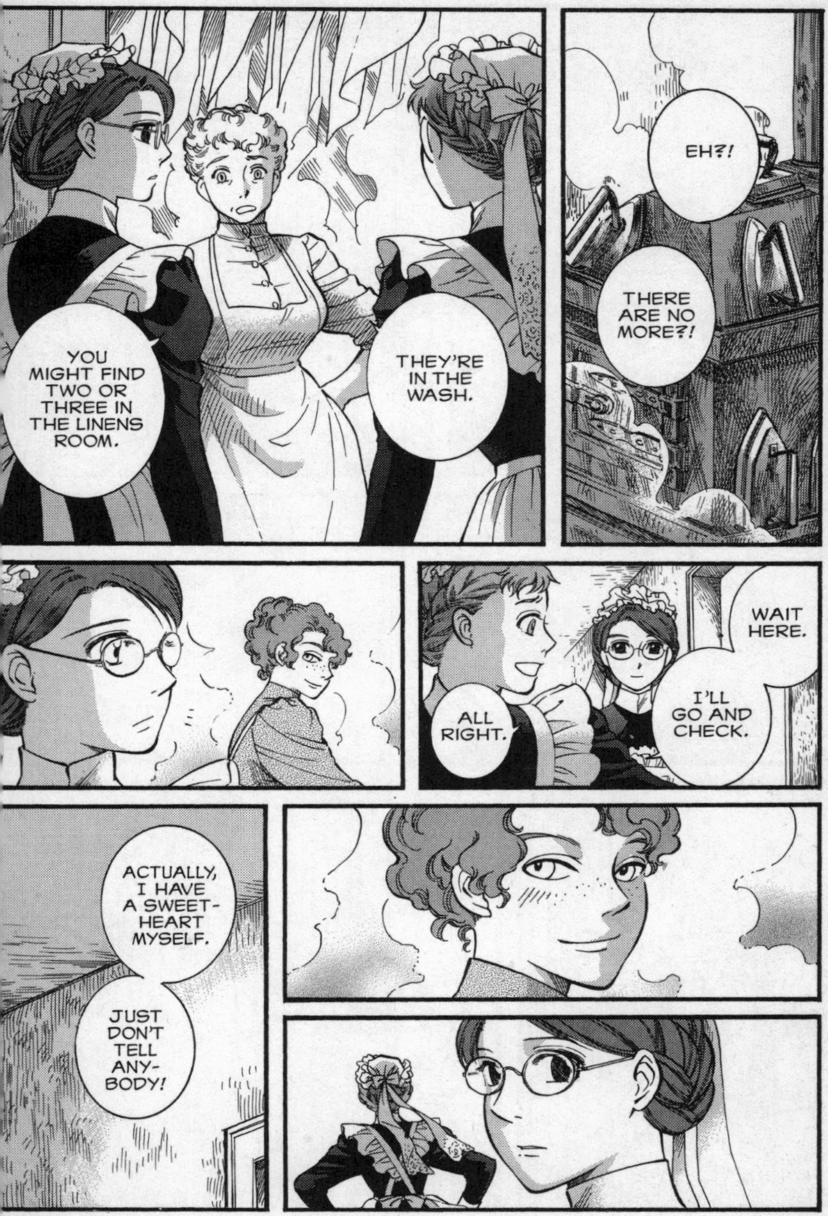
EH?!
THERE ARE NO MORE?!
THEY'RE IN THE WASH.
YOU MIGHT FIND TWO OR THREE IN THE LINENS ROOM.
WAIT HERE.
I'LL GO AND CHECK.
ALL RIGHT.
ACTUALLY, I HAVE A SWEET-HEART MYSELF.
JUST DON'T TELL ANY-BODY!

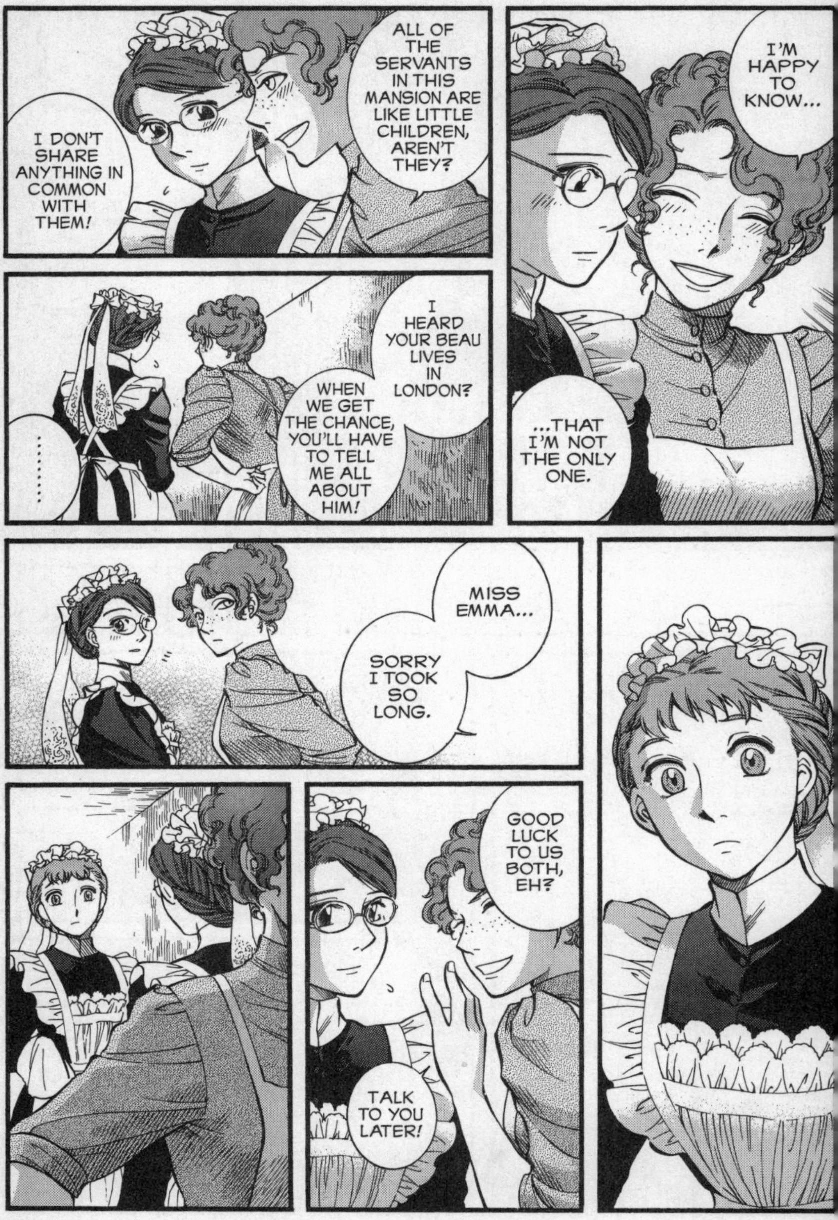
ALL OF THE SERVANTS IN THIS MANSION ARE LIKE LITTLE CHILDREN, AREN'T THEY?
I DON'T SHARE ANYTHING IN COMMON WITH THEM!
I HEARD YOUR BEAU LIVES IN LONDON?
WHEN WE GET THE CHANCE, YOU'LL HAVE TO TELL ME ALL ABOUT HIM!
......
I'M HAPPY TO KNOW...
...THAT I'M NOT THE ONLY ONE.
MISS EMMA...
SORRY I TOOK SO LONG.
GOOD LUCK TO US BOTH, EH?
TALK TO YOU LATER!

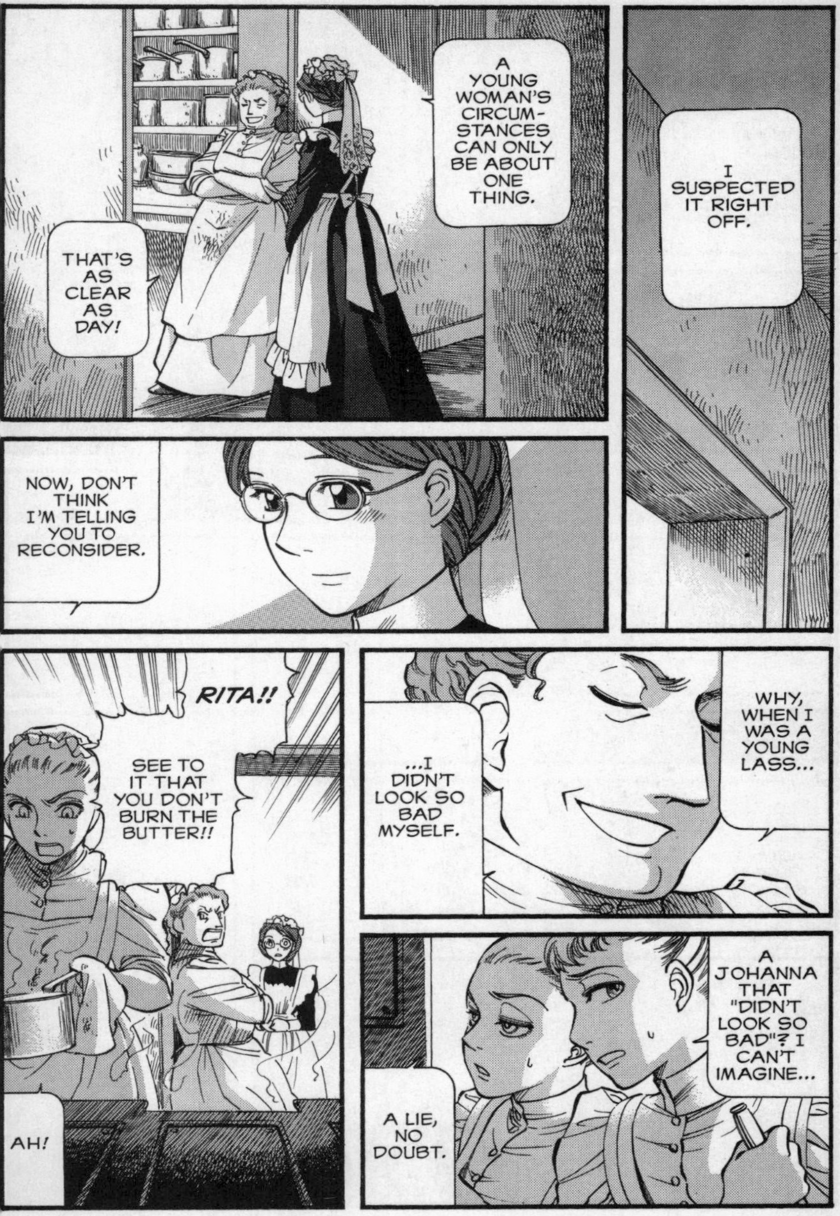
I SUSPECTED IT RIGHT OFF.
A YOUNG WOMAN'S CIRCUM-STANCES CAN ONLY BE ABOUT ONE THING.
THAT'S AS CLEAR AS DAY!
NOW, DON'T THINK I'M TELLING YOU TO RECONSIDER.
WHY, WHEN I WAS A YOUNG LASS...
...I DIDN'T LOOK SO BAD MYSELF.
A JOHANNA THAT "DIDN'T LOOK SO BAD"? I CAN'T IMAGINE...
A LIE, NO DOUBT.
RITA!!
SEE TO IT THAT YOU DON'T BURN THE BUTTER!!
AH!

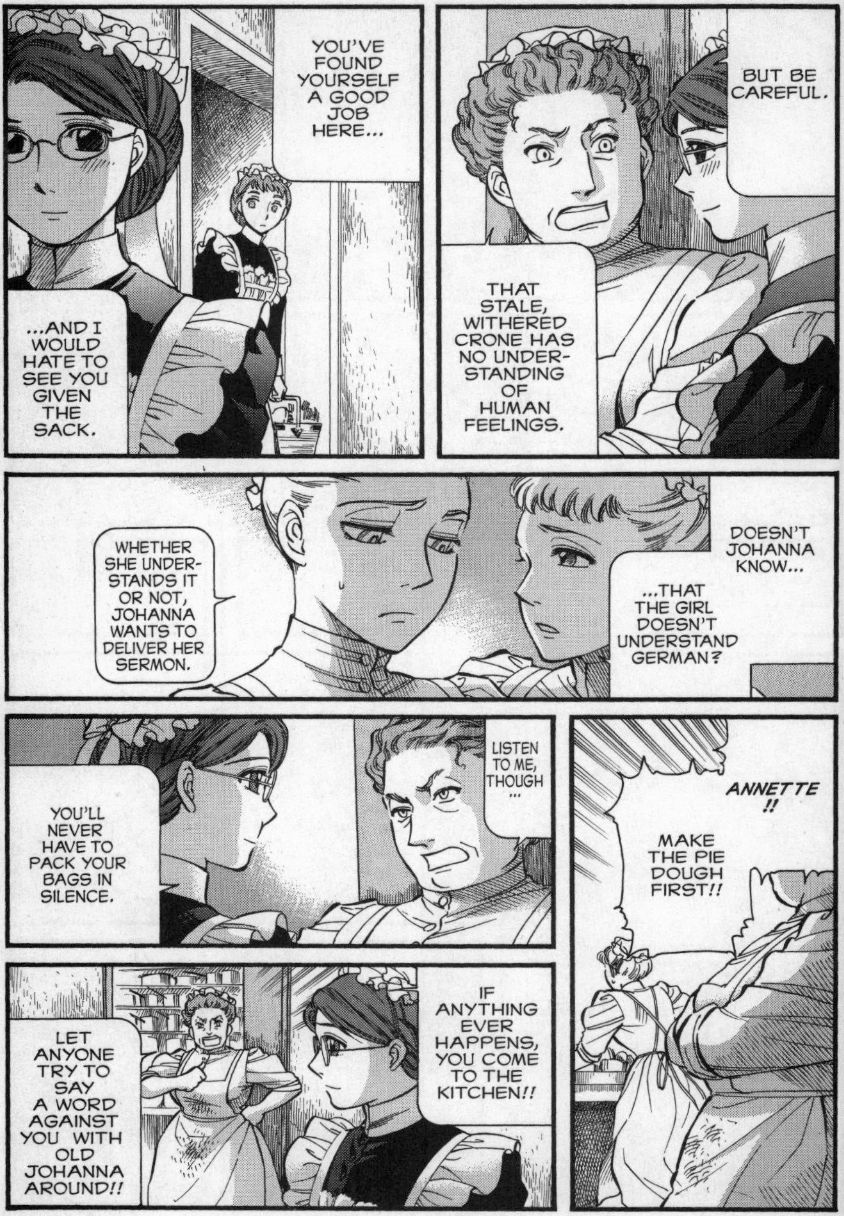
BUT BE CAREFUL.
THAT STALE, WITHERED CRONE HAS NO UNDER-STANDING OF HUMAN FEELINGS.
YOU'VE FOUND YOURSELF A GOOD JOB HERE...
...AND I WOULD HATE TO SEE YOU GIVEN THE SACK.
DOESN'T JOHANNA KNOW...
...THAT THE GIRL DOESN'T UNDERSTAND GERMAN?
WHETHER SHE UNDER-STANDS IT OR NOT, JOHANNA WANTS TO DELIVER HER SERMON.
ANNETTE !!
MAKE THE PIE DOUGH FIRST!!
LISTEN TO ME, THOUGH ...
YOU'LL NEVER HAVE TO PACK YOUR BAGS IN SILENCE.
IF ANYTHING EVER HAPPENS, YOU COME TO THE KITCHEN!!
LET ANYONE TRY TO SAY A WORD AGAINST YOU WITH OLD JOHANNA AROUND!!

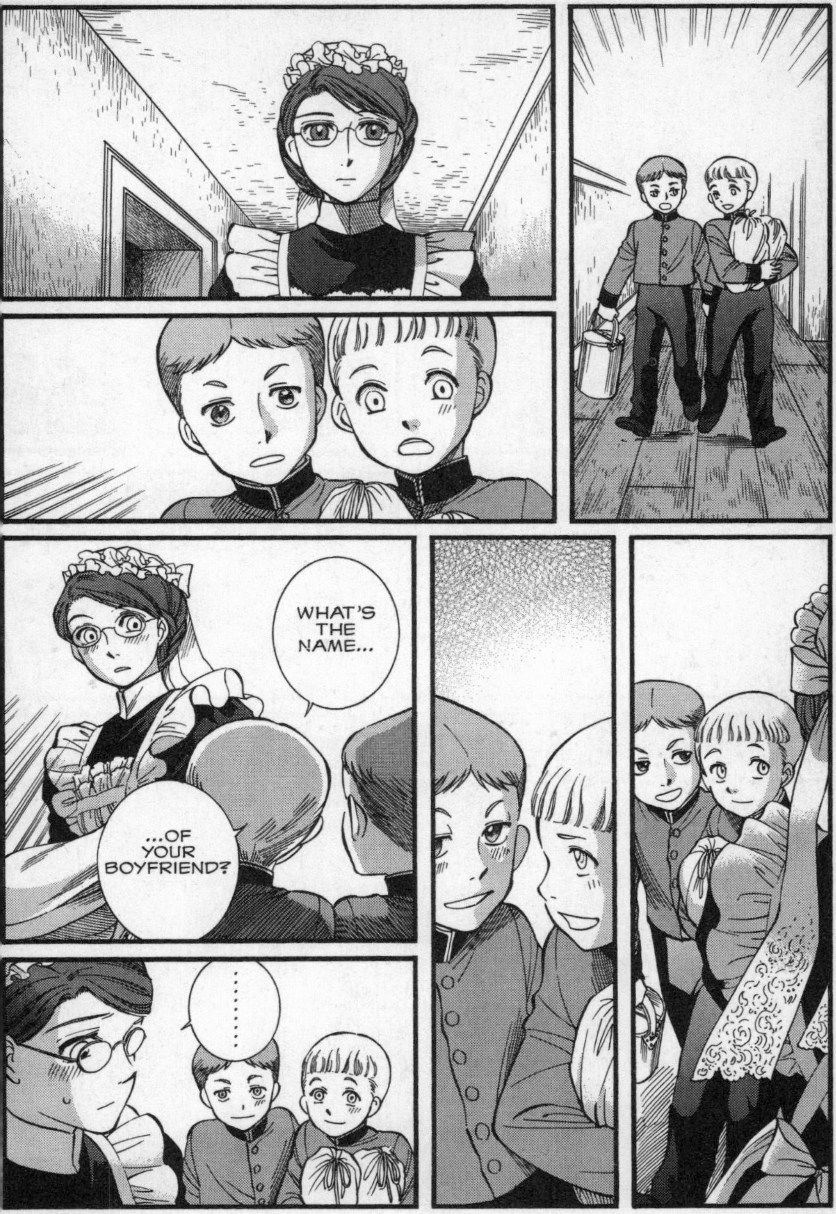
WHAT'S THE NAME...
...OF YOUR BOYFRIEND?
......

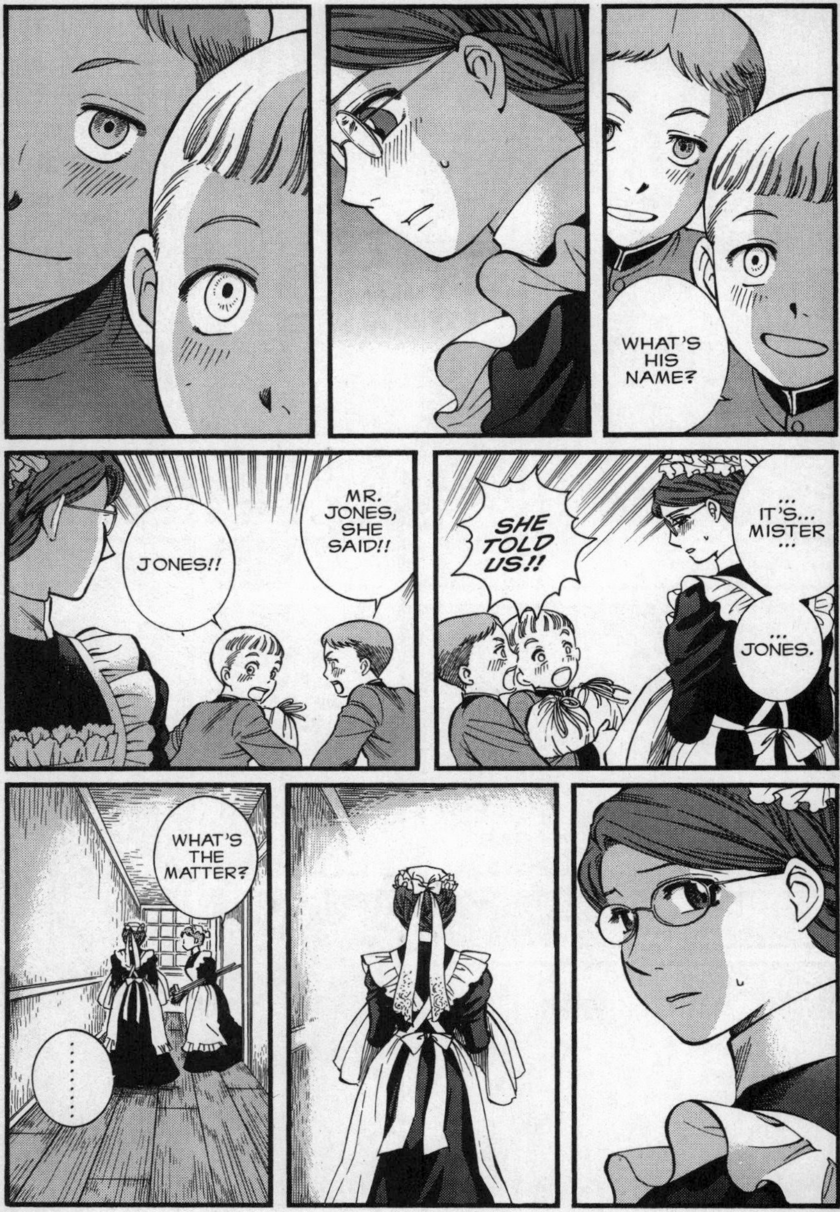
WHAT'S HIS NAME?
... IT'S... MISTER ...
... JONES.
SHE TOLD US!!
MR. JONES, SHE SAID!!
JONES!!
WHAT'S THE MATTER?
......

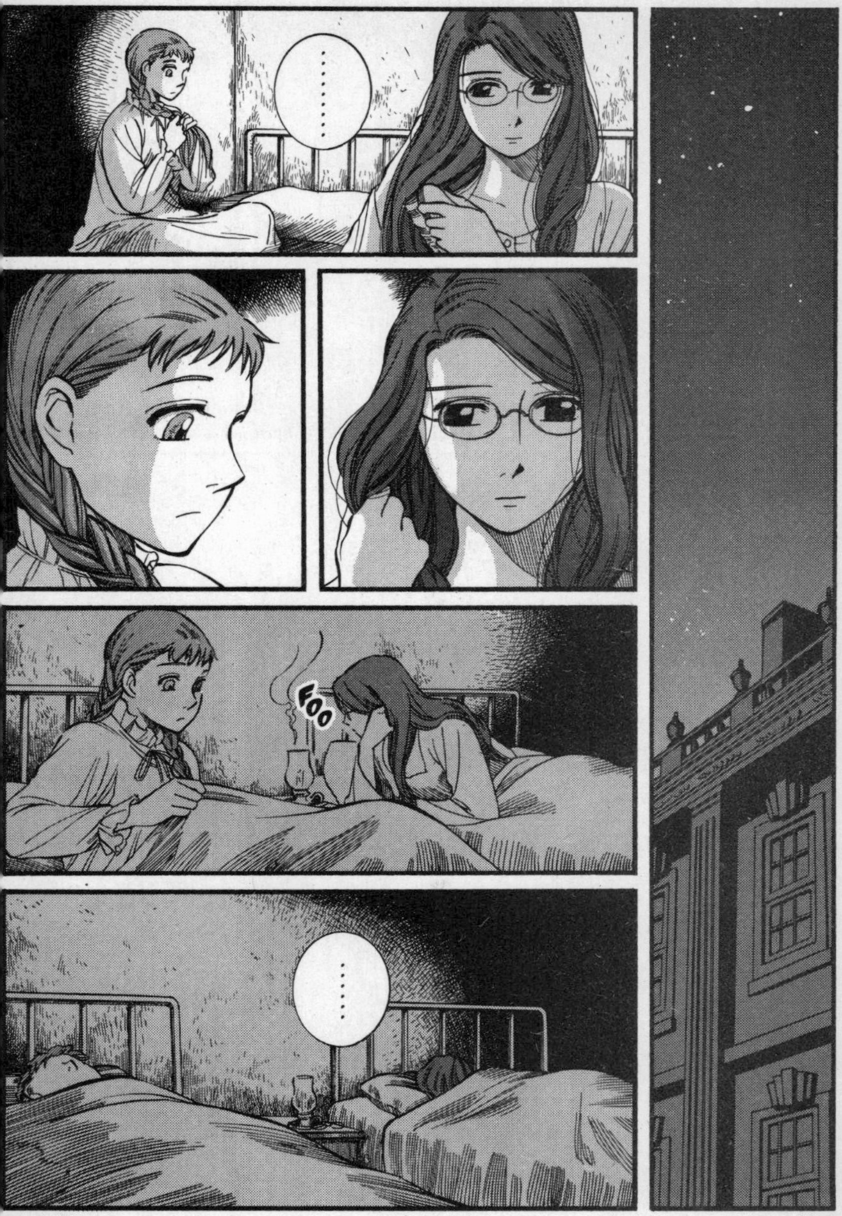
……
FOO
……

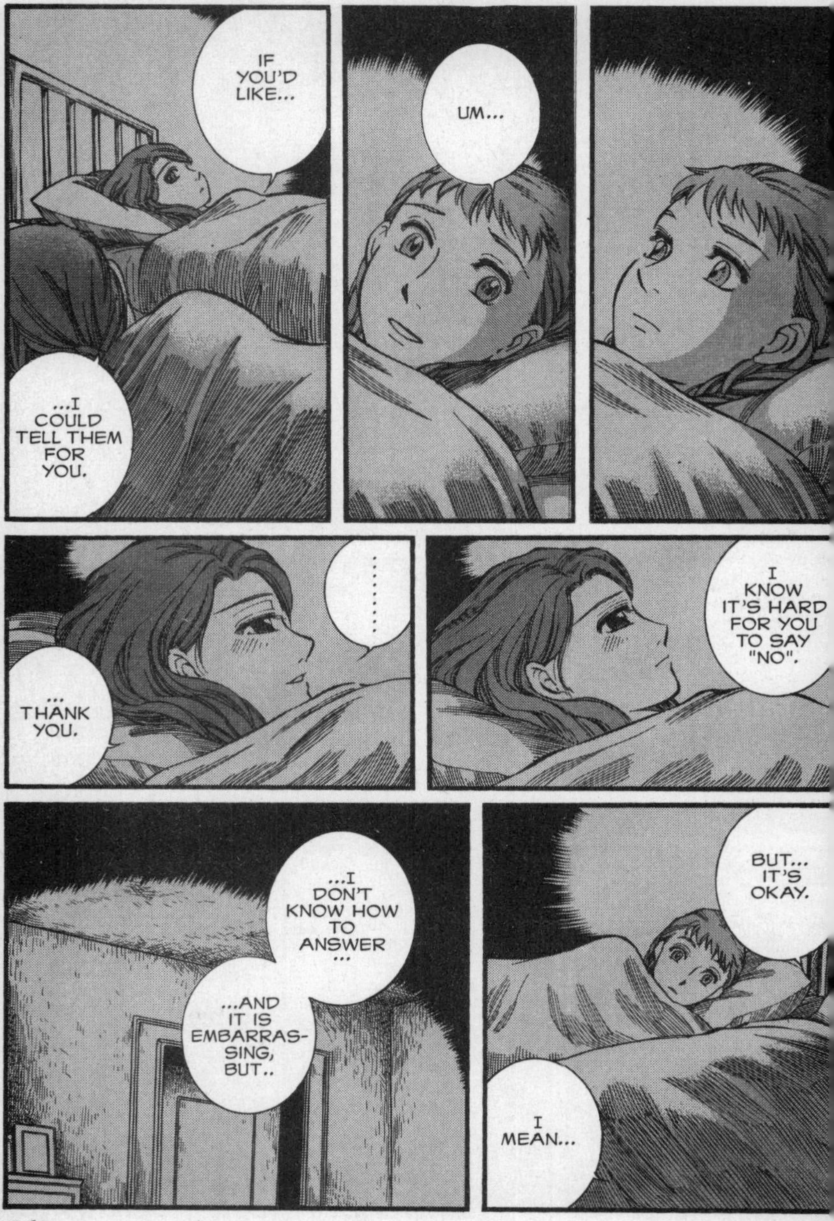
UM...
IF YOU'D LIKE...
...I COULD TELL THEM FOR YOU.
I KNOW IT'S HARD FOR YOU TO SAY "NO".
......
... THANK YOU.
BUT... IT'S OKAY.
I MEAN...
...I DON'T KNOW HOW TO ANSWER ...
...AND IT IS EMBARRAS-SING, BUT..

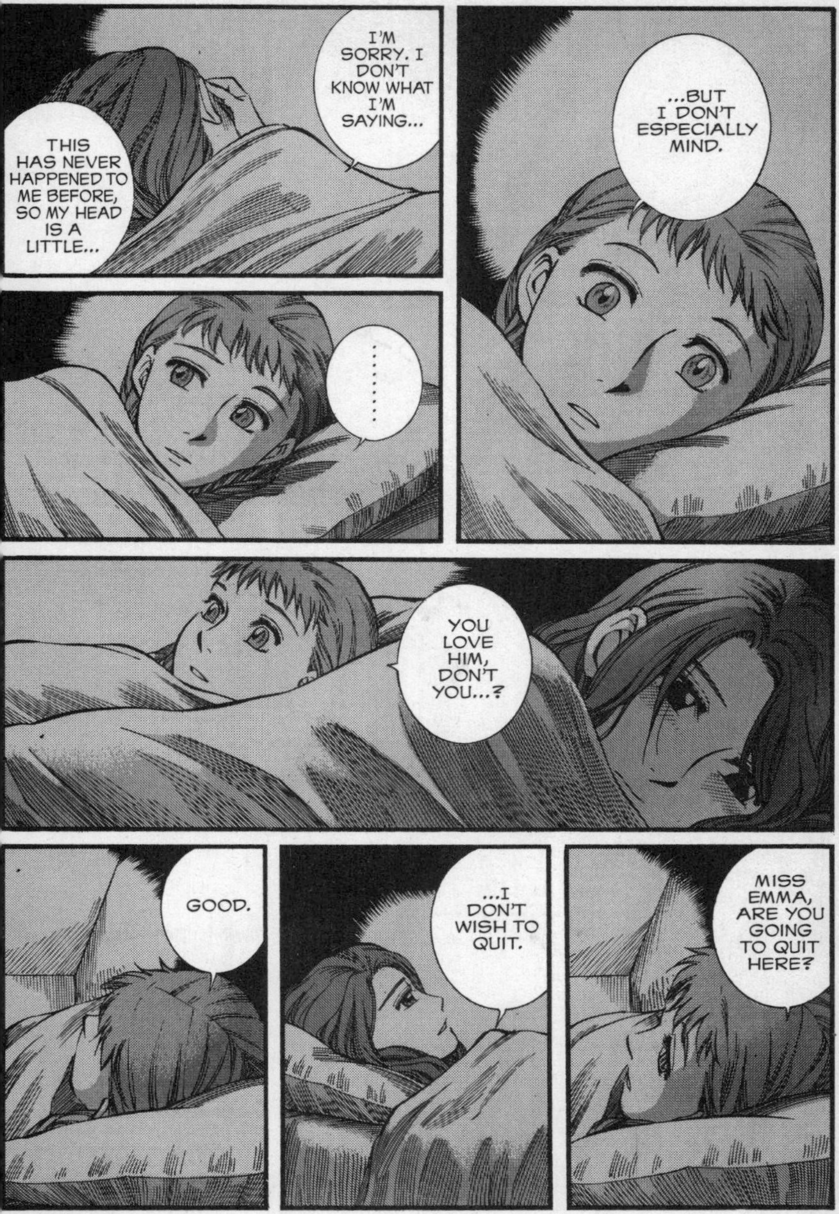
...BUT I DON'T ESPECIALLY MIND.
I'M SORRY. I DON'T KNOW WHAT I'M SAYING...
THIS HAS NEVER HAPPENED TO ME BEFORE, SO MY HEAD IS A LITTLE...
......
YOU LOVE HIM, DON'T YOU...?
MISS EMMA, ARE YOU GOING TO QUIT HERE?
...I DON'T WISH TO QUIT.
GOOD.

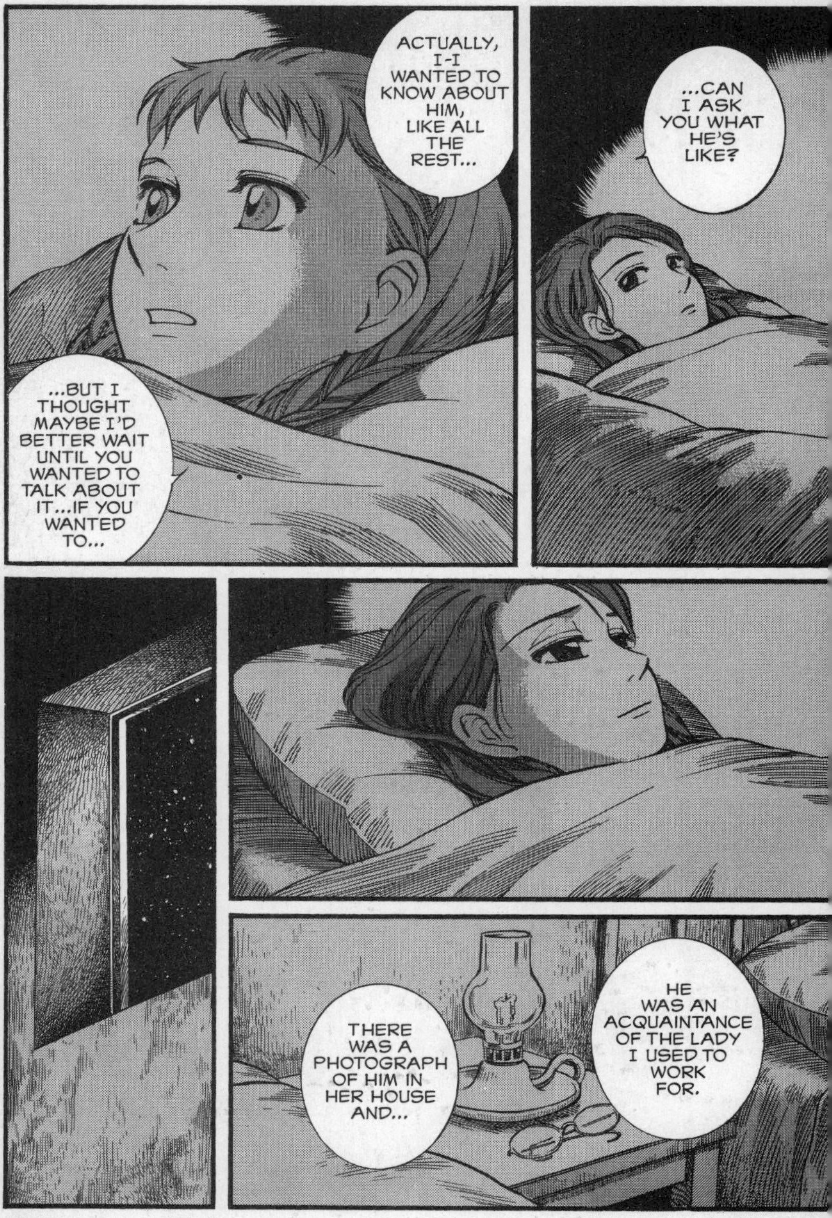
...CAN I ASK YOU WHAT HE'S LIKE?
ACTUALLY, I-I WANTED TO KNOW ABOUT HIM, LIKE ALL THE REST...
...BUT I THOUGHT MAYBE I'D BETTER WAIT UNTIL YOU WANTED TO TALK ABOUT IT...IF YOU WANTED TO...
HE WAS AN ACQUAINTANCE OF THE LADY I USED TO WORK FOR.
THERE WAS A PHOTOGRAPH OF HIM IN HER HOUSE AND...

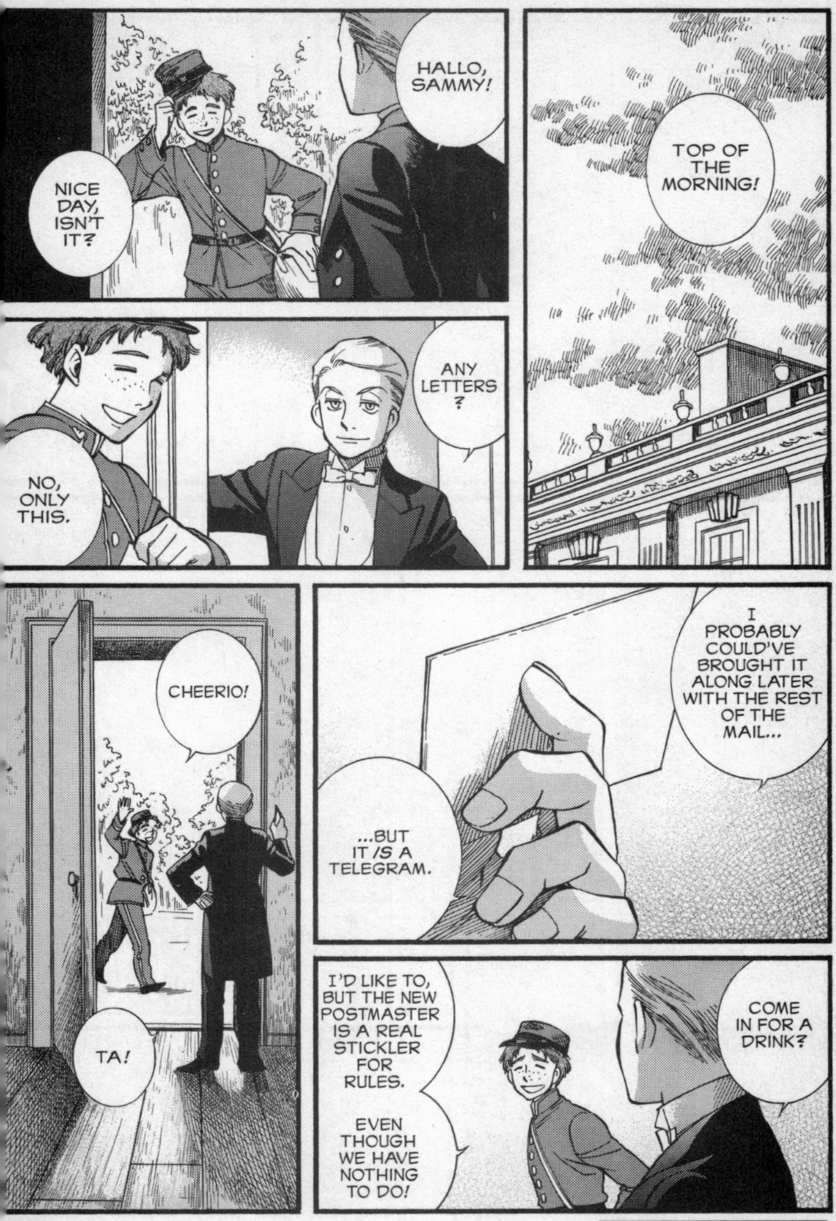
TOP OF THE MORNING!
HALLO, SAMMY!
NICE DAY, ISN'T IT?
ANY LETTERS?
NO, ONLY THIS.
I PROBABLY COULD'VE BROUGHT IT ALONG LATER WITH THE REST OF THE MAIL...
...BUT IT *IS* A TELEGRAM.
COME IN FOR A DRINK?
I'D LIKE TO, BUT THE NEW POSTMASTER IS A REAL STICKLER FOR RULES.
EVEN THOUGH WE HAVE NOTHING TO DO!
CHEERIO!
TA!

Chapter Thirty Nine: The End

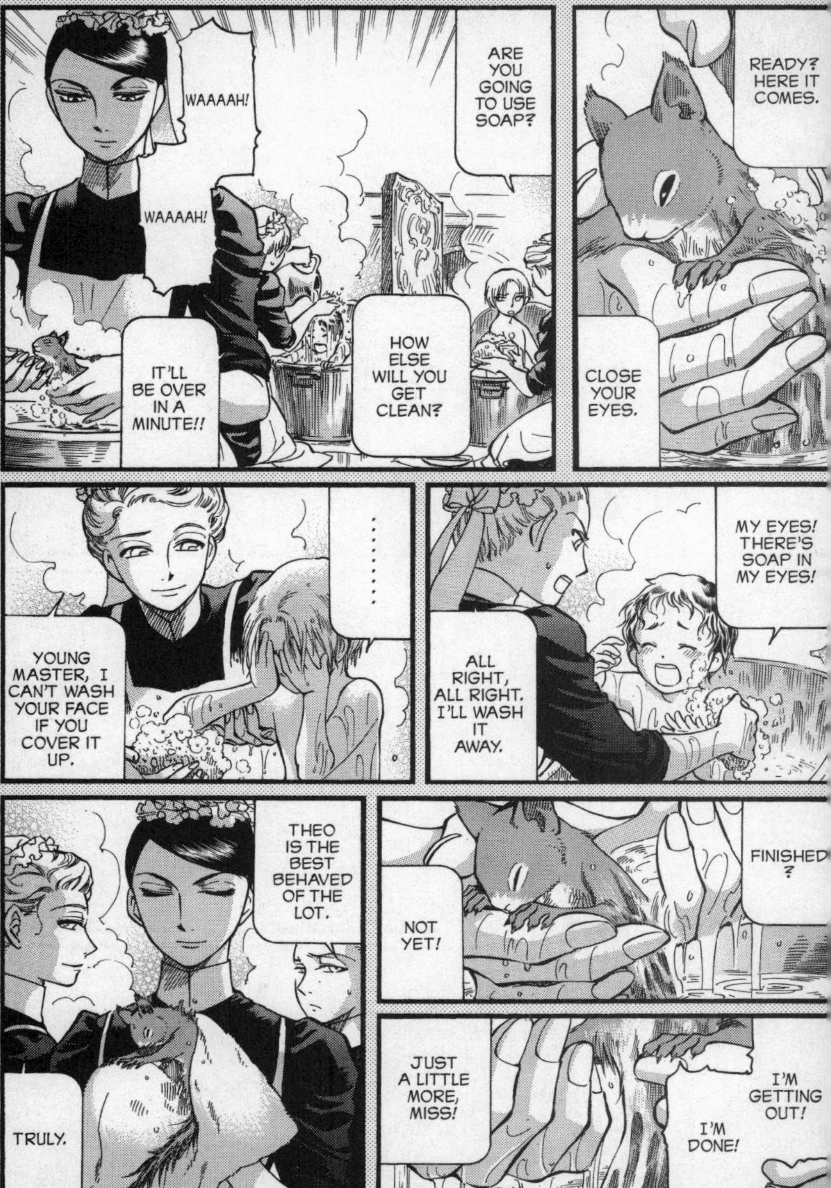
READY? HERE IT COMES.
CLOSE YOUR EYES.
ARE YOU GOING TO USE SOAP?
HOW ELSE WILL YOU GET CLEAN?
WAAAAH!
WAAAAH!
IT'LL BE OVER IN A MINUTE!!
MY EYES! THERE'S SOAP IN MY EYES!
ALL RIGHT, ALL RIGHT. I'LL WASH IT AWAY.
......
YOUNG MASTER, I CAN'T WASH YOUR FACE IF YOU COVER IT UP.
FINISHED?
NOT YET!
I'M GETTING OUT!
I'M DONE!
JUST A LITTLE MORE, MISS!
THEO IS THE BEST BEHAVED OF THE LOT.
TRULY.

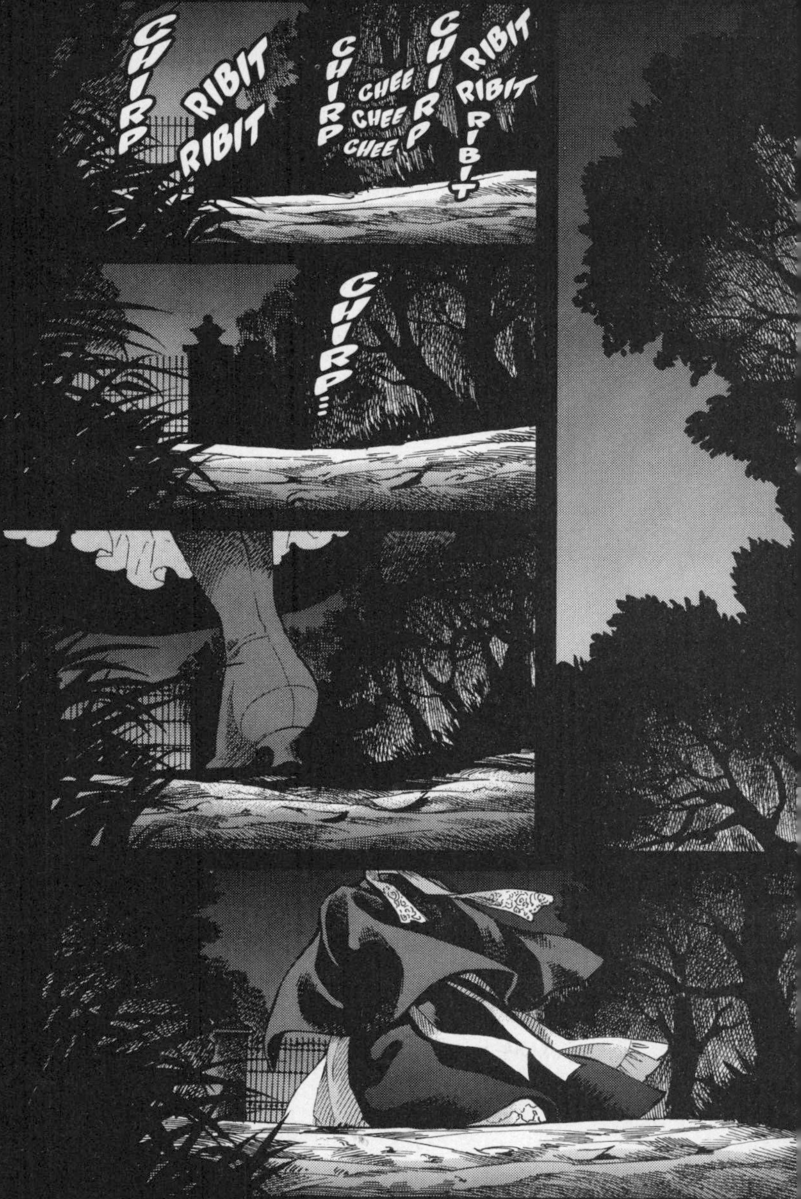
RIBIT
RIBIT
RIBIT
CHIRP
CHEE
CHEE
CHEE
CHIRP
RIBIT
RIBIT
CHIRP
CHIRP...

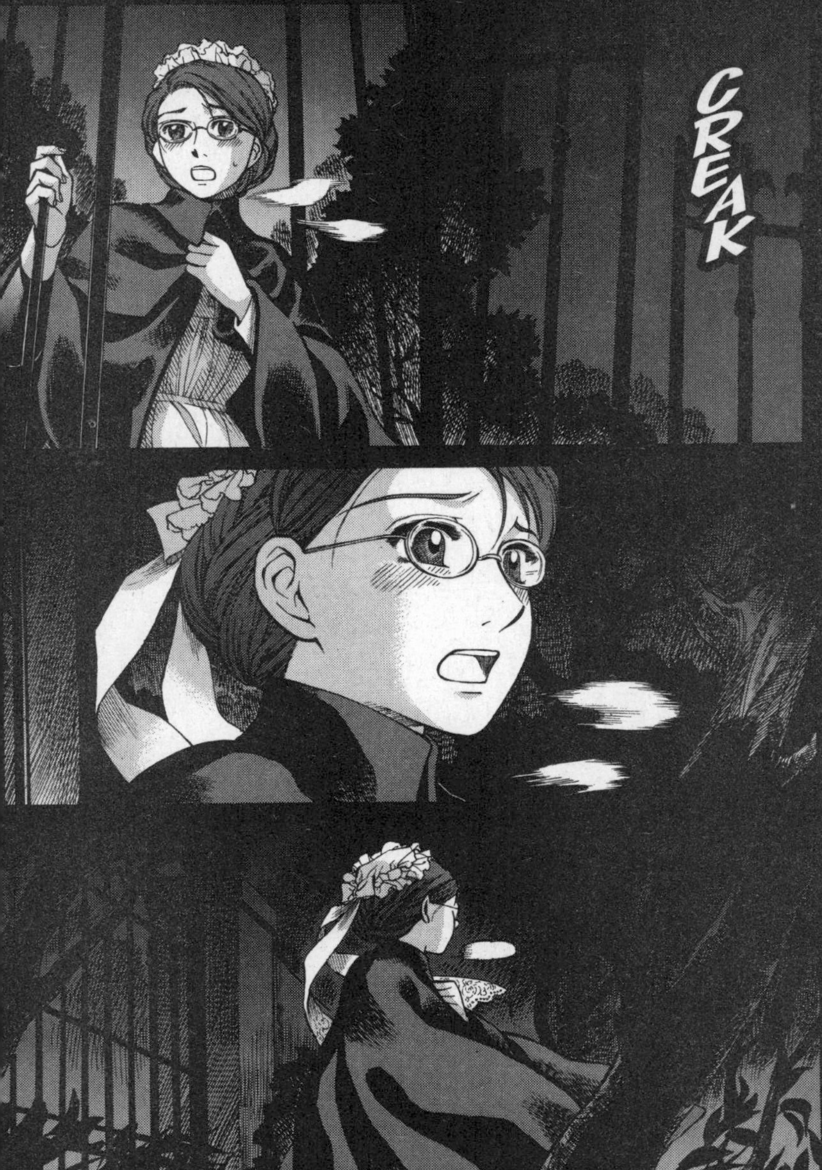
CREAK

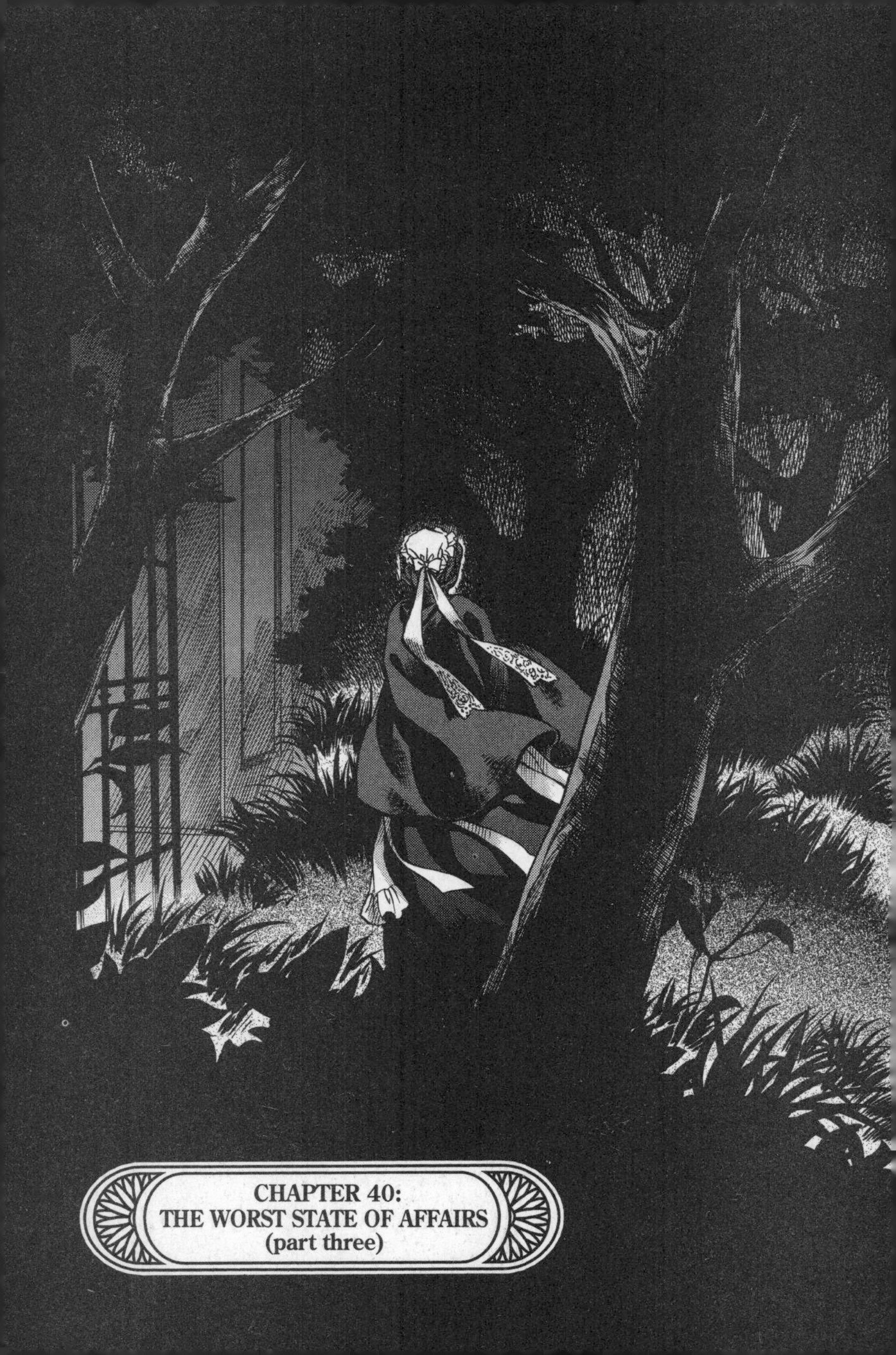
CHAPTER 40:
THE WORST STATE OF AFFAIRS
(part three)

THERE'S A TELEGRAM ...

... FOR YOU.

... THANK YOU.

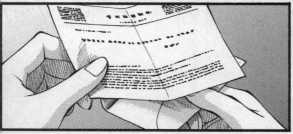

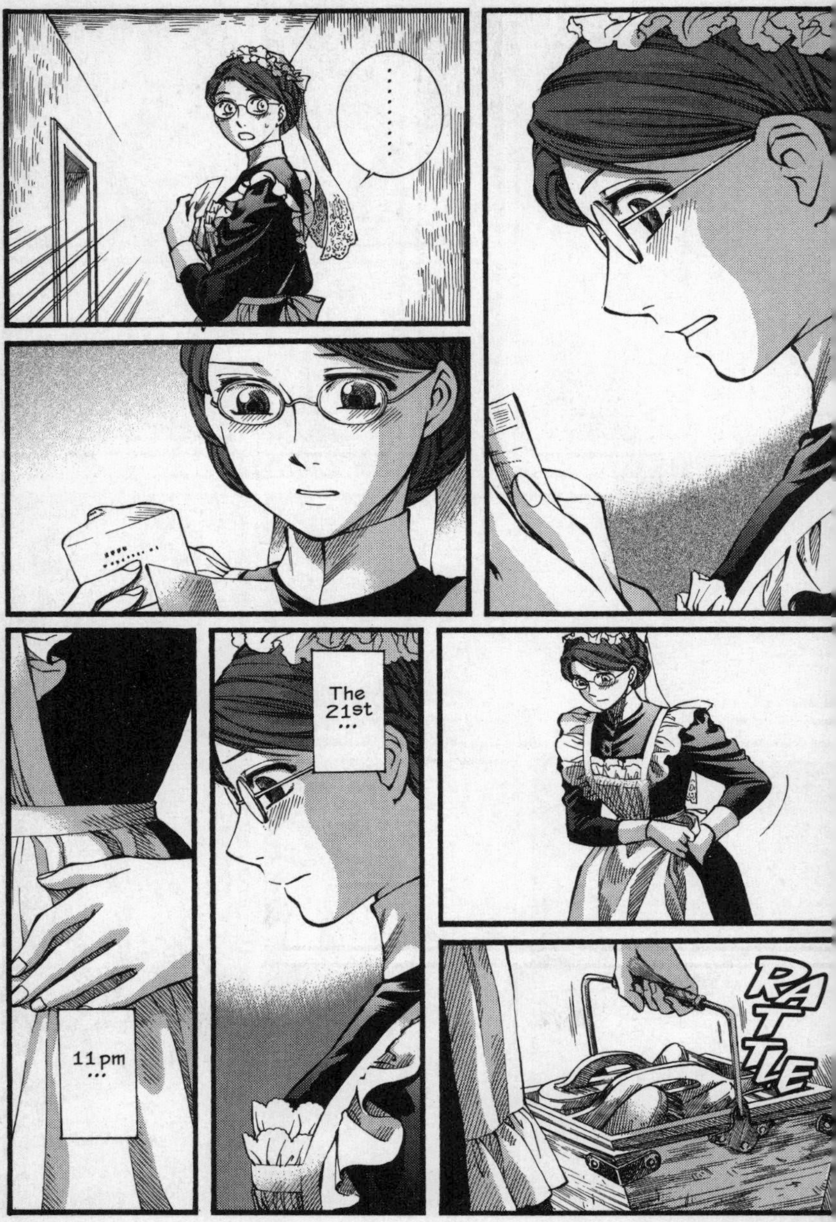
......
RATTLE
The 21st ...
11pm ...

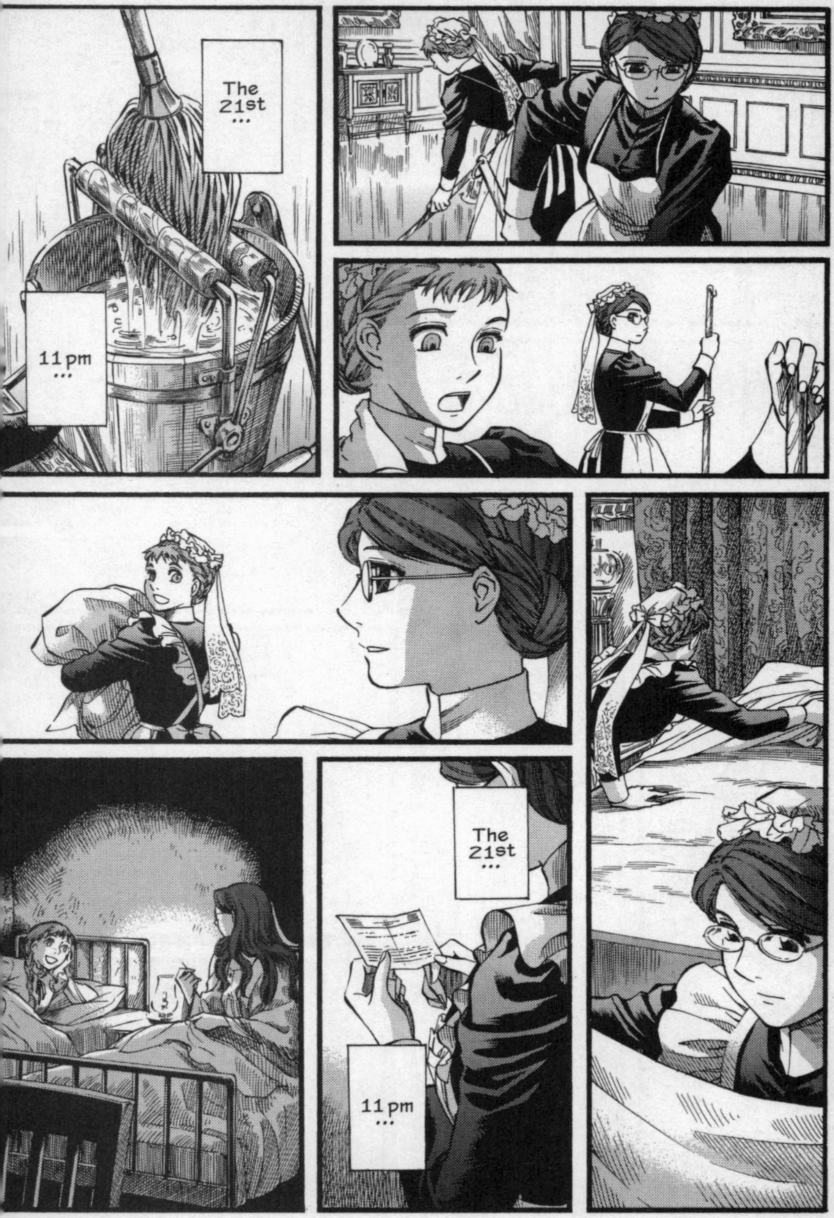
The 21st ...
11 pm ...
The 21st ...
11 pm ...

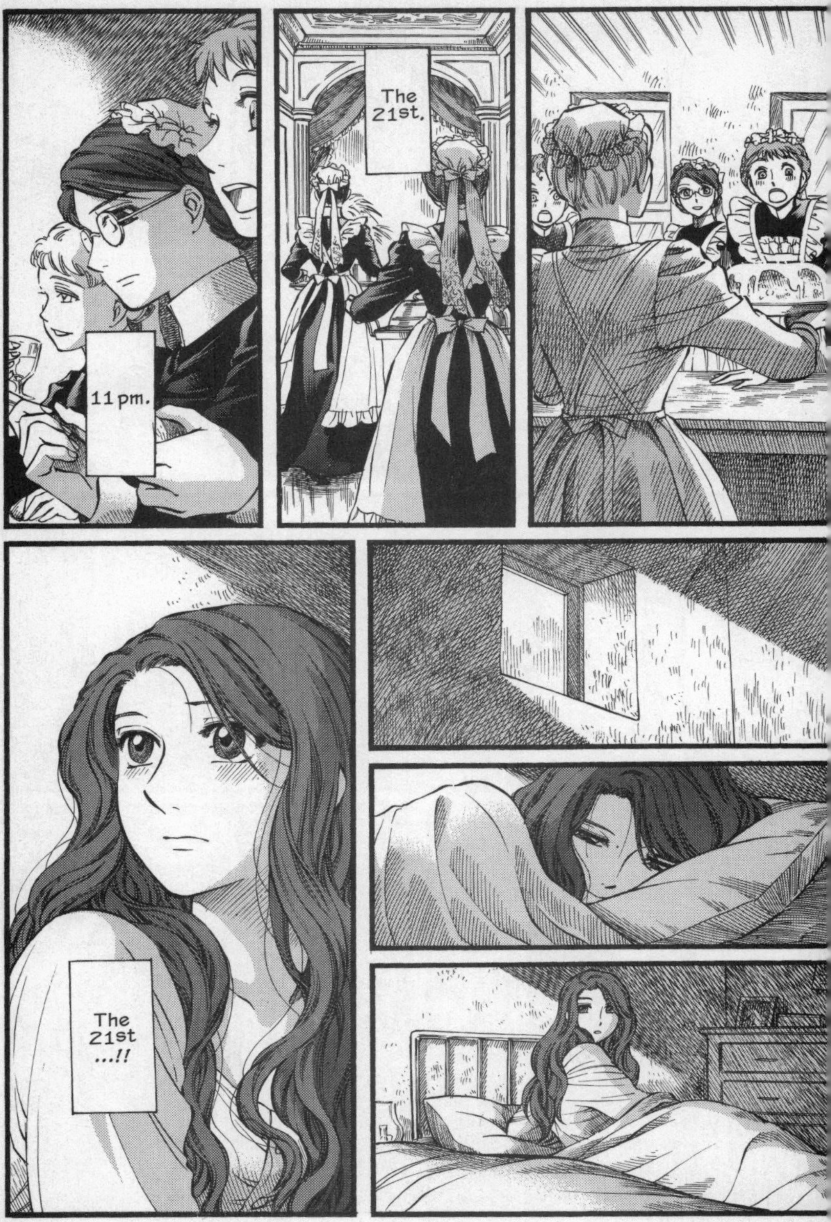
The 21st.
11 pm.
The 21st ...!!

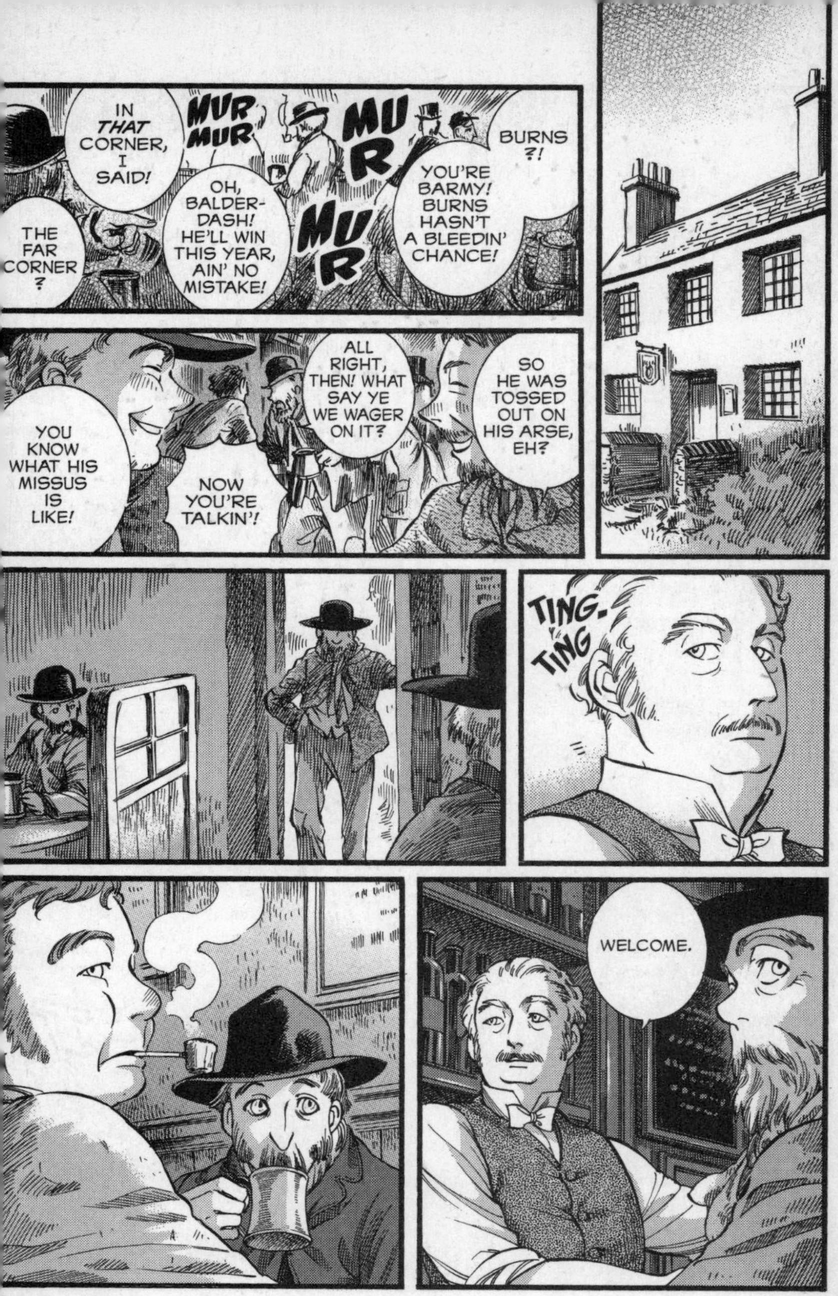
BURNS ?!
YOU'RE BARMY! BURNS HASN'T A BLEEDIN' CHANCE!
MUR MUR
MUR MUR
MUR MUR
OH, BALDER-DASH! HE'LL WIN THIS YEAR, AIN' NO MISTAKE!
IN THAT CORNER, I SAID!
THE FAR CORNER?
SO HE WAS TOSSED OUT ON HIS ARSE, EH?
ALL RIGHT, THEN! WHAT SAY YE WE WAGER ON IT?
NOW YOU'RE TALKIN'!
YOU KNOW WHAT HIS MISSUS IS LIKE!
TING. TING
WELCOME.

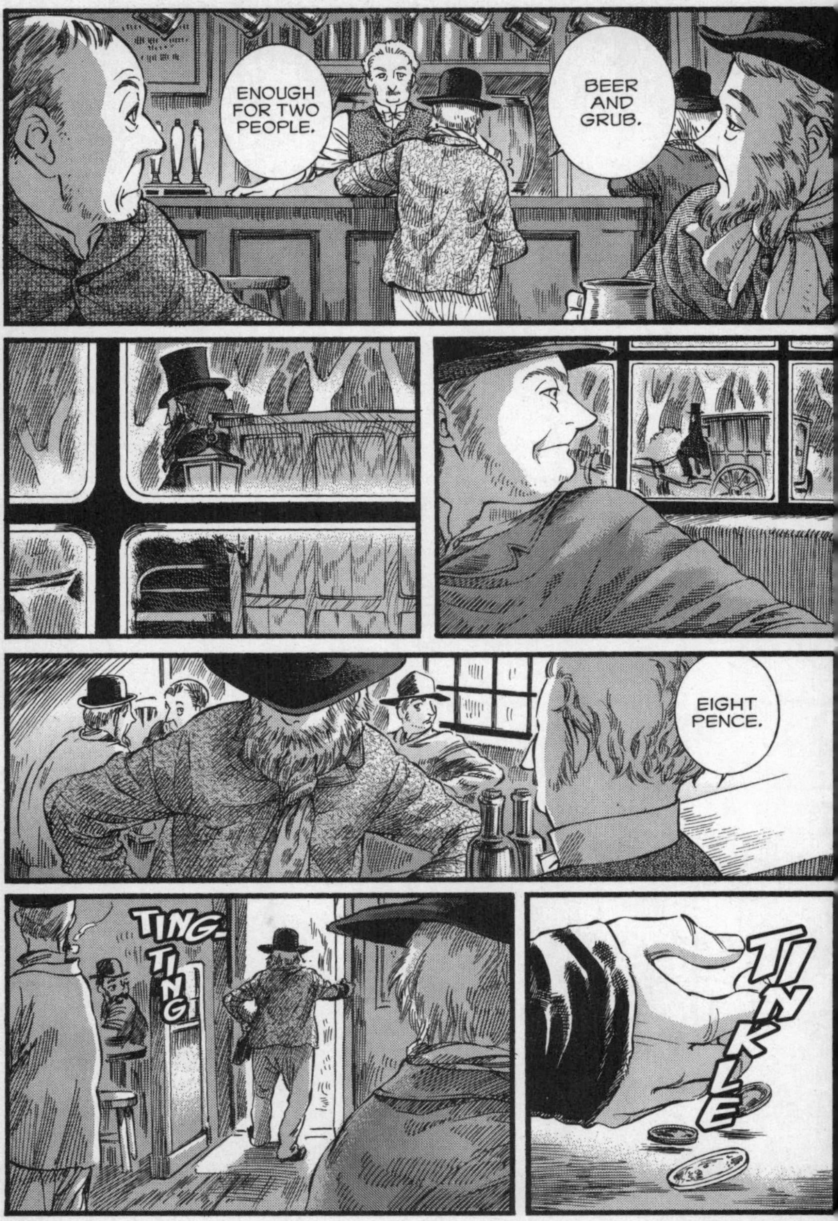
BEER AND GRUB.
ENOUGH FOR TWO PEOPLE.
EIGHT PENCE.
TINKLE
TING-TING TING

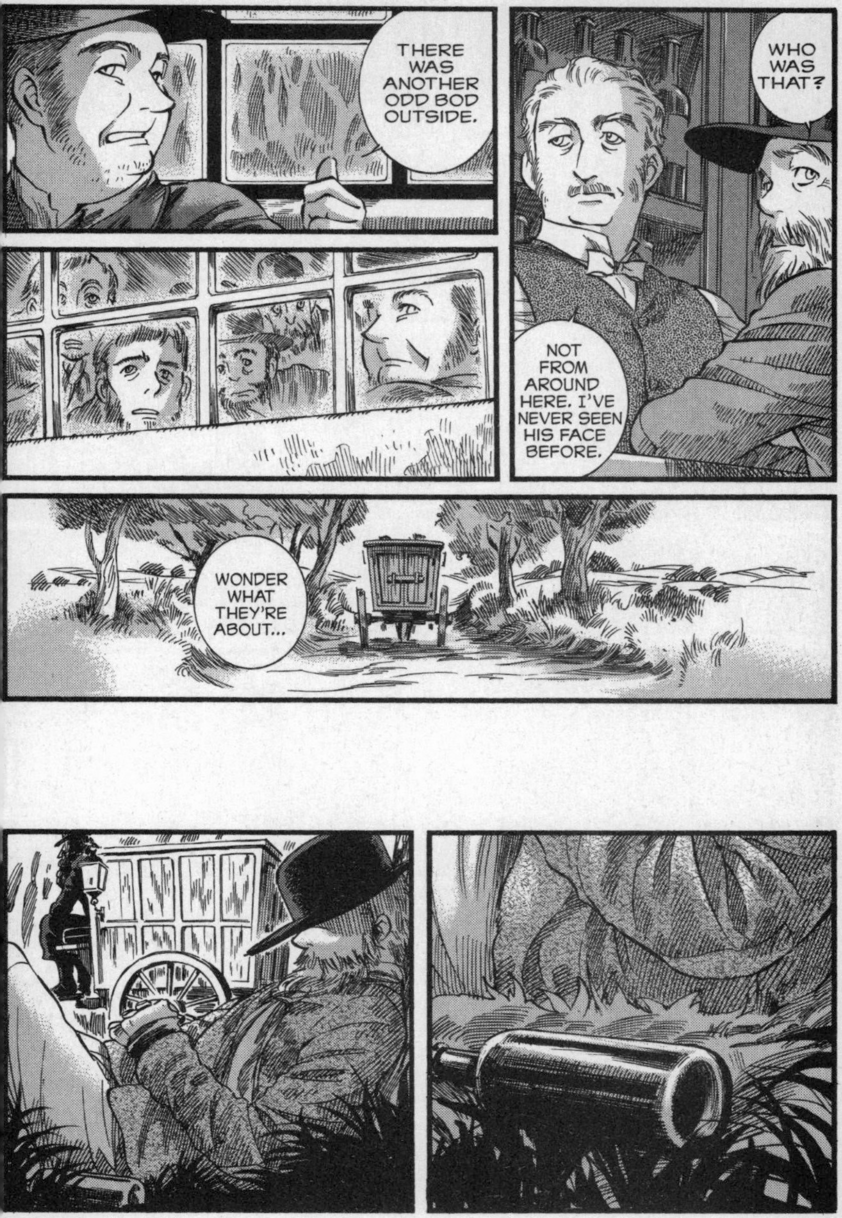
THERE WAS ANOTHER ODD BOD OUTSIDE.
WHO WAS THAT?
NOT FROM AROUND HERE. I'VE NEVER SEEN HIS FACE BEFORE.
WONDER WHAT THEY'RE ABOUT...

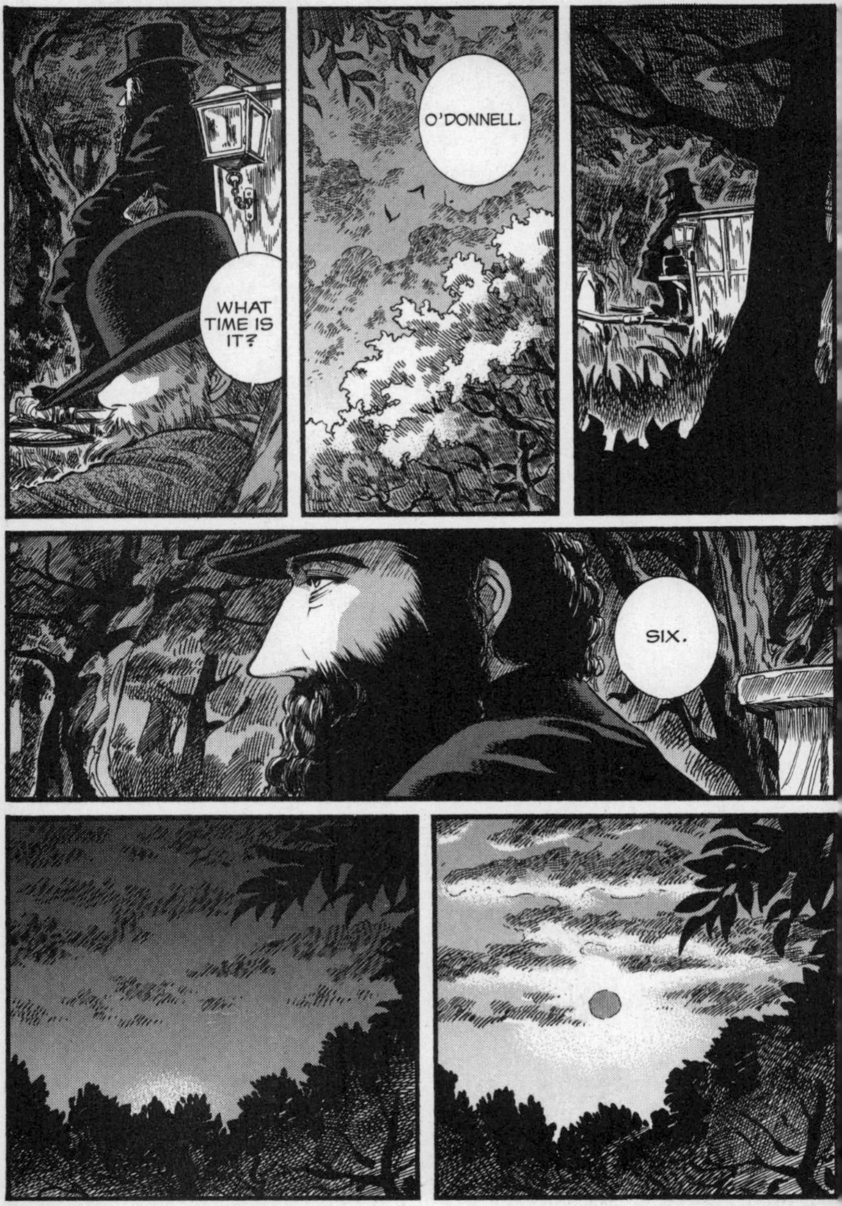
O'DONNELL.
WHAT TIME IS IT?
SIX.

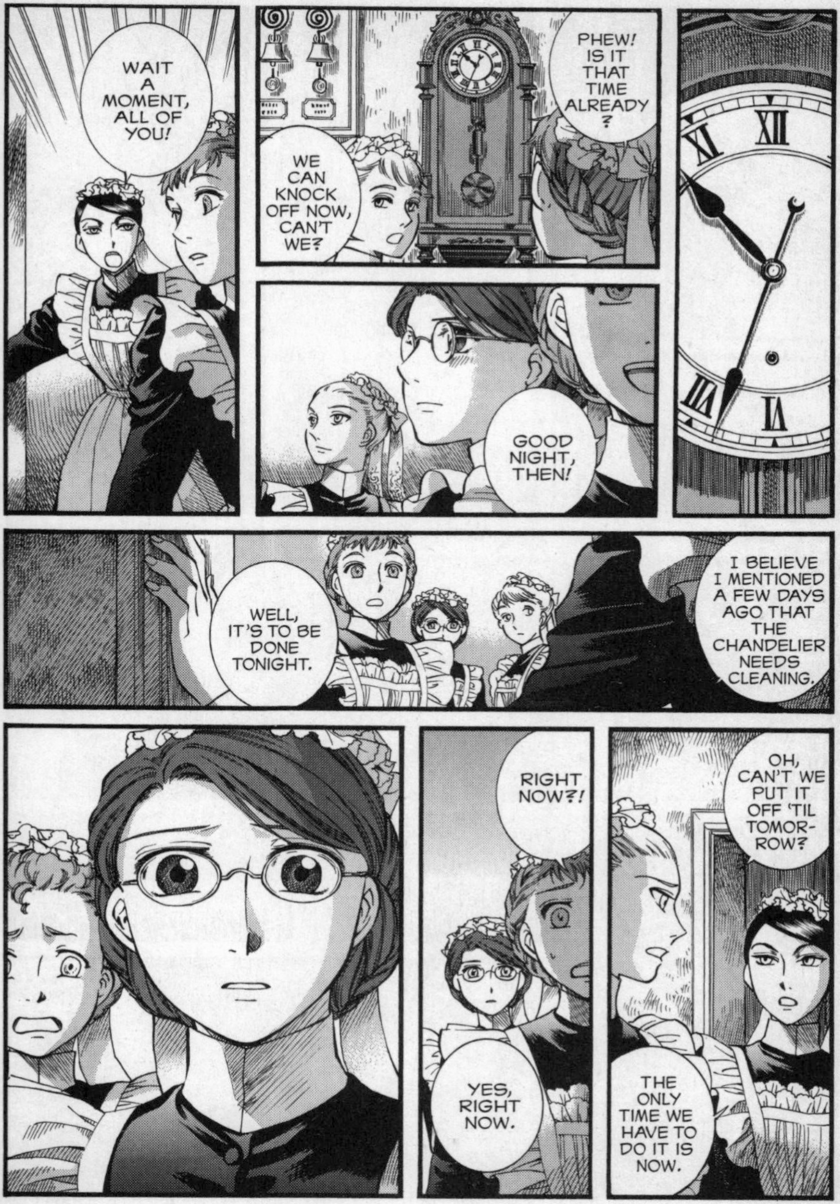
PHEW! IS IT THAT TIME ALREADY?
WE CAN KNOCK OFF NOW, CAN'T WE?
GOOD NIGHT, THEN!
WAIT A MOMENT, ALL OF YOU!
I BELIEVE I MENTIONED A FEW DAYS AGO THAT THE CHANDELIER NEEDS CLEANING.
WELL, IT'S TO BE DONE TONIGHT.
OH, CAN'T WE PUT IT OFF 'TIL TOMOR-ROW?
THE ONLY TIME WE HAVE TO DO IT IS NOW.
RIGHT NOW?!
YES, RIGHT NOW.

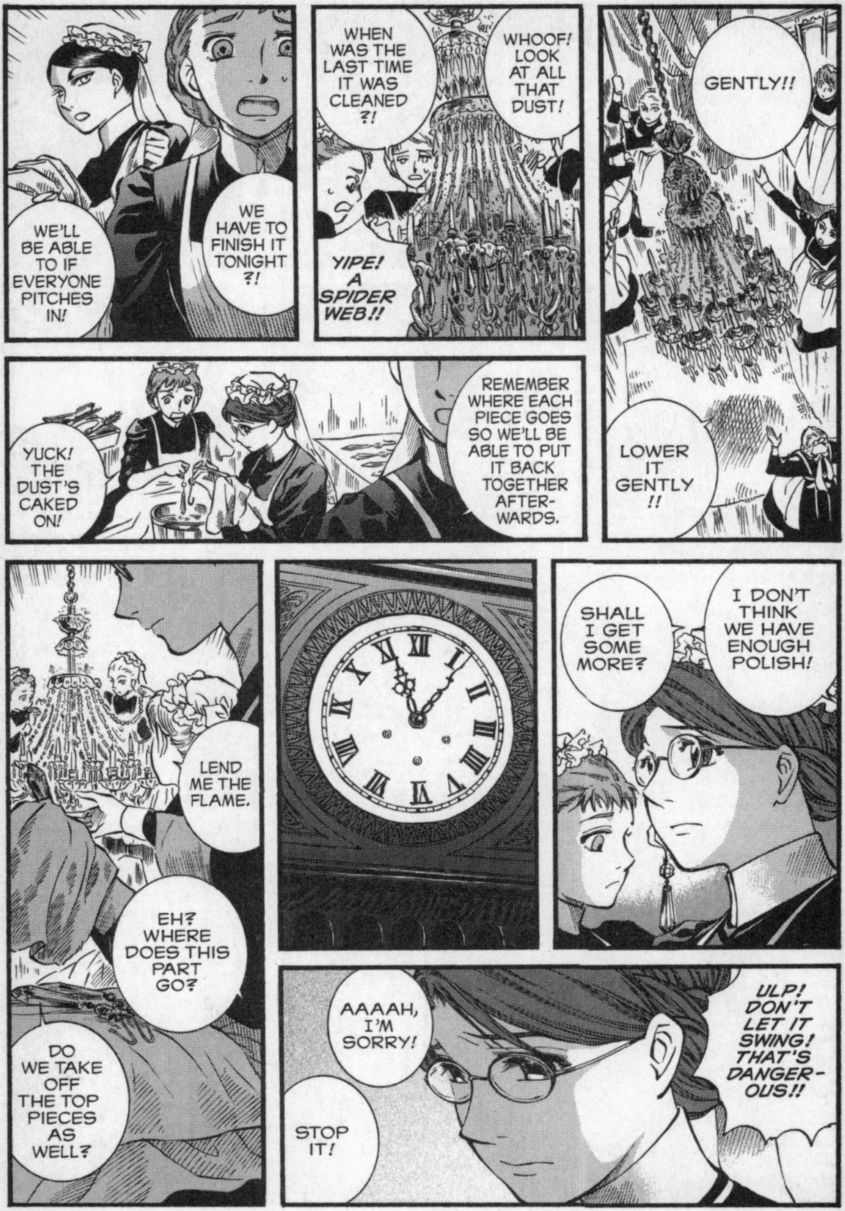
GENTLY!!
LOWER IT GENTLY!!
WHOOF! LOOK AT ALL THAT DUST!
WHEN WAS THE LAST TIME IT WAS CLEANED?!
YIPE! A SPIDER WEB!!
WE HAVE TO FINISH IT TONIGHT?!
WE'LL BE ABLE TO IF EVERYONE PITCHES IN!
REMEMBER WHERE EACH PIECE GOES SO WE'LL BE ABLE TO PUT IT BACK TOGETHER AFTER-WARDS.
YUCK! THE DUST'S CAKED ON!
I DON'T THINK WE HAVE ENOUGH POLISH!
SHALL I GET SOME MORE?
ULP! DON'T LET IT SWING! THAT'S DANGER-OUS!!
AAAAH, I'M SORRY!
STOP IT!
LEND ME THE FLAME.
EH? WHERE DOES THIS PART GO?
DO WE TAKE OFF THE TOP PIECES AS WELL?

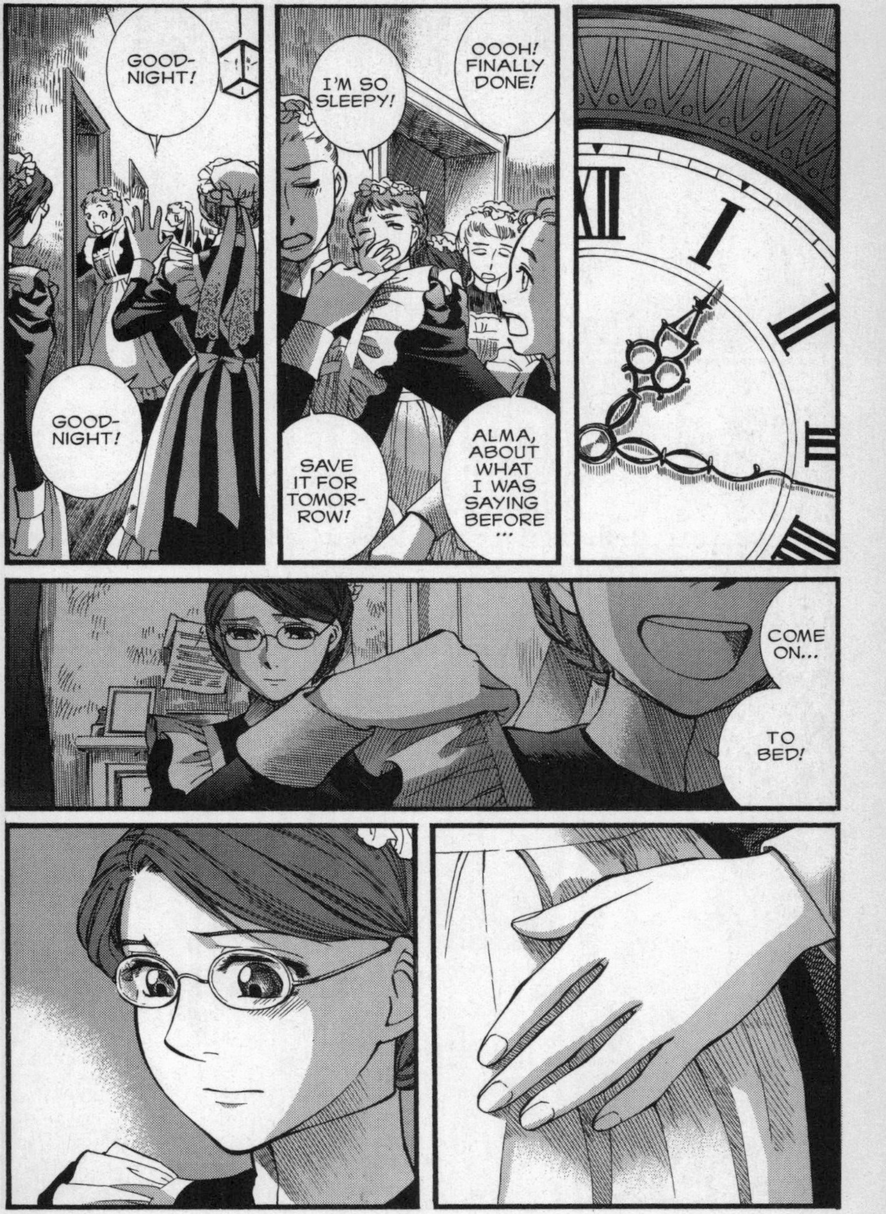
OOOH! FINALLY DONE!
I'M SO SLEEPY!
ALMA, ABOUT WHAT I WAS SAYING BEFORE...
SAVE IT FOR TOMORROW!
GOOD-NIGHT!
GOOD-NIGHT!
COME ON...
TO BED!

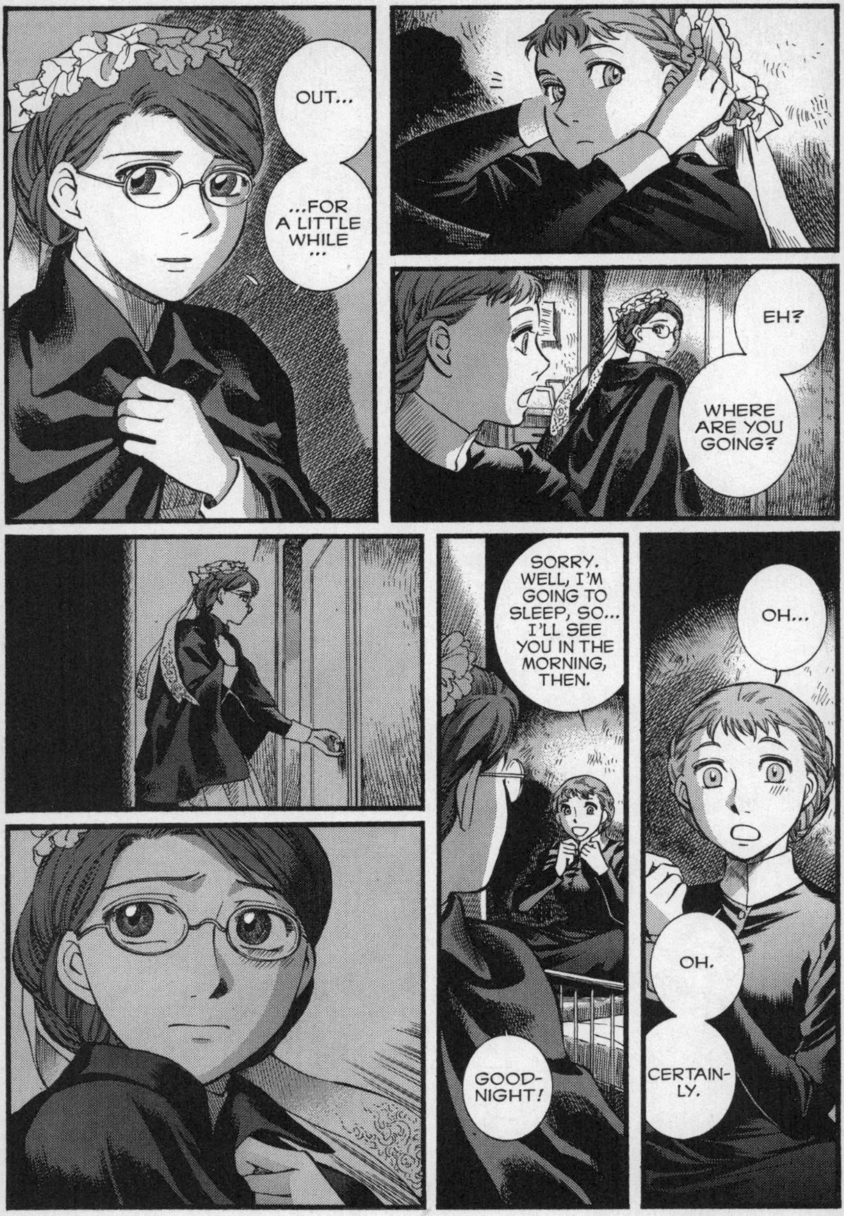
EH?
WHERE ARE YOU GOING?
OUT...
...FOR A LITTLE WHILE ...
OH...
OH.
CERTAIN-LY.
SORRY. WELL, I'M GOING TO SLEEP, SO... I'LL SEE YOU IN THE MORNING, THEN.
GOOD-NIGHT!

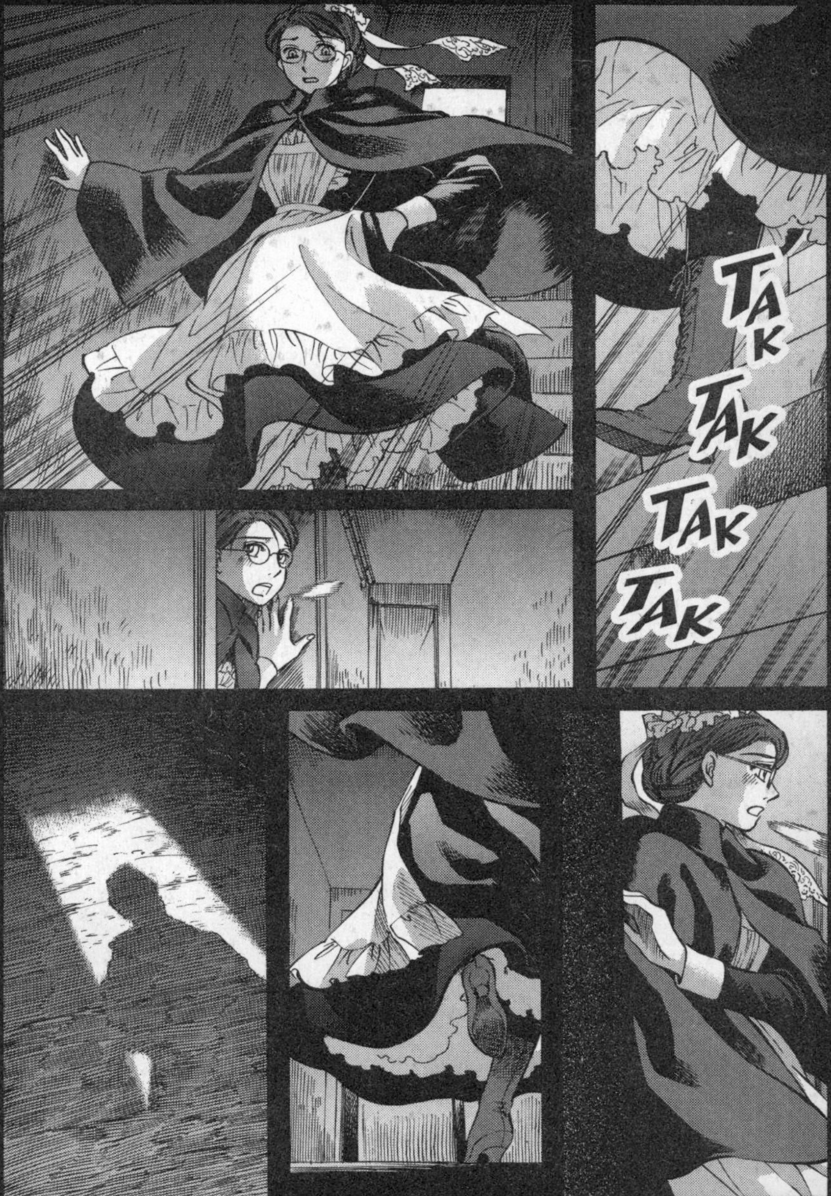
TAK
TAK
TAK
TAK

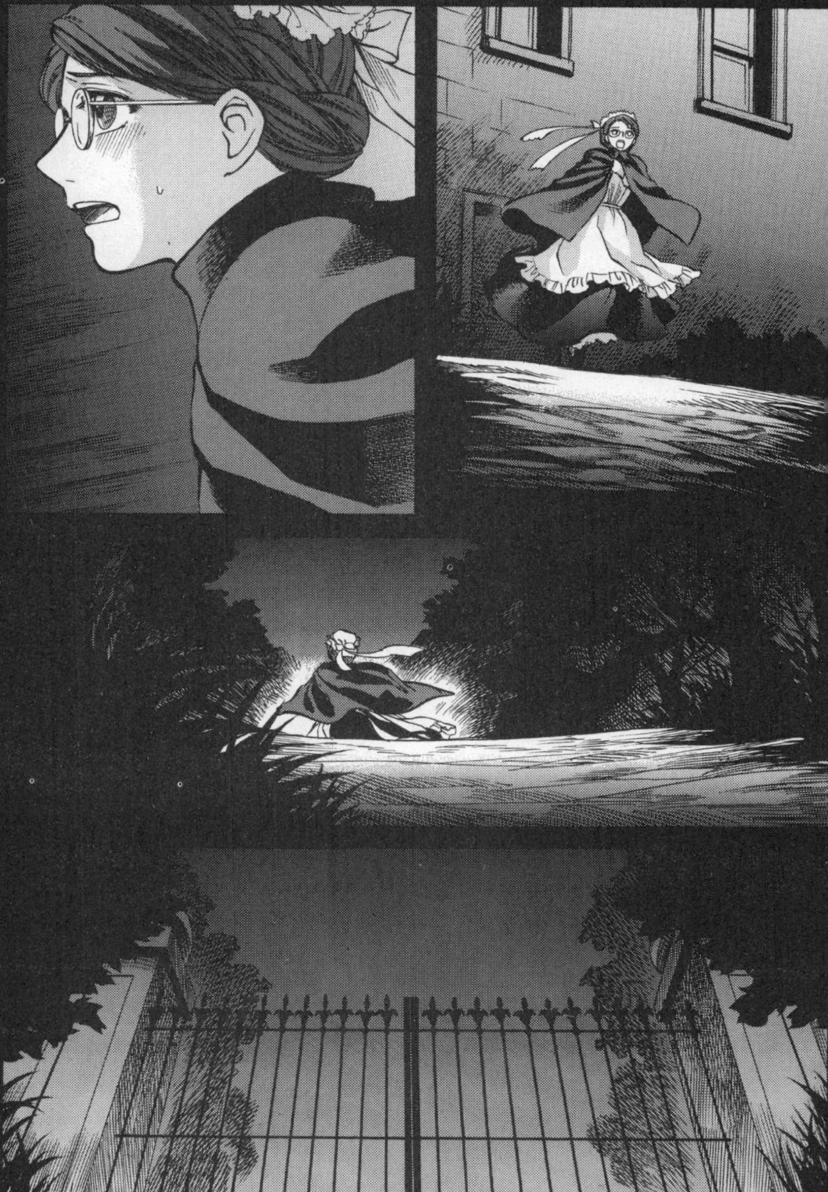

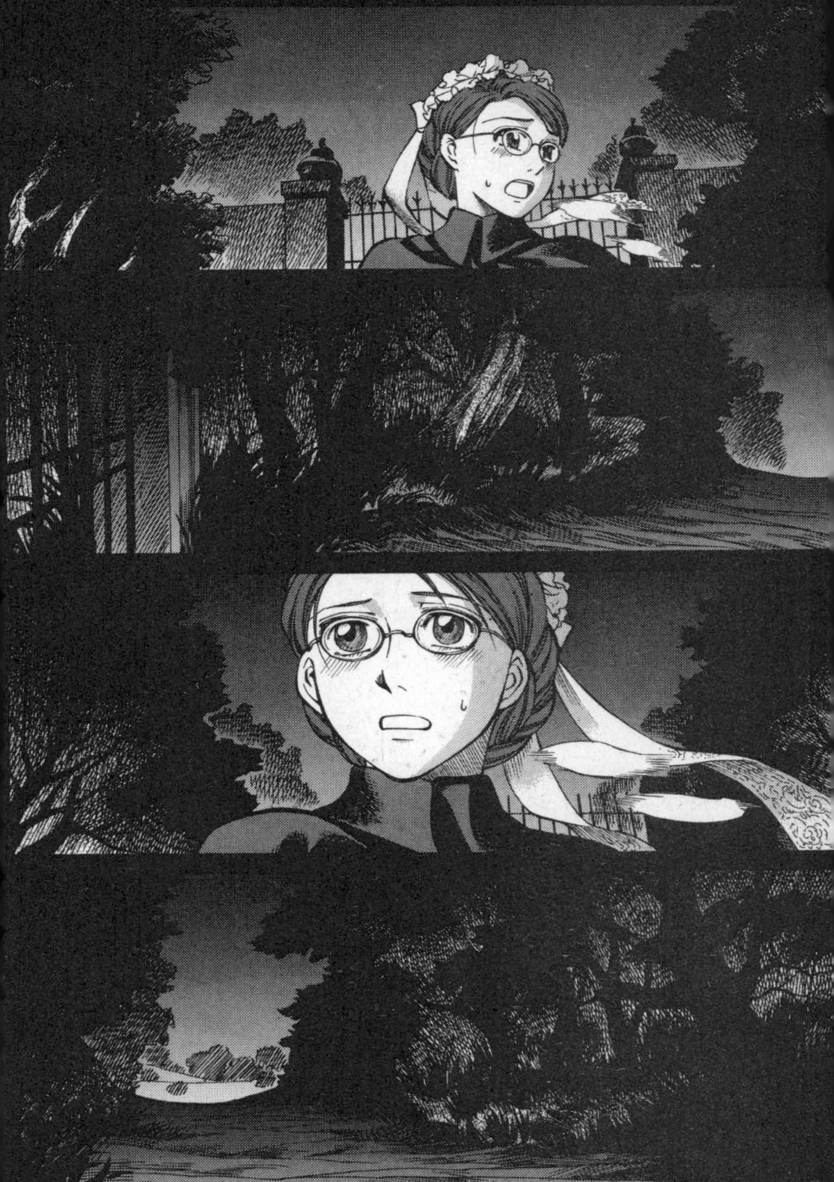

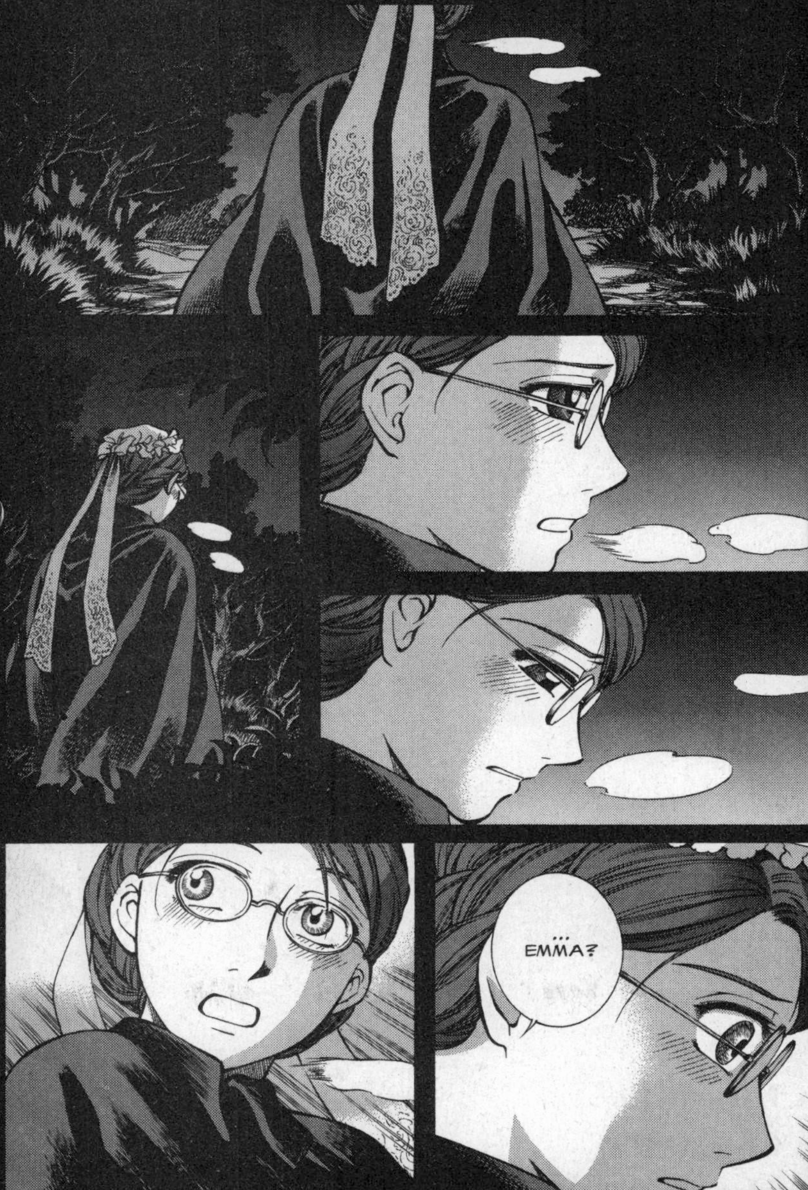
...EMMA?

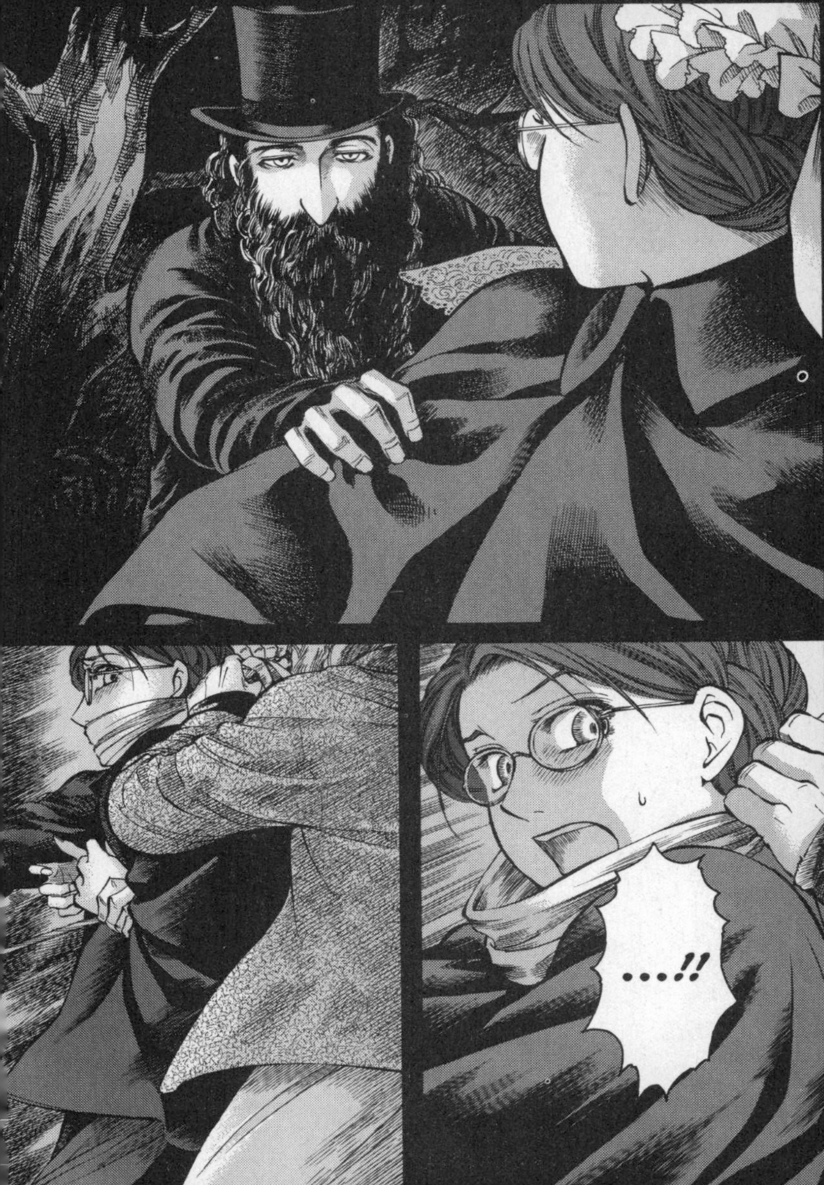
...!!

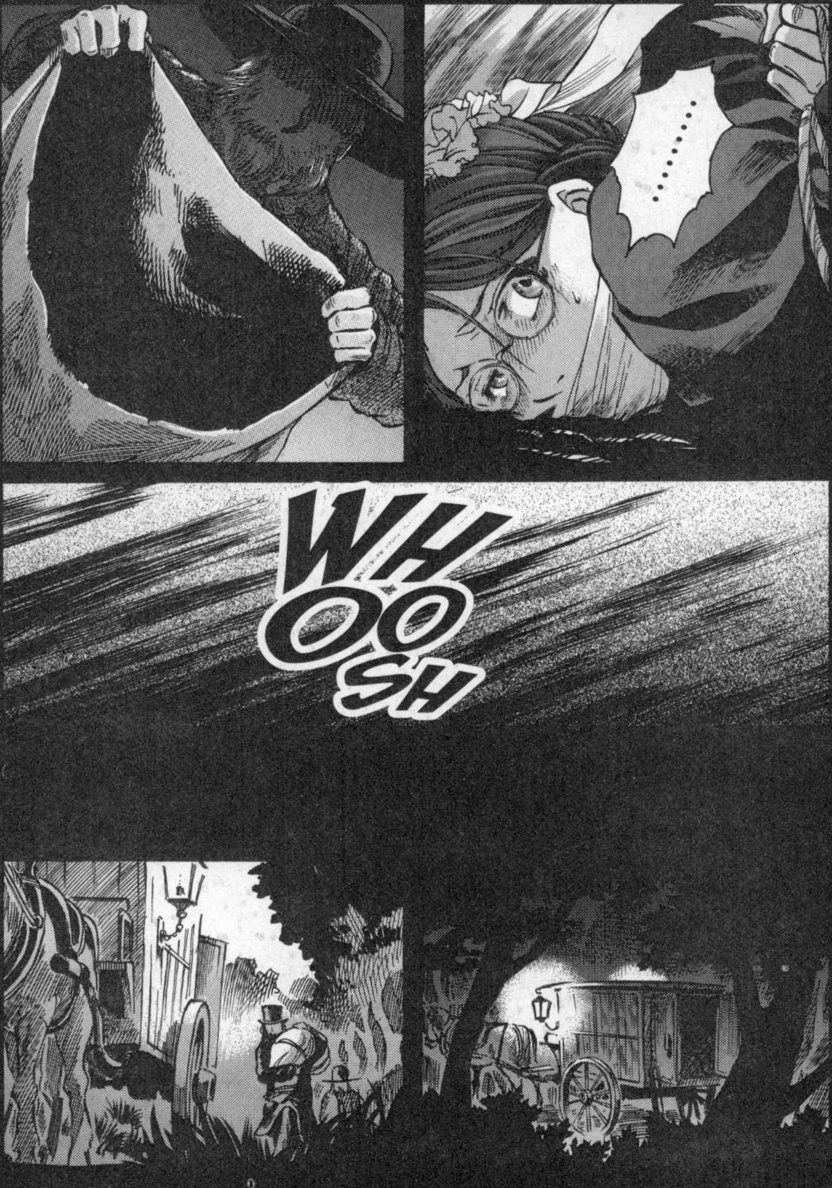
......
WHOOSH

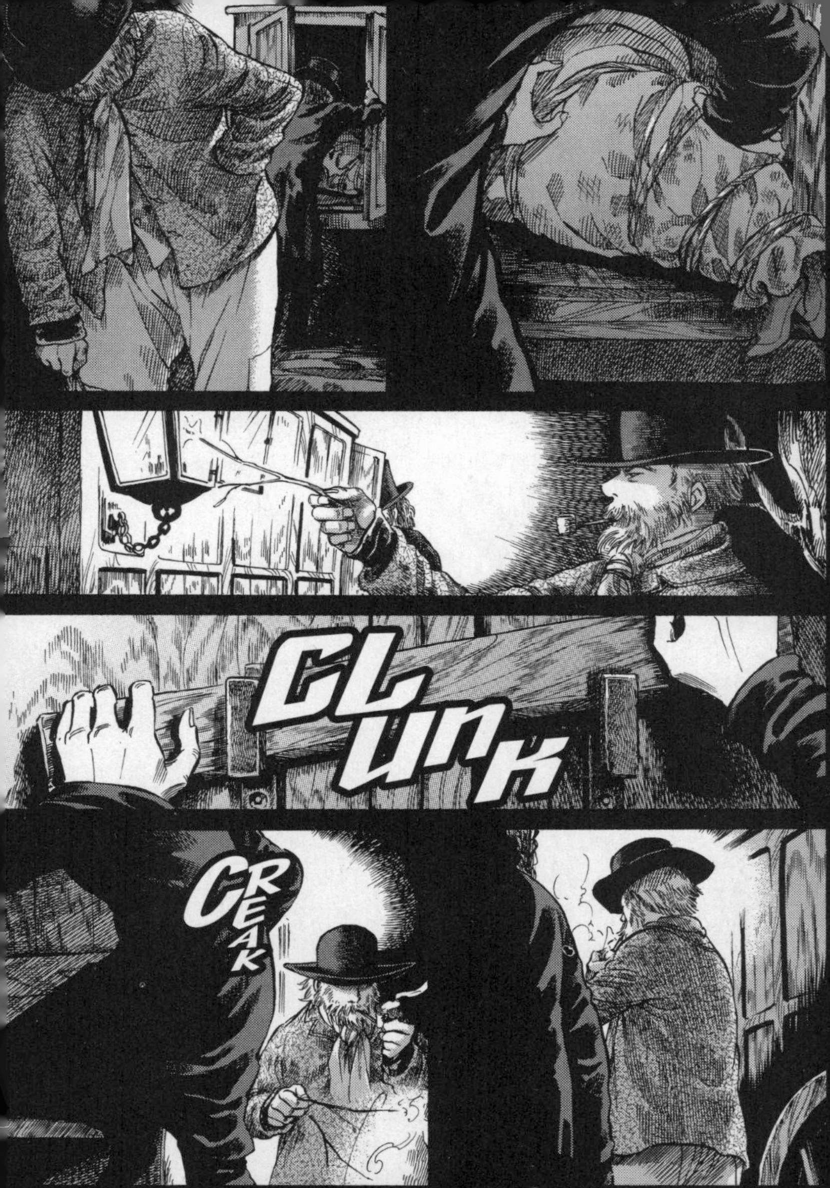
CLUNK
CREAK

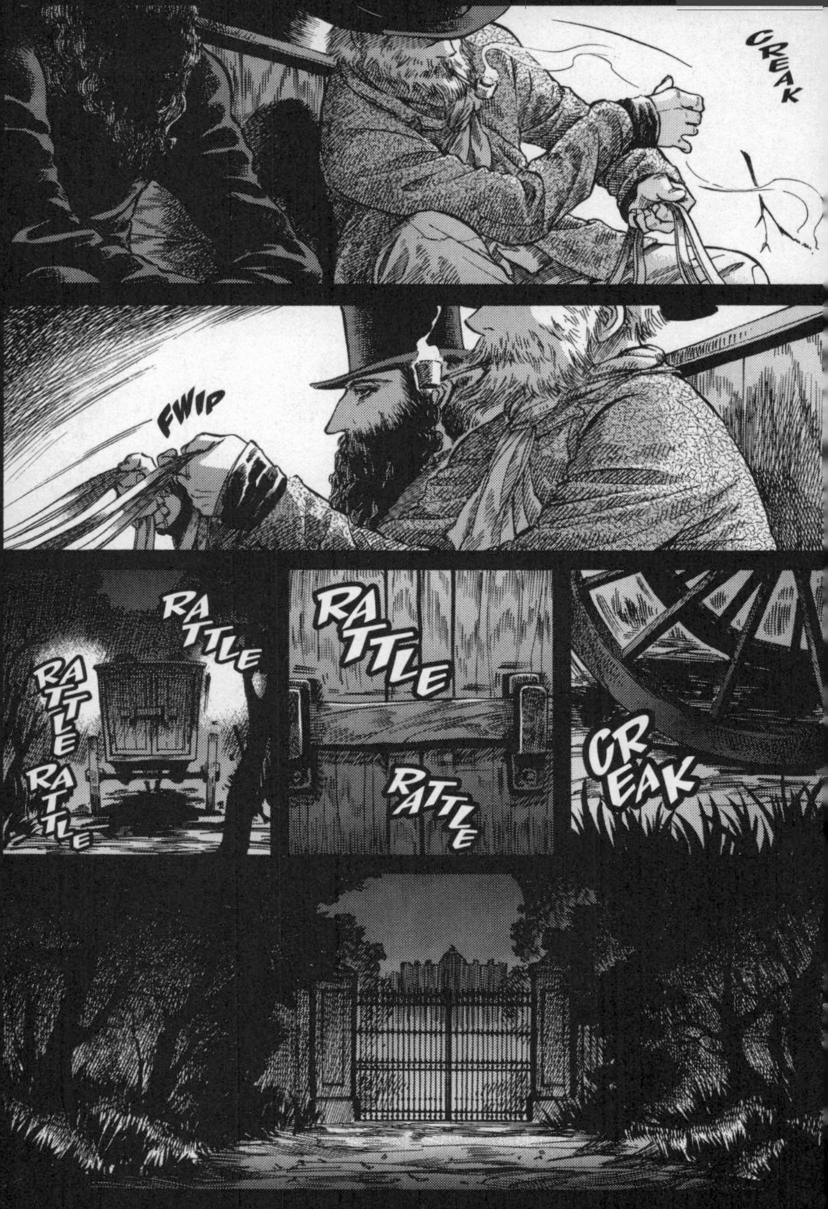
CREAK
FWIP
CREAK
RATTLE
RATTLE
RATTLE
RATTLE
RATTLE
RATTLE

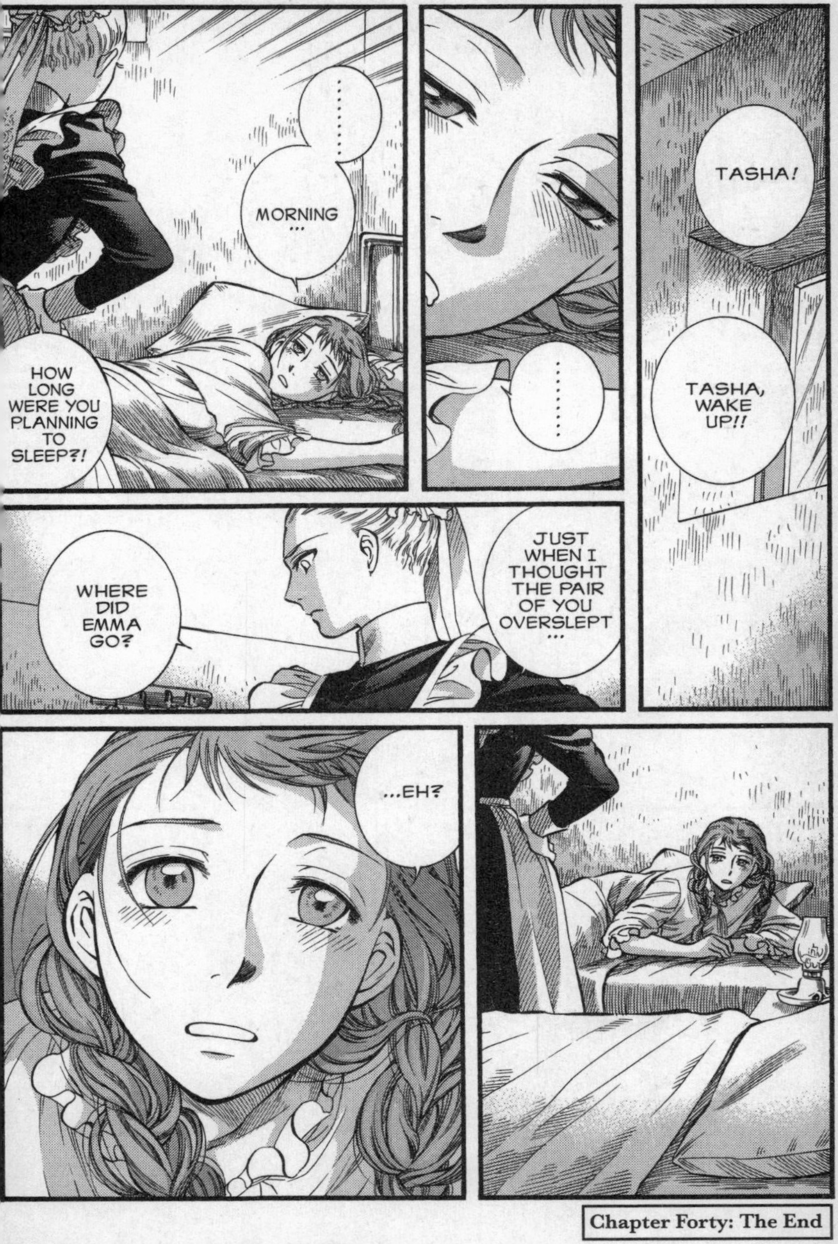
TASHA!
TASHA, WAKE UP!!
......
......
MORNING ...
HOW LONG WERE YOU PLANNING TO SLEEP?!
JUST WHEN I THOUGHT THE PAIR OF YOU OVERSLEPT ...
WHERE DID EMMA GO?
...EH?

Chapter Forty: The End

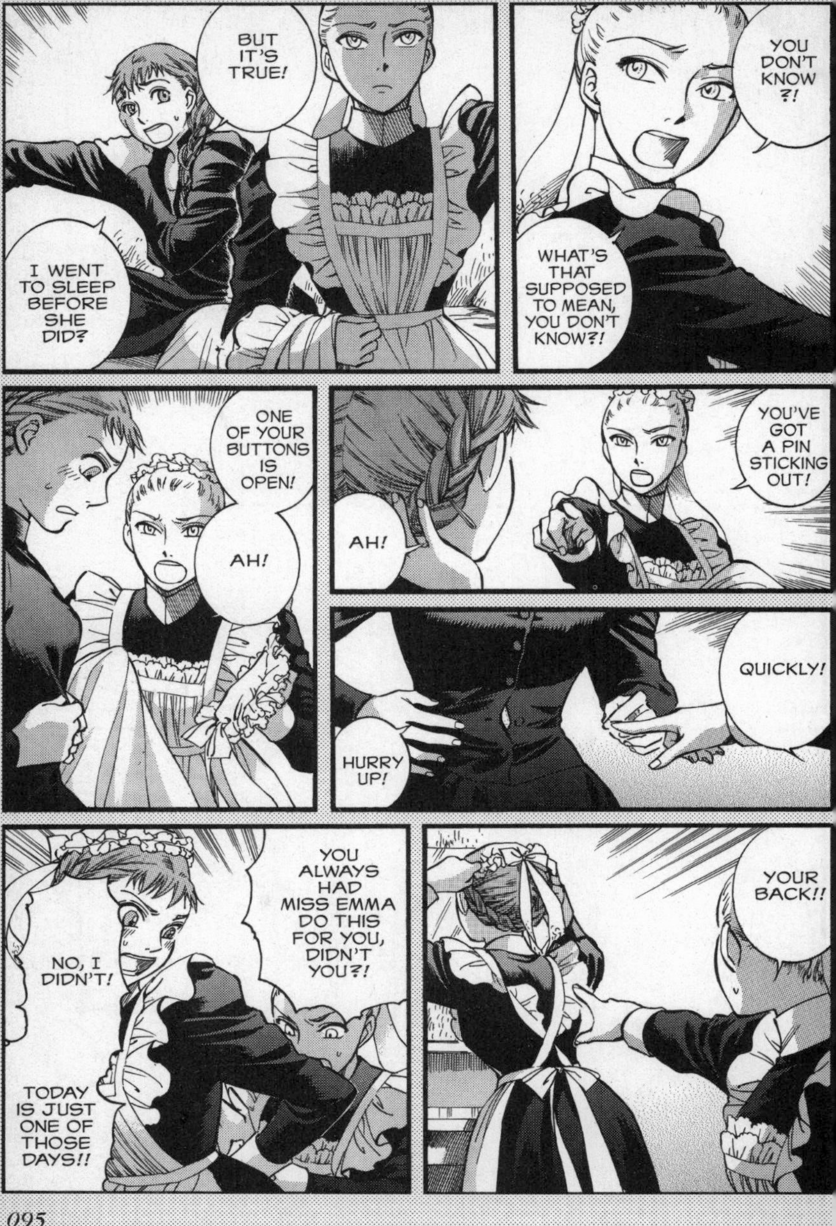
YOU DON'T KNOW ?!
WHAT'S THAT SUPPOSED TO MEAN, YOU DON'T KNOW?!
BUT IT'S TRUE!
I WENT TO SLEEP BEFORE SHE DID?
YOU'VE GOT A PIN STICKING OUT!
AH!
QUICKLY!
HURRY UP!
ONE OF YOUR BUTTONS IS OPEN!
AH!
YOUR BACK!!
YOU ALWAYS HAD MISS EMMA DO THIS FOR YOU, DIDN'T YOU?!
NO, I DIDN'T!
TODAY IS JUST ONE OF THOSE DAYS!!

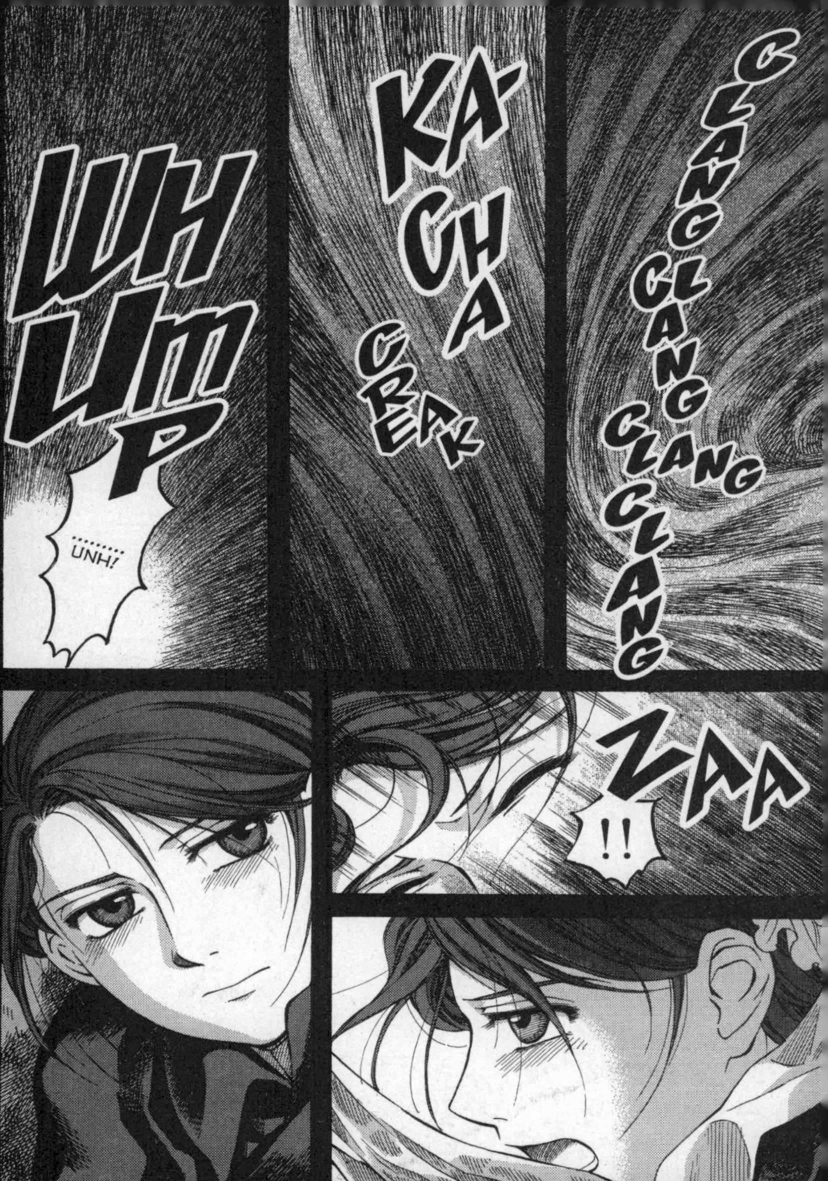
CLANG CLANG CLANG CLANG CLANG CLANG
KA-CHA
CREAK
WHUMP
..........UNH!
ZAA
!!

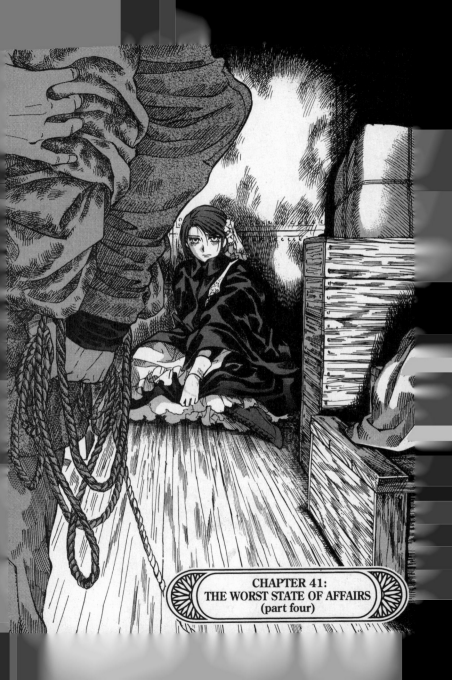

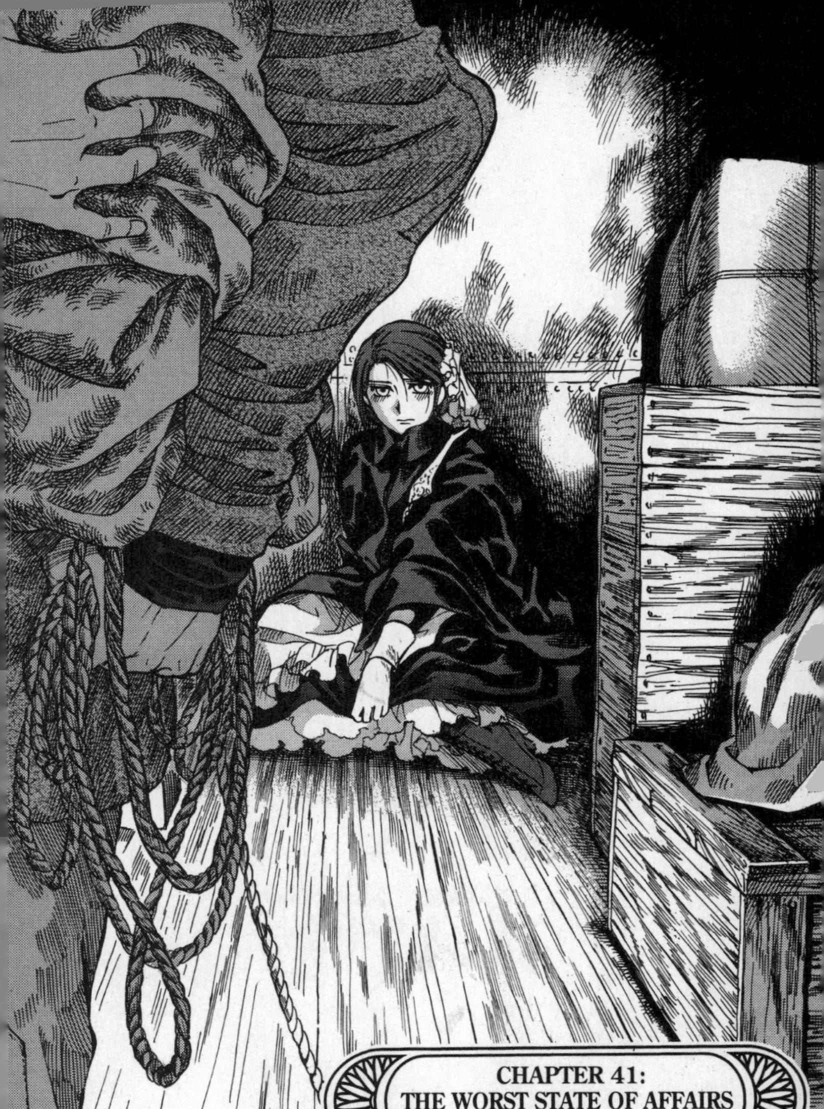
CHAPTER 41:
THE WORST STATE OF AFFAIRS
(part four)

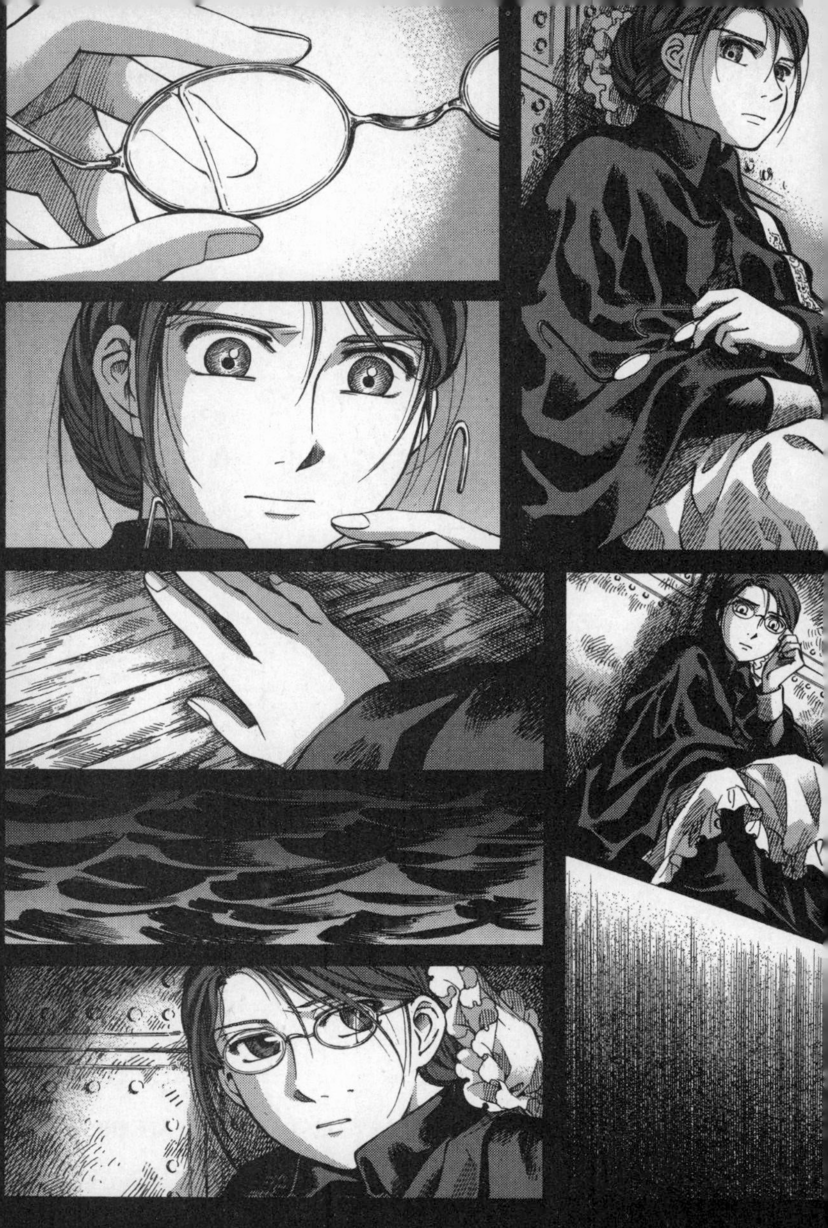

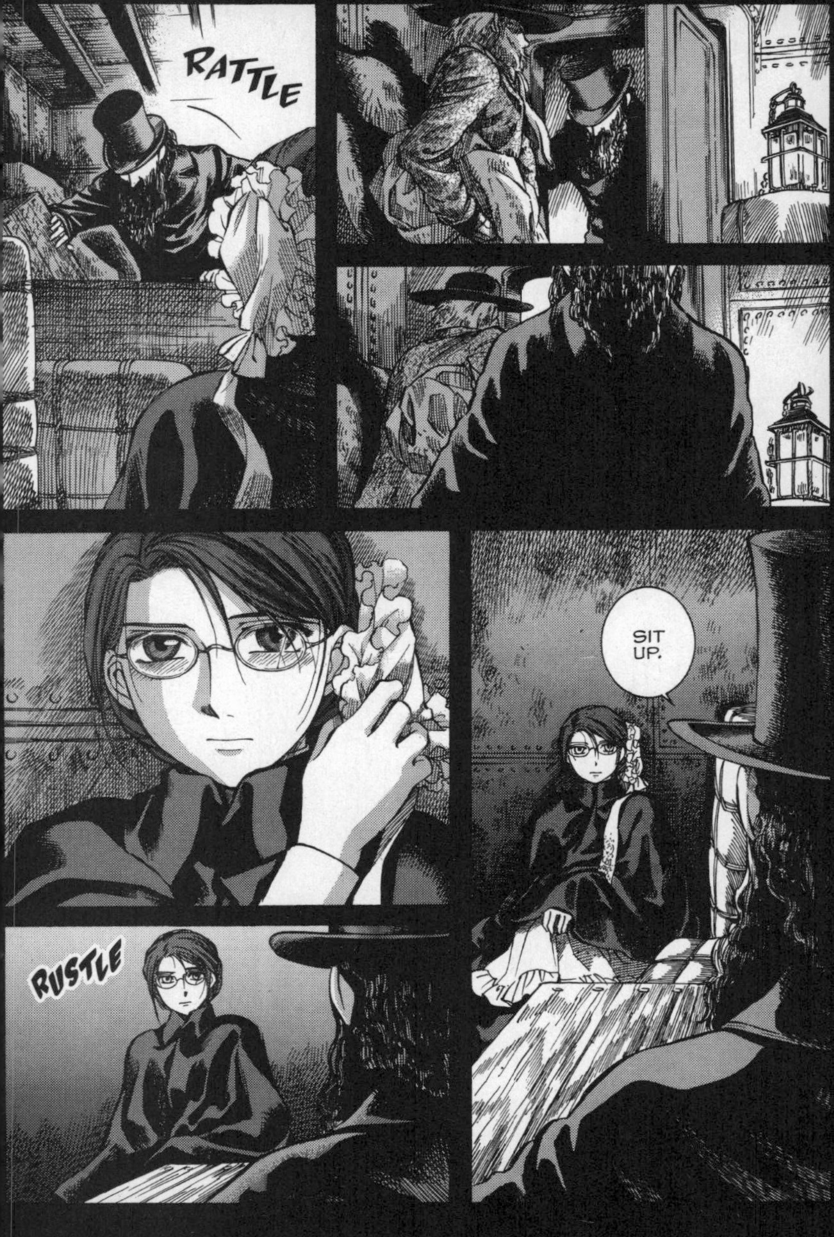
RATTLE
SIT UP.
RUSTLE

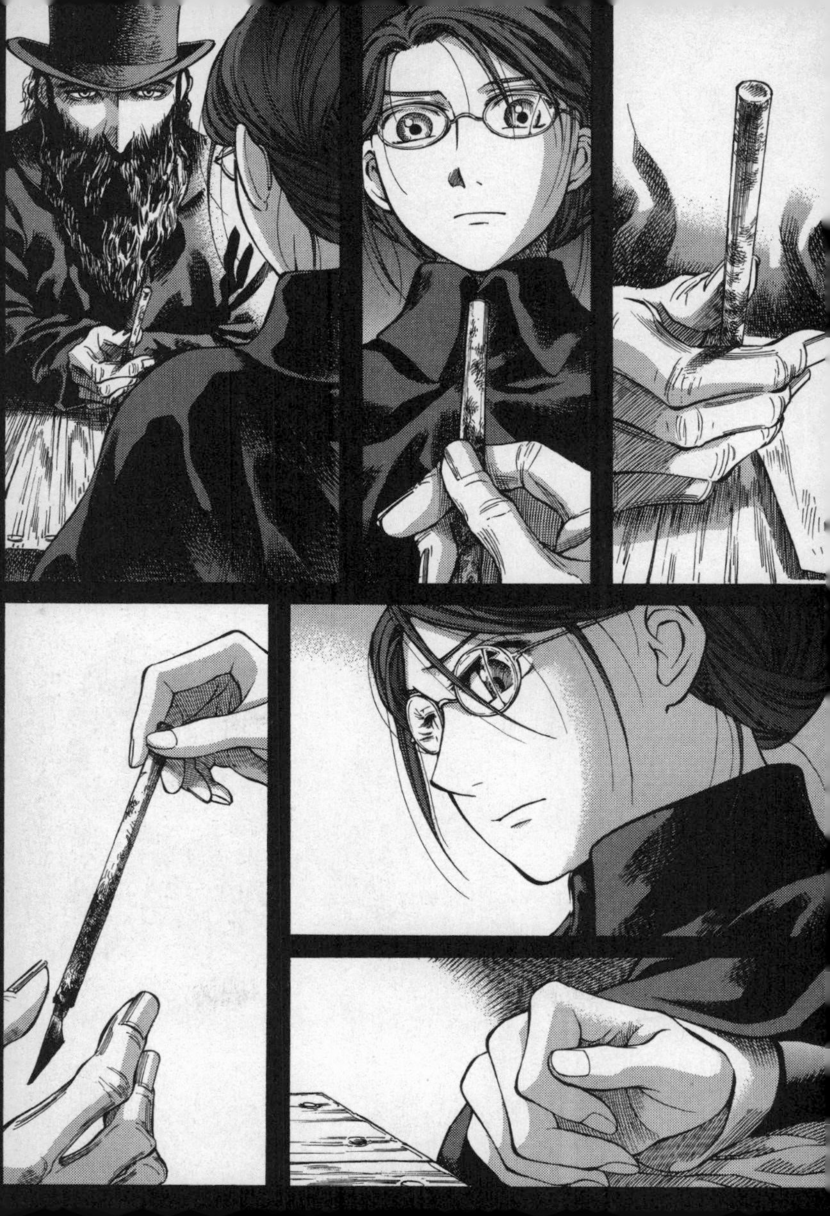

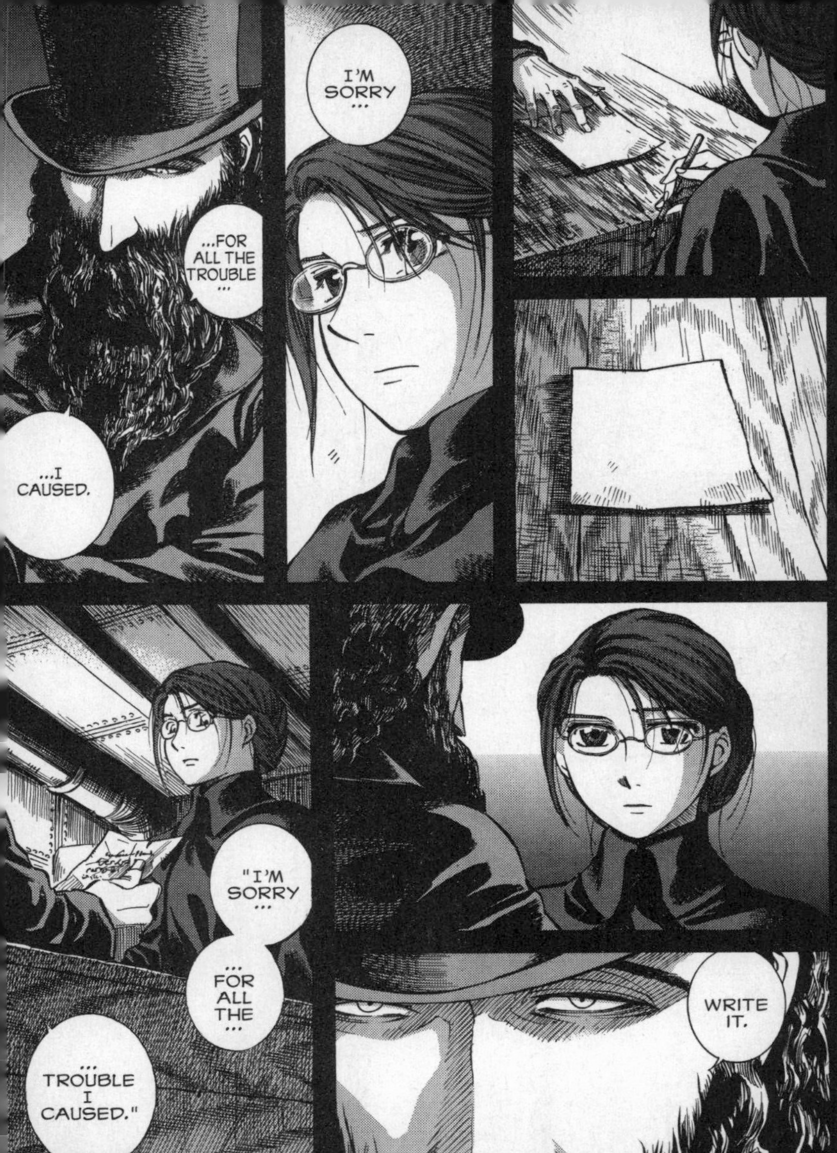
I'M SORRY ...
...FOR ALL THE TROUBLE ...
...I CAUSED.
WRITE IT.
"I'M SORRY ...
... FOR ALL THE ...
... TROUBLE I CAUSED."

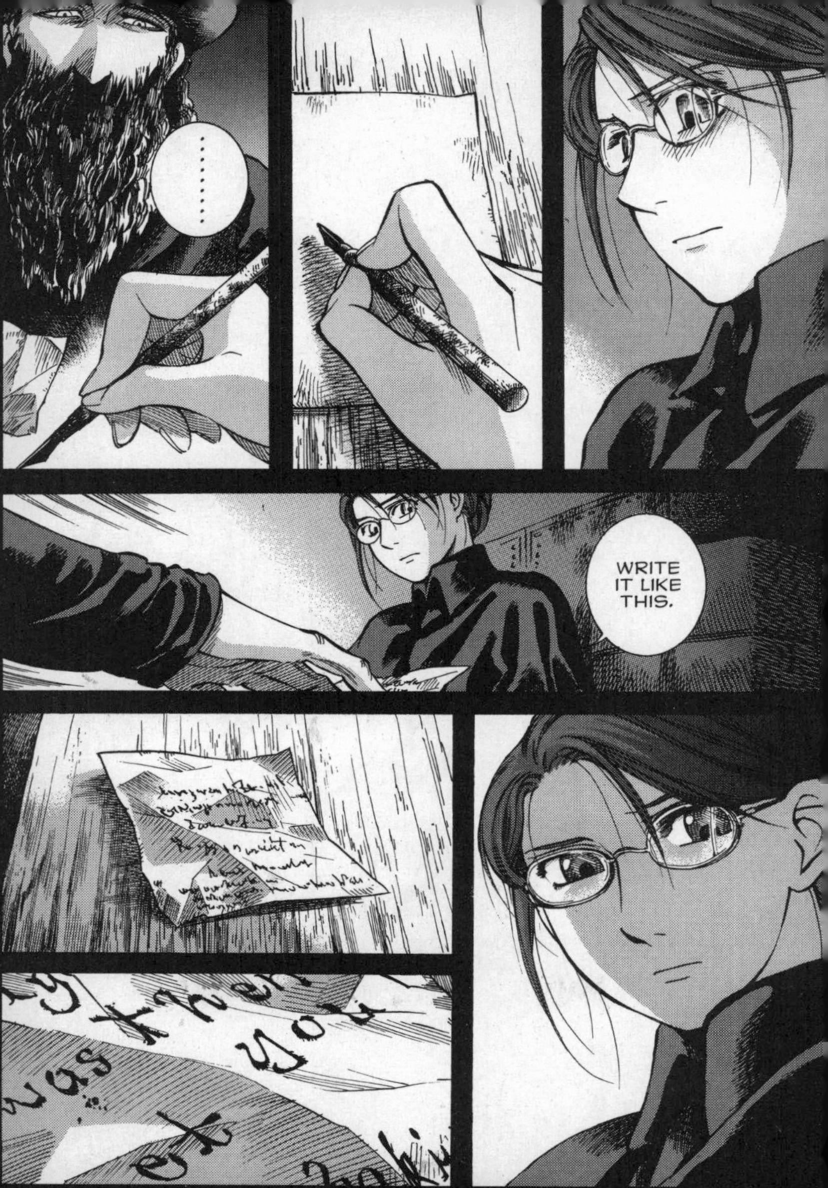
......
WRITE IT LIKE THIS.

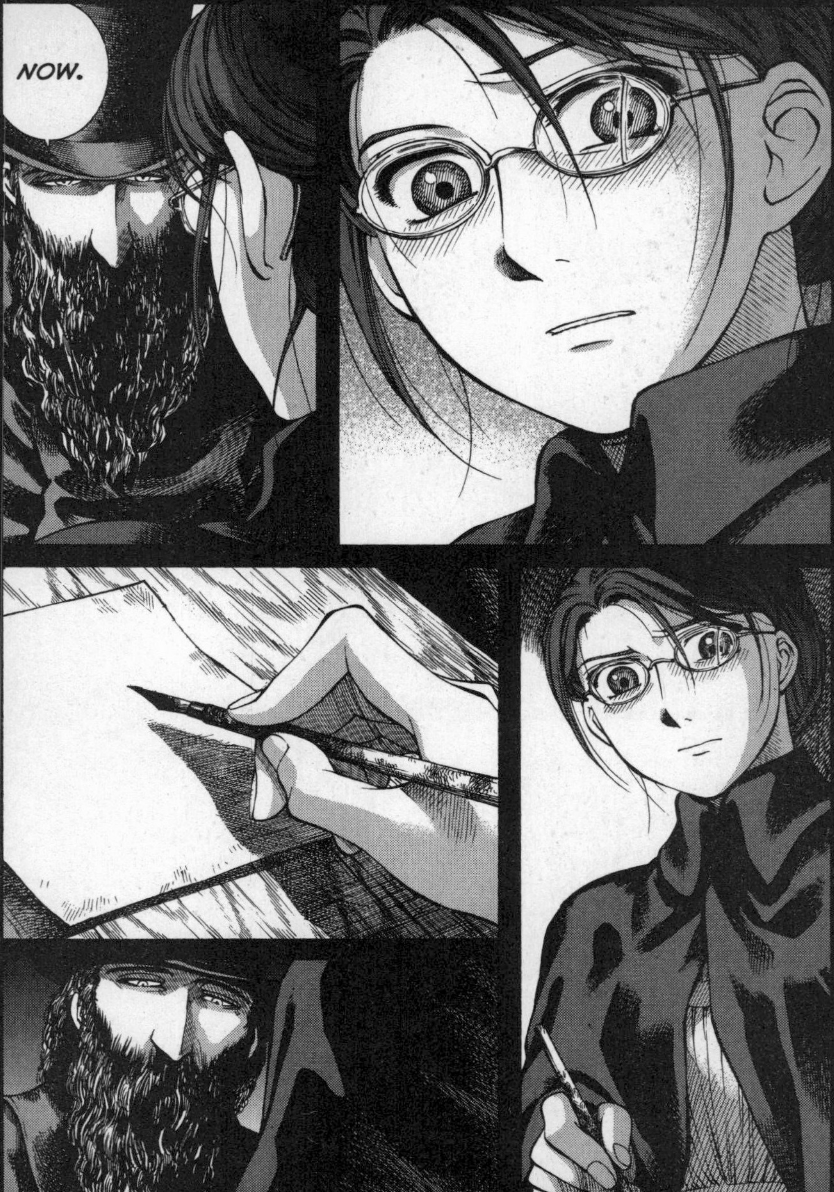
NOW.

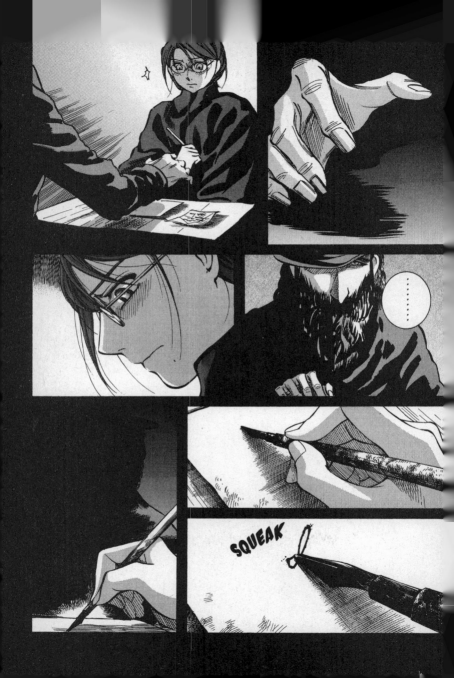

SQUEAK

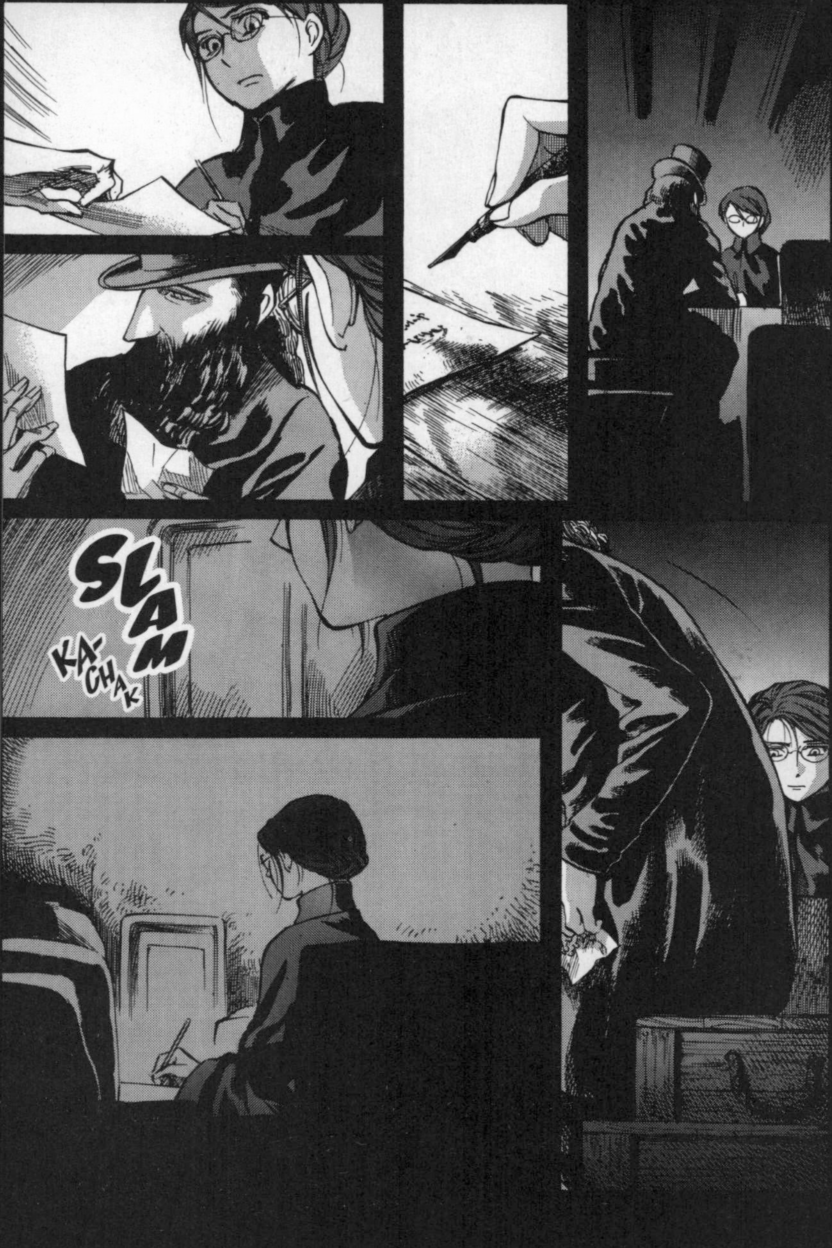
SLAM
KA-CHAK

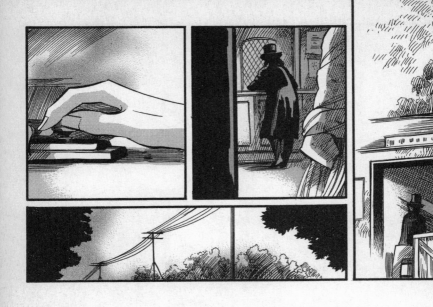

IT'S
ENTITLED
"THE JOY
OF
LOVE".

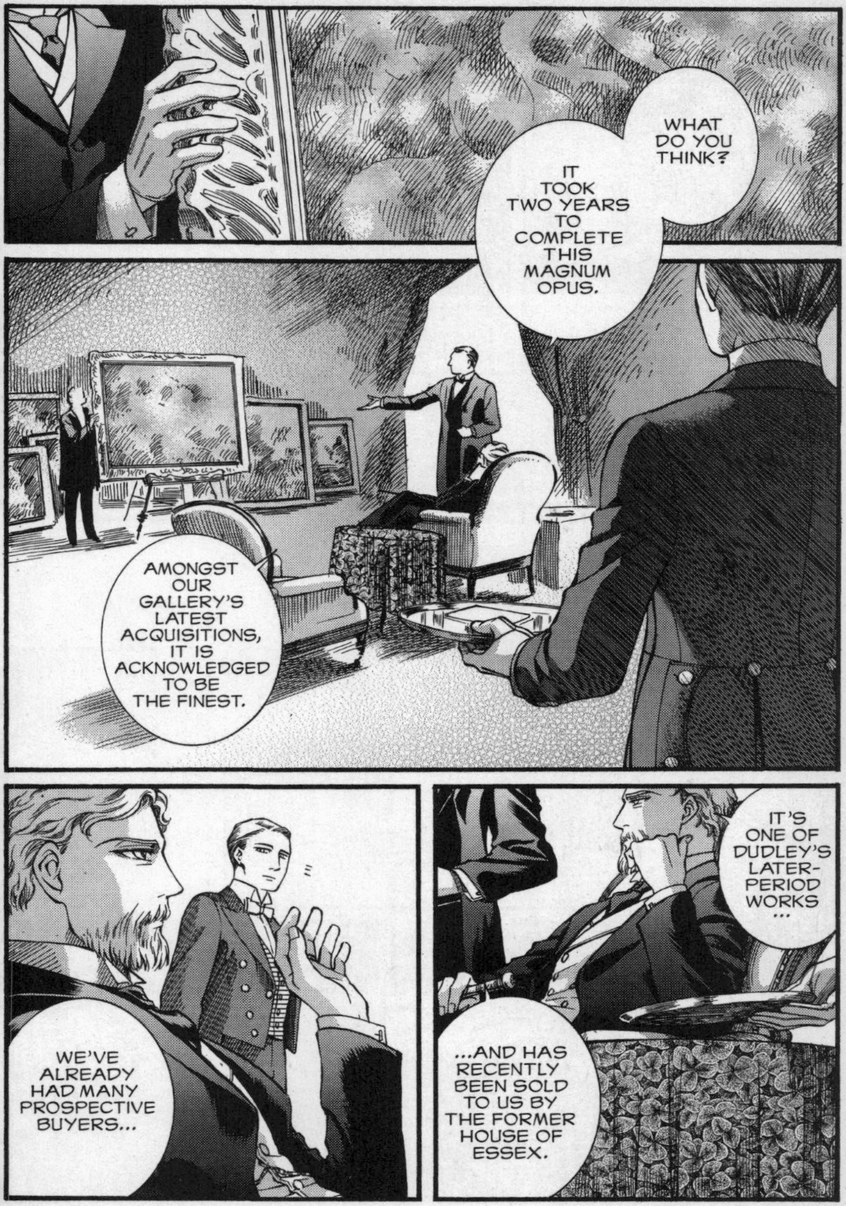
WHAT DO YOU THINK?
IT TOOK TWO YEARS TO COMPLETE THIS MAGNUM OPUS.
AMONGST OUR GALLERY'S LATEST ACQUISITIONS, IT IS ACKNOWLEDGED TO BE THE FINEST.
IT'S ONE OF DUDLEY'S LATER-PERIOD WORKS...
...AND HAS RECENTLY BEEN SOLD TO US BY THE FORMER HOUSE OF ESSEX.
WE'VE ALREADY HAD MANY PROSPECTIVE BUYERS...

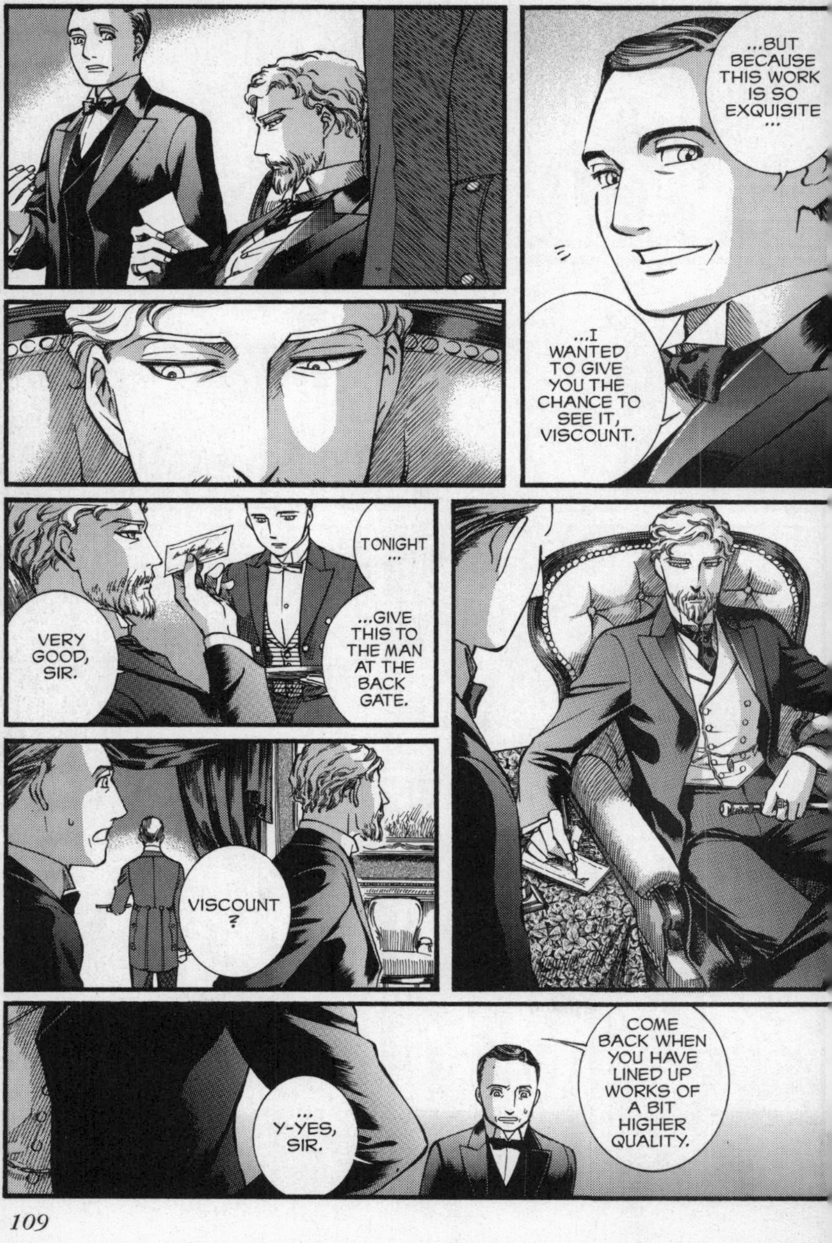
...BUT BECAUSE THIS WORK IS SO EXQUISITE ...
...I WANTED TO GIVE YOU THE CHANCE TO SEE IT, VISCOUNT.
TONIGHT ...
...GIVE THIS TO THE MAN AT THE BACK GATE.
VERY GOOD, SIR.
VISCOUNT ?
COME BACK WHEN YOU HAVE LINED UP WORKS OF A BIT HIGHER QUALITY.
... Y-YES, SIR.

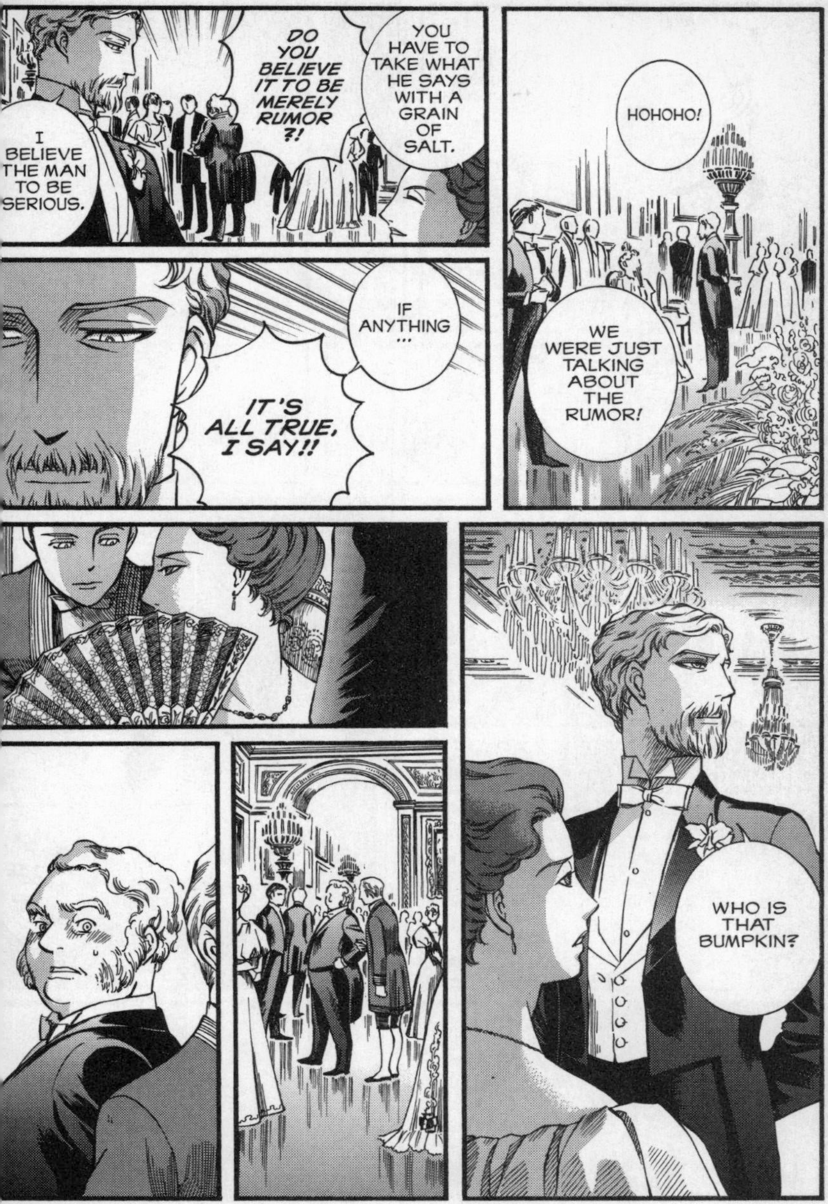
HOHOHO!
WE WERE JUST TALKING ABOUT THE RUMOR!
YOU HAVE TO TAKE WHAT HE SAYS WITH A GRAIN OF SALT.
DO YOU BELIEVE IT TO BE MERELY RUMOR?!
I BELIEVE THE MAN TO BE SERIOUS.
IF ANYTHING...
IT'S ALL TRUE, I SAY!!
WHO IS THAT BUMPKIN?

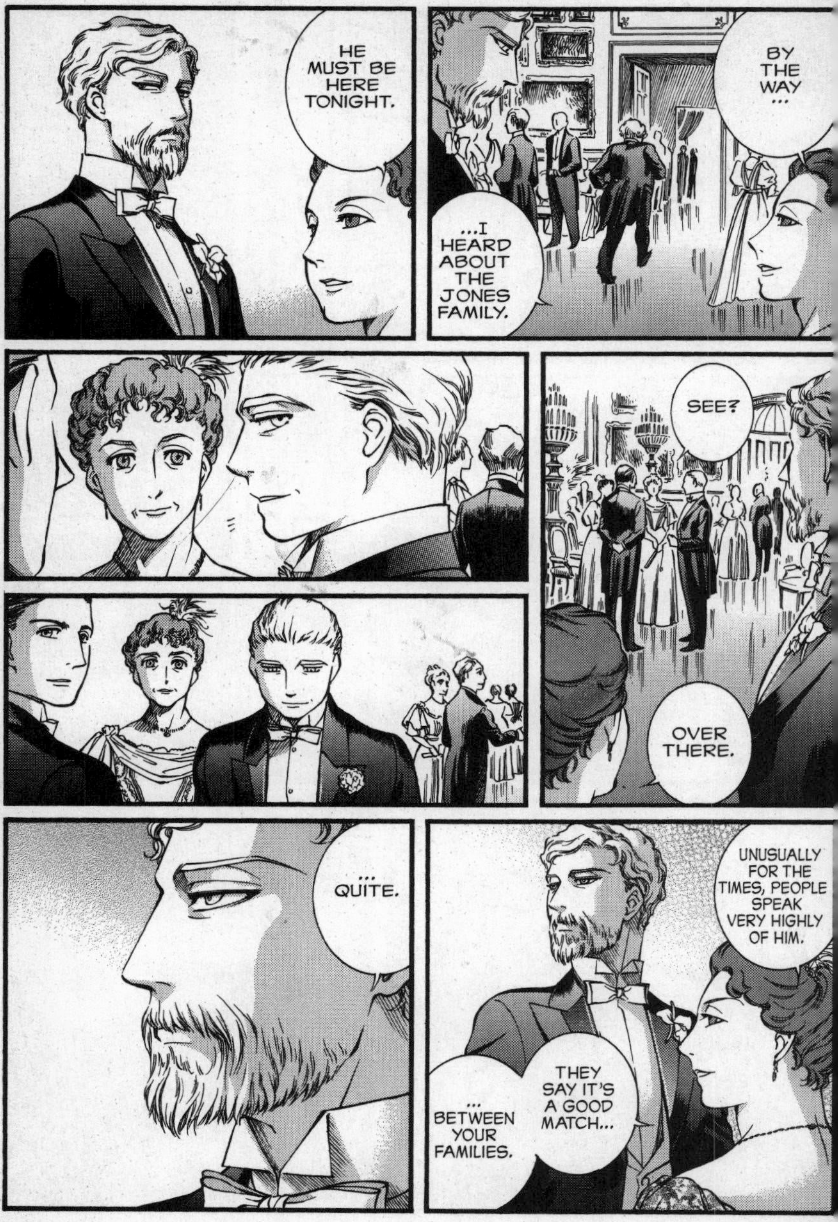
BY THE WAY ...
...I HEARD ABOUT THE JONES FAMILY.
HE MUST BE HERE TONIGHT.
SEE?
OVER THERE.
UNUSUALLY FOR THE TIMES, PEOPLE SPEAK VERY HIGHLY OF HIM.
THEY SAY IT'S A GOOD MATCH...
... BETWEEN YOUR FAMILIES.
... QUITE.

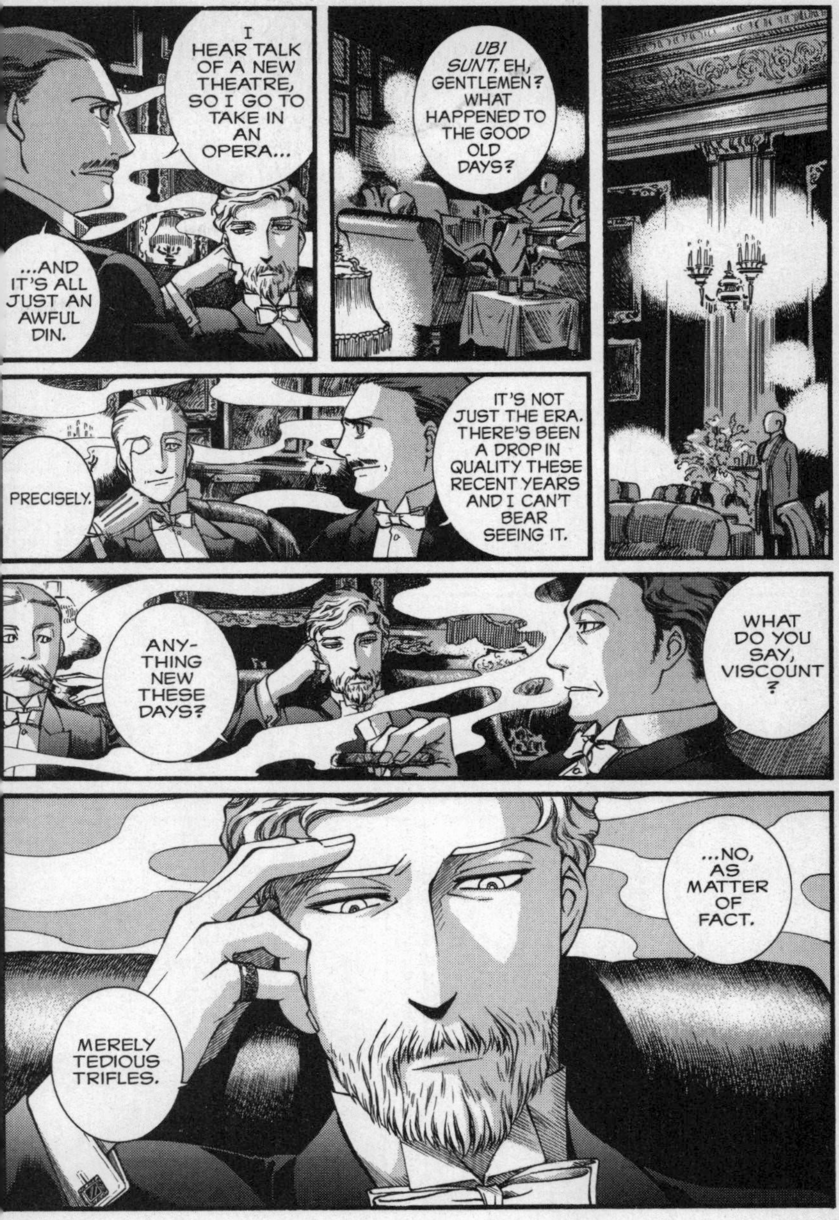
UBI SUNT, EH, GENTLEMEN? WHAT HAPPENED TO THE GOOD OLD DAYS?
I HEAR TALK OF A NEW THEATRE, SO I GO TO TAKE IN AN OPERA...
...AND IT'S ALL JUST AN AWFUL DIN.
IT'S NOT JUST THE ERA. THERE'S BEEN A DROP IN QUALITY THESE RECENT YEARS AND I CAN'T BEAR SEEING IT.
PRECISELY.
WHAT DO YOU SAY, VISCOUNT?
ANY-THING NEW THESE DAYS?
...NO, AS MATTER OF FACT.
MERELY TEDIOUS TRIFLES.

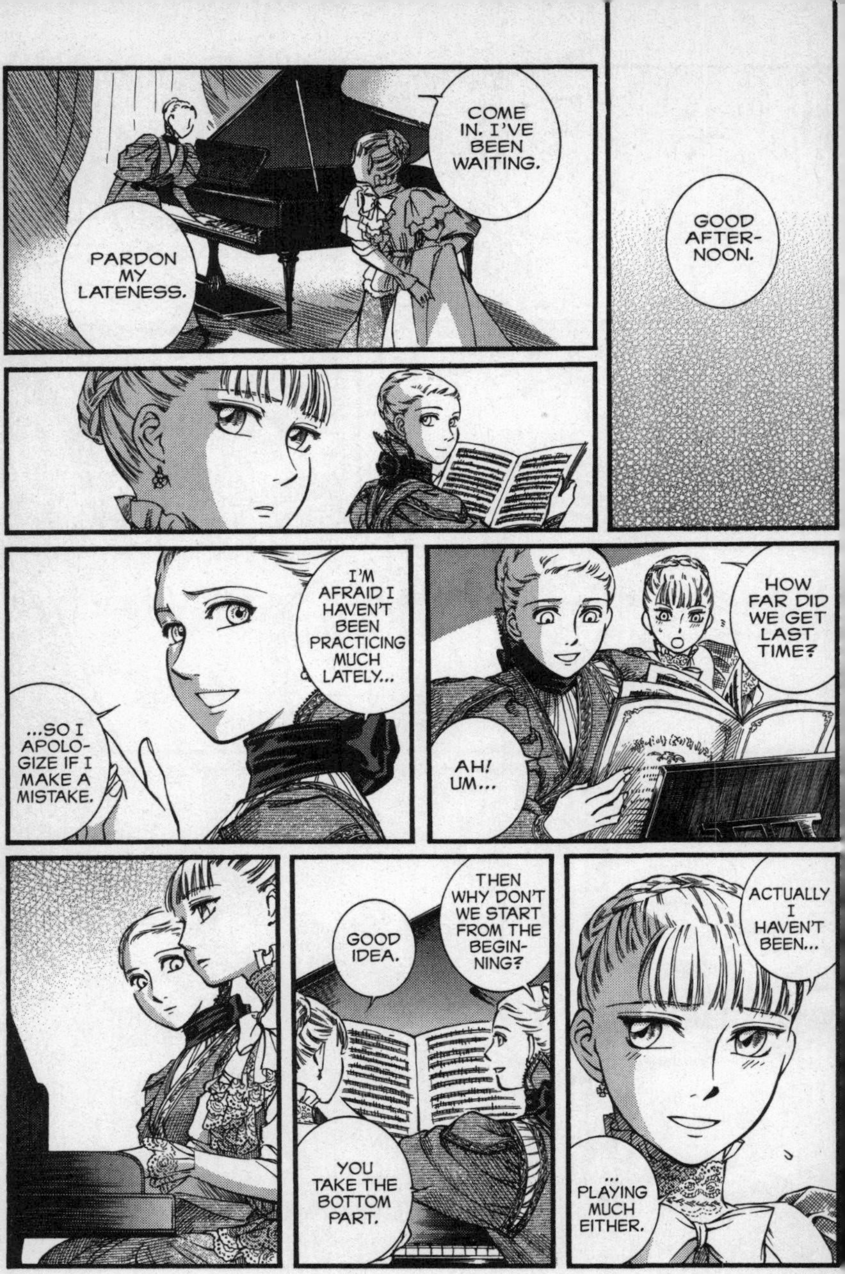
GOOD AFTER-NOON.
COME IN. I'VE BEEN WAITING.
PARDON MY LATENESS.
HOW FAR DID WE GET LAST TIME?
AH! UM...
I'M AFRAID I HAVEN'T BEEN PRACTICING MUCH LATELY...
...SO I APOLO-GIZE IF I MAKE A MISTAKE.
ACTUALLY I HAVEN'T BEEN...
...PLAYING MUCH EITHER.
THEN WHY DON'T WE START FROM THE BEGIN-NING?
GOOD IDEA.
YOU TAKE THE BOTTOM PART.

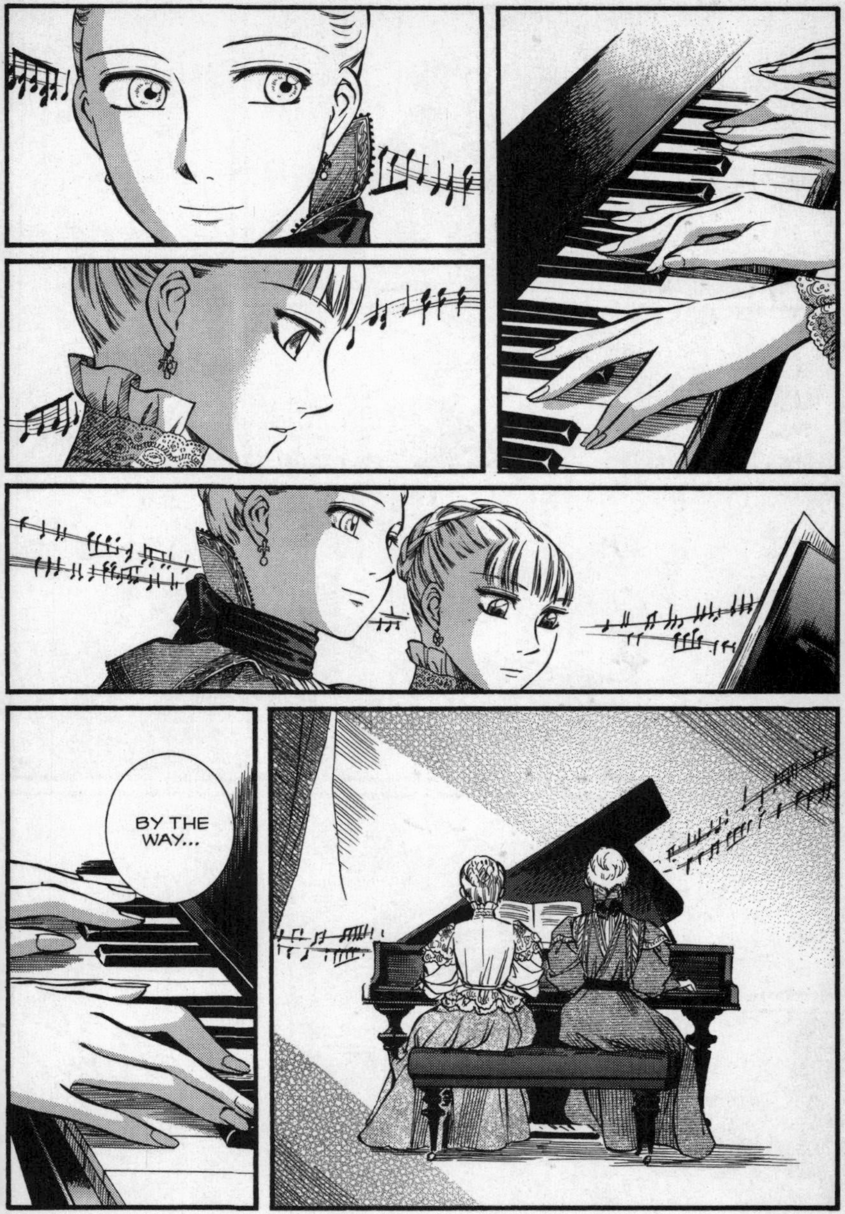
BY THE WAY...

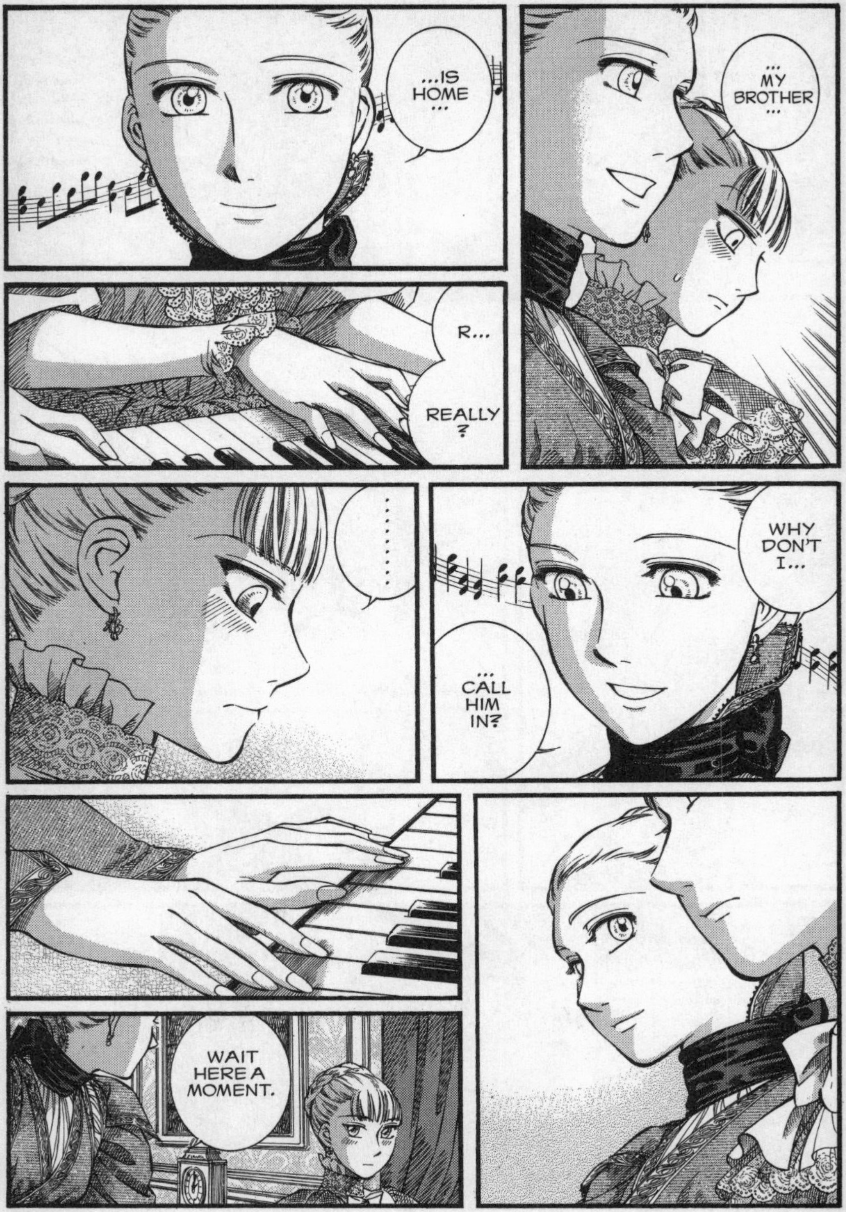
... MY BROTHER ...
...IS HOME ...
R... REALLY?
WHY DON'T I...
... CALL HIM IN?
......
WAIT HERE A MOMENT.

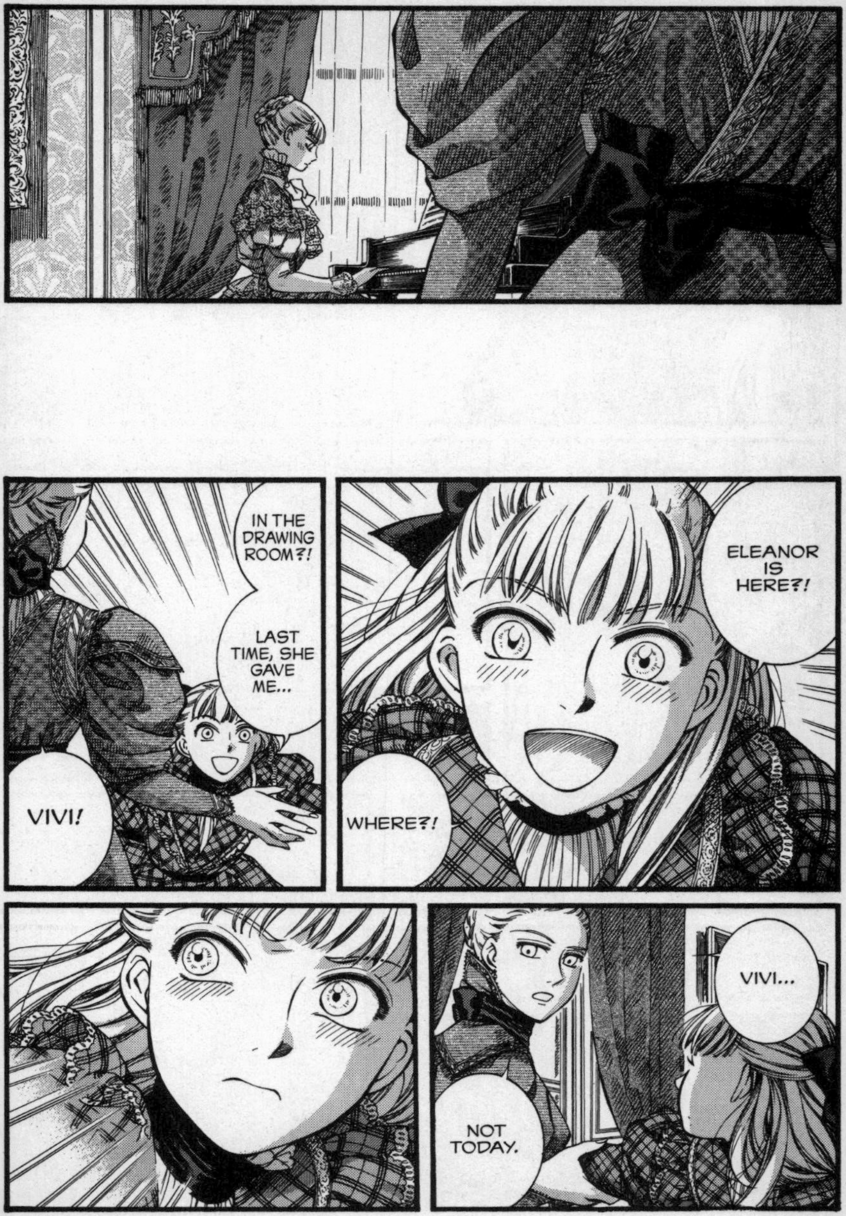
ELEANOR IS HERE?!
WHERE?!
IN THE DRAWING ROOM?!
LAST TIME, SHE GAVE ME...
VIVI!
VIVI...
NOT TODAY.

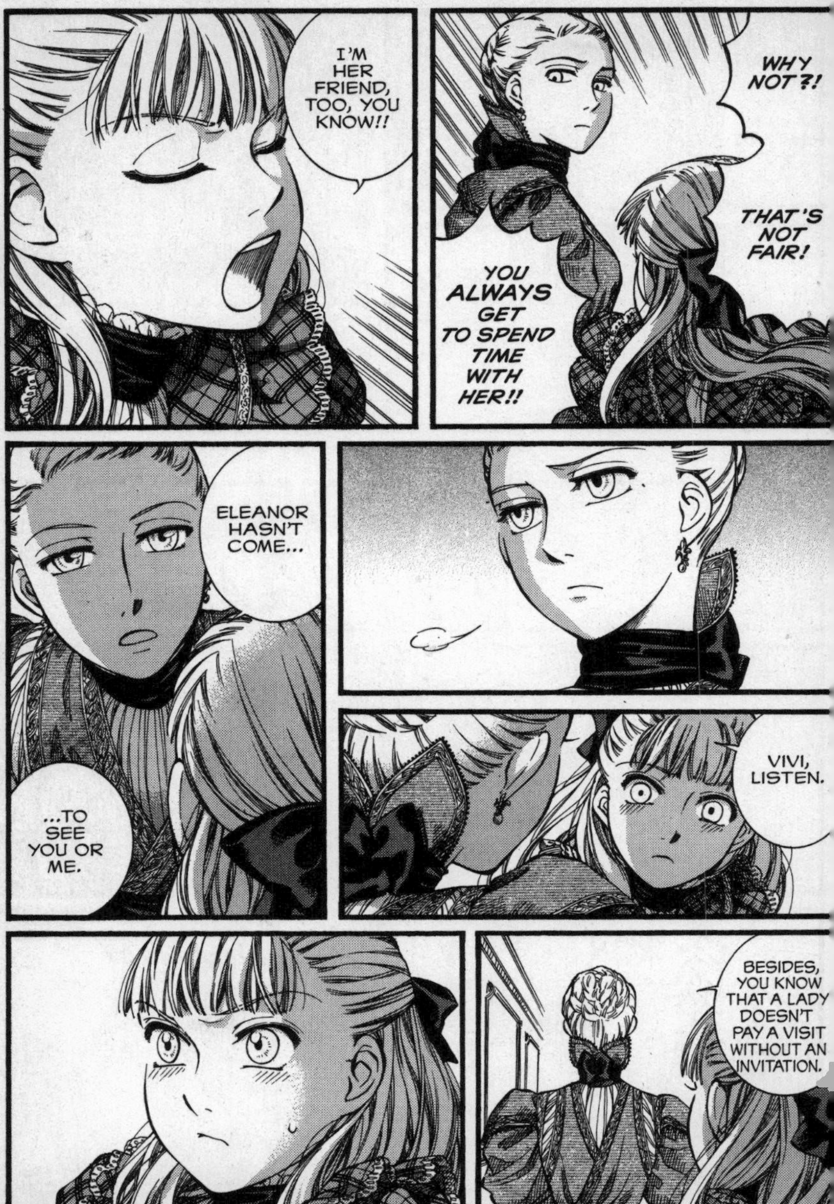
WHY NOT?!
THAT'S NOT FAIR!
YOU ALWAYS GET TO SPEND TIME WITH HER!!
I'M HER FRIEND, TOO, YOU KNOW!!
VIVI, LISTEN.
ELEANOR HASN'T COME...
...TO SEE YOU OR ME.
BESIDES, YOU KNOW THAT A LADY DOESN'T PAY A VISIT WITHOUT AN INVITATION.

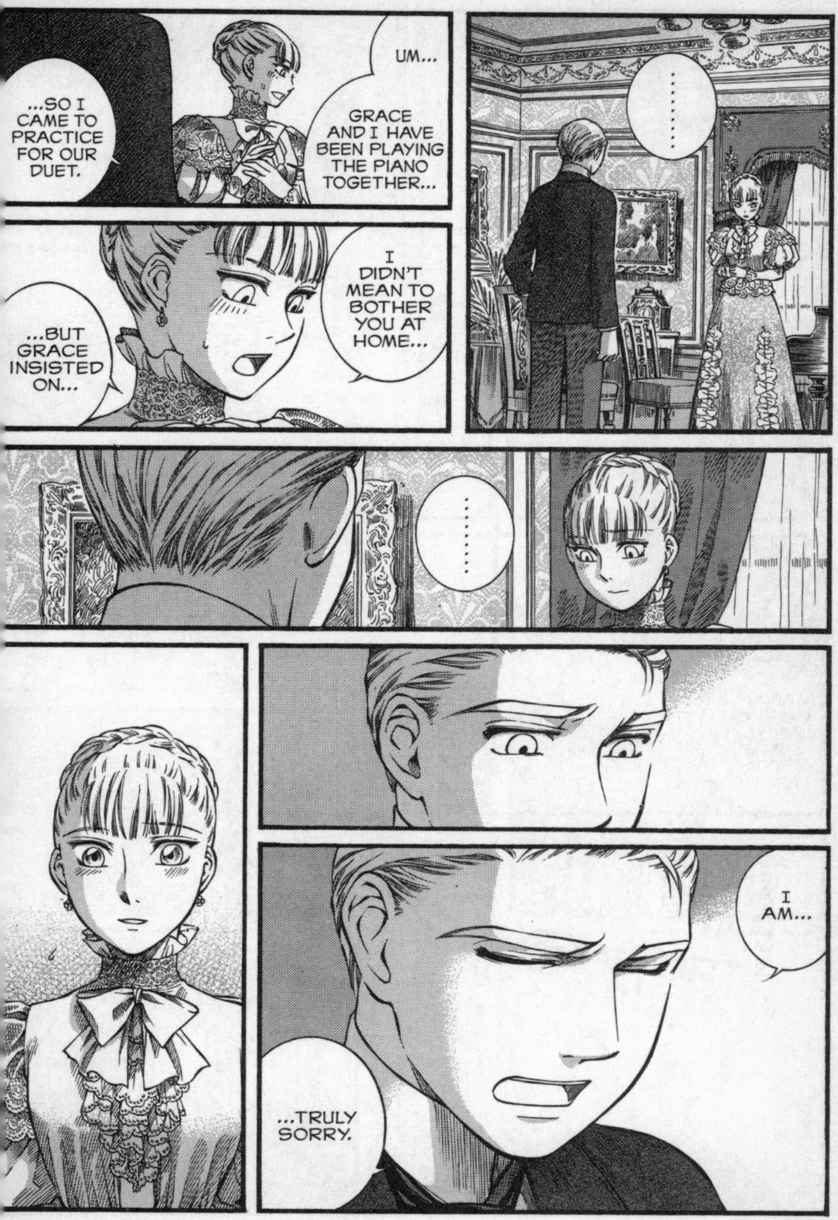
......
UM...
GRACE AND I HAVE BEEN PLAYING THE PIANO TOGETHER...
...SO I CAME TO PRACTICE FOR OUR DUET.
I DIDN'T MEAN TO BOTHER YOU AT HOME...
...BUT GRACE INSISTED ON...
......
I AM...
...TRULY SORRY.

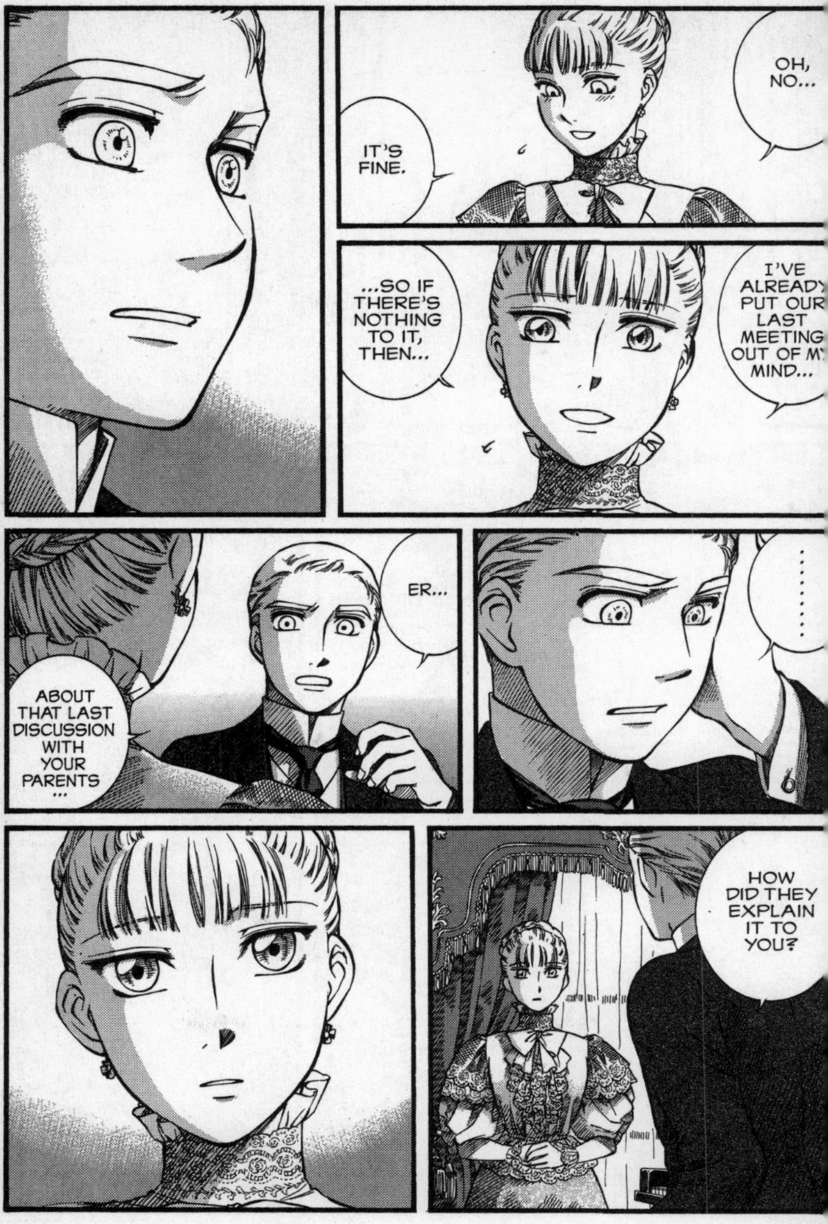
OH, NO...
IT'S FINE.
I'VE ALREADY PUT OUR LAST MEETING OUT OF MY MIND...
...SO IF THERE'S NOTHING TO IT, THEN...
......
ER...
ABOUT THAT LAST DISCUSSION WITH YOUR PARENTS ...
HOW DID THEY EXPLAIN IT TO YOU?

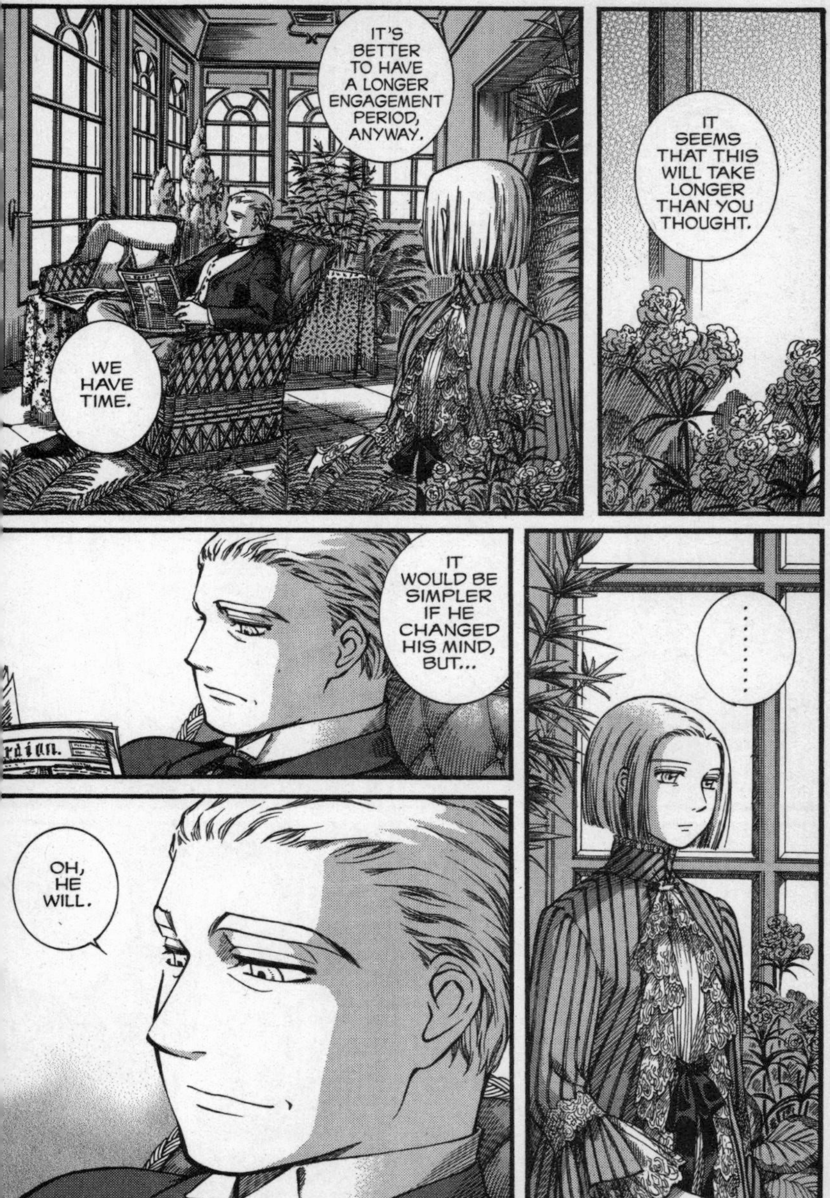
IT SEEMS THAT THIS WILL TAKE LONGER THAN YOU THOUGHT.
IT'S BETTER TO HAVE A LONGER ENGAGEMENT PERIOD, ANYWAY.
WE HAVE TIME.
......
IT WOULD BE SIMPLER IF HE CHANGED HIS MIND, BUT...
OH, HE WILL.

Chapter Forty One: The End

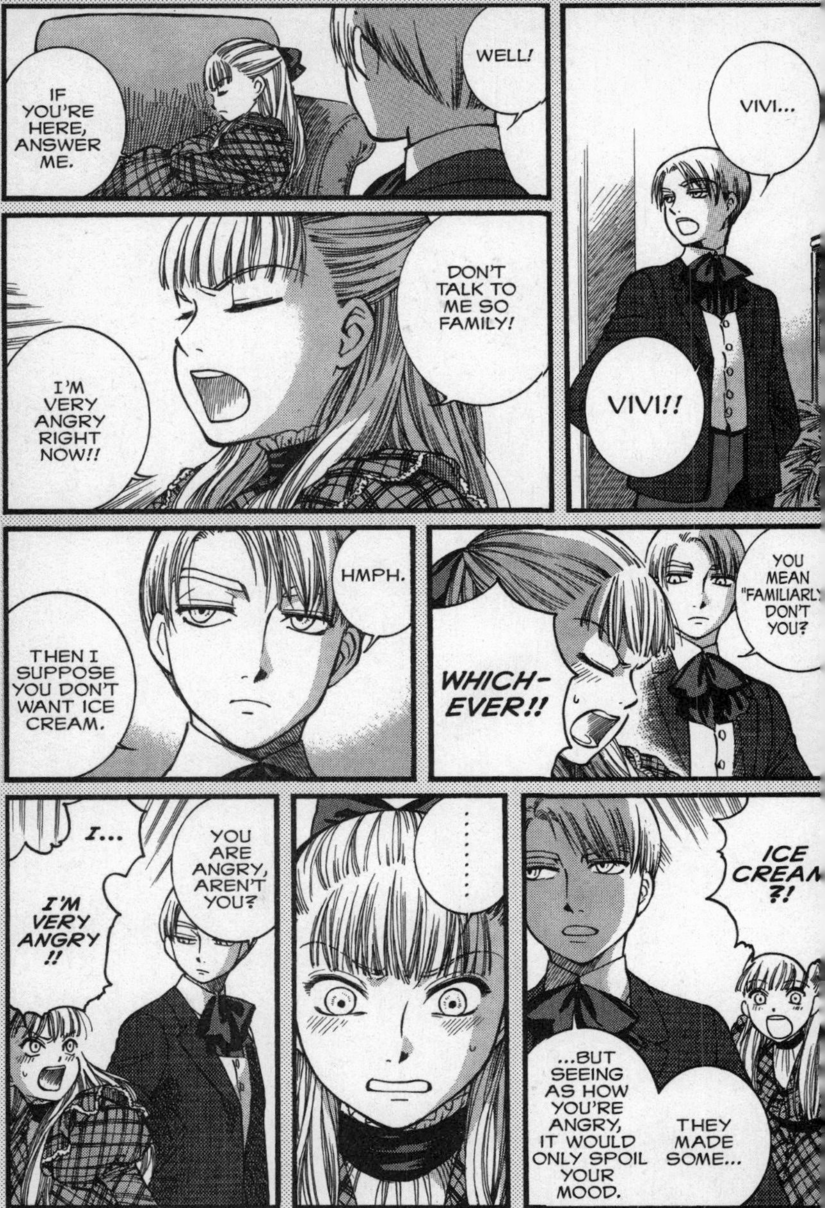
VIVI...
VIVI!!
WELL!
IF YOU'RE HERE, ANSWER ME.
DON'T TALK TO ME SO FAMILY!
I'M VERY ANGRY RIGHT NOW!!
YOU MEAN "FAMILIARLY" DON'T YOU?
WHICH-EVER!!
HMPH.
THEN I SUPPOSE YOU DON'T WANT ICE CREAM.
ICE CREAM ?!
THEY MADE SOME...
...BUT SEEING AS HOW YOU'RE ANGRY, IT WOULD ONLY SPOIL YOUR MOOD.
......
YOU ARE ANGRY, AREN'T YOU?
I...
I'M VERY ANGRY!!

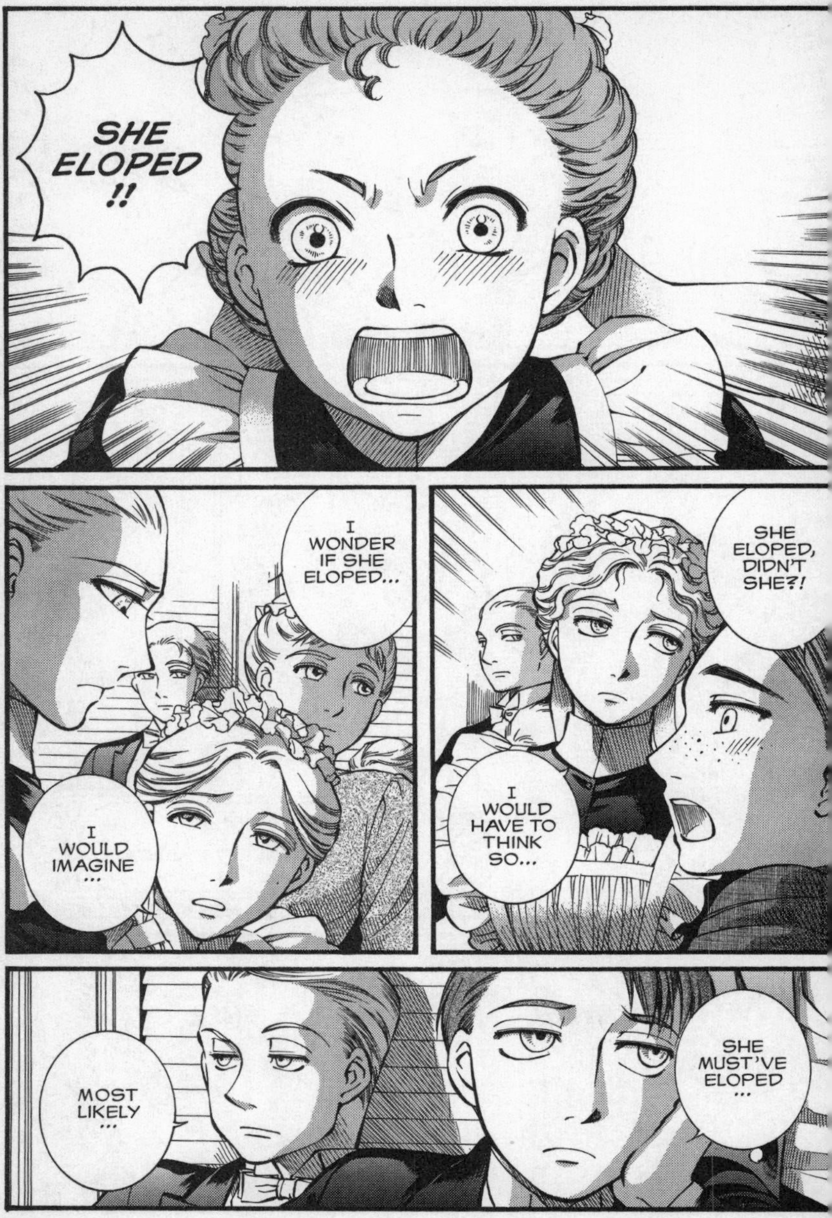
SHE ELOPED !!
SHE ELOPED, DIDN'T SHE?!
I WOULD HAVE TO THINK SO...
I WONDER IF SHE ELOPED...
I WOULD IMAGINE...
SHE MUST'VE ELOPED...
MOST LIKELY...

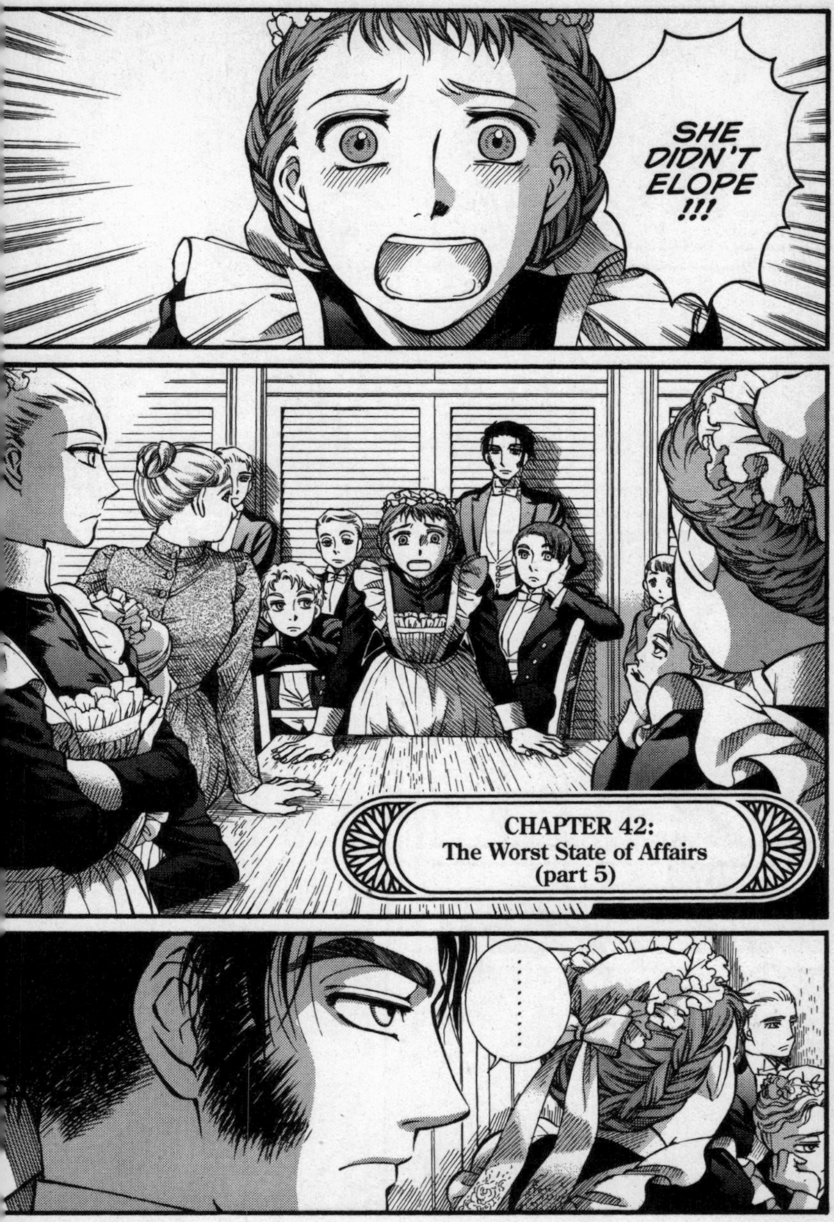
SHE DIDN'T ELOPE !!!
CHAPTER 42:
The Worst State of Affairs
(part 5)
......

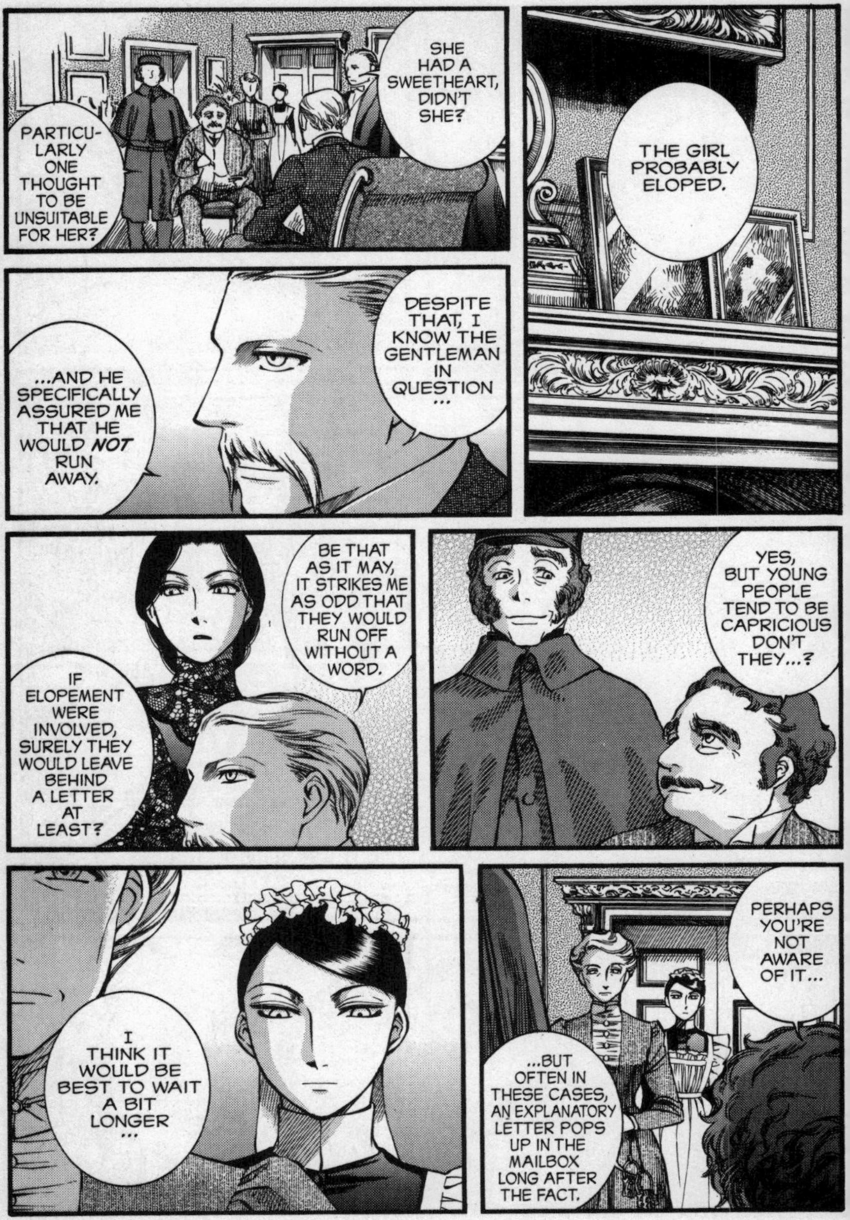
THE GIRL PROBABLY ELOPED.
SHE HAD A SWEETHEART, DIDN'T SHE?
PARTICU-LARLY ONE THOUGHT TO BE UNSUITABLE FOR HER?
DESPITE THAT, I KNOW THE GENTLEMAN IN QUESTION...
...AND HE SPECIFICALLY ASSURED ME THAT HE WOULD *NOT* RUN AWAY.
YES, BUT YOUNG PEOPLE TEND TO BE CAPRICIOUS DON'T THEY...?
BE THAT AS IT MAY, IT STRIKES ME AS ODD THAT THEY WOULD RUN OFF WITHOUT A WORD.
IF ELOPEMENT WERE INVOLVED, SURELY THEY WOULD LEAVE BEHIND A LETTER AT LEAST?
PERHAPS YOU'RE NOT AWARE OF IT...
...BUT OFTEN IN THESE CASES, AN EXPLANATORY LETTER POPS UP IN THE MAILBOX LONG AFTER THE FACT.
I THINK IT WOULD BE BEST TO WAIT A BIT LONGER...

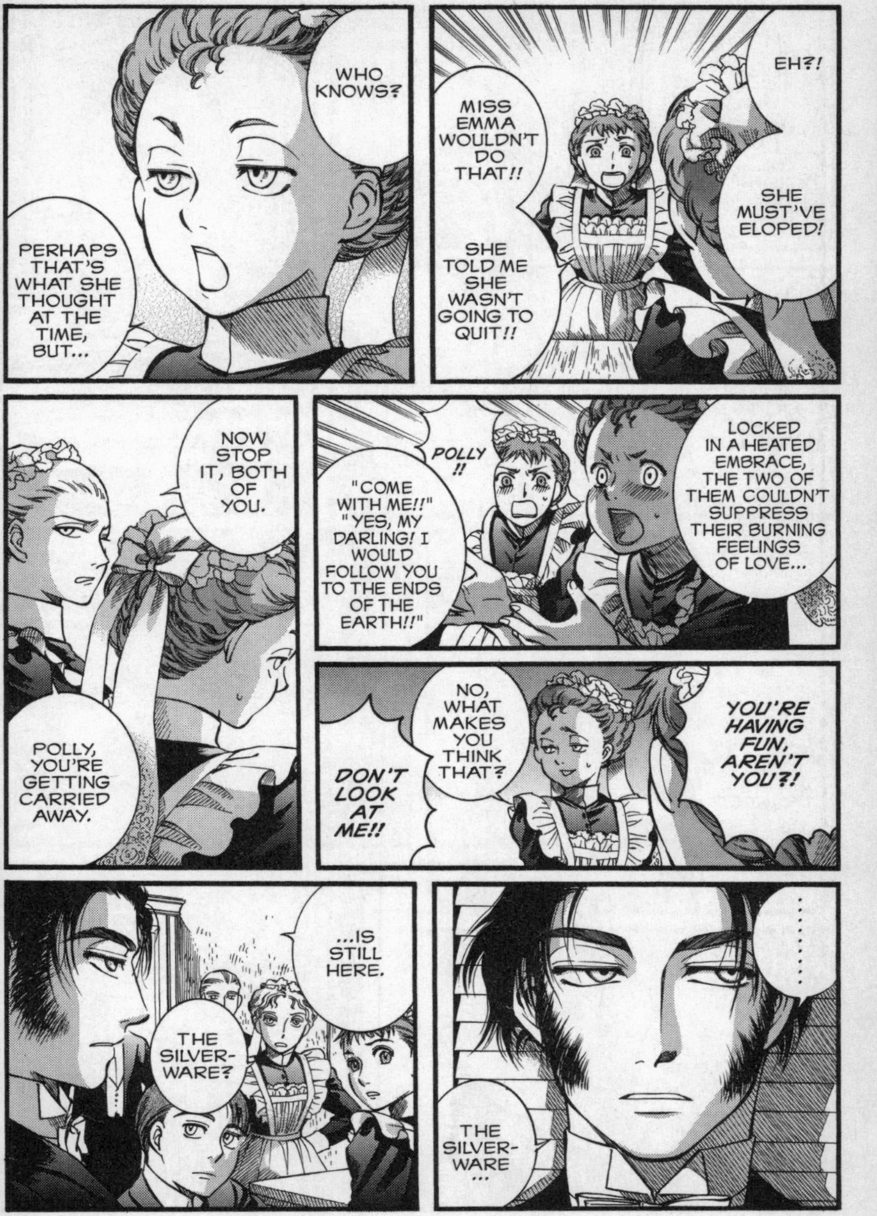
EH?!
SHE MUST'VE ELOPED!
MISS EMMA WOULDN'T DO THAT!!
SHE TOLD ME SHE WASN'T GOING TO QUIT!!
WHO KNOWS?
PERHAPS THAT'S WHAT SHE THOUGHT AT THE TIME, BUT...
LOCKED IN A HEATED EMBRACE, THE TWO OF THEM COULDN'T SUPPRESS THEIR BURNING FEELINGS OF LOVE...
"COME WITH ME!!" "YES, MY DARLING! I WOULD FOLLOW YOU TO THE ENDS OF THE EARTH!!"
POLLY!!
YOU'RE HAVING FUN, AREN'T YOU?!
NO, WHAT MAKES YOU THINK THAT?
DON'T LOOK AT ME!!
NOW STOP IT, BOTH OF YOU.
POLLY, YOU'RE GETTING CARRIED AWAY.
......
THE SILVERWARE...
THE SILVERWARE?
...IS STILL HERE.

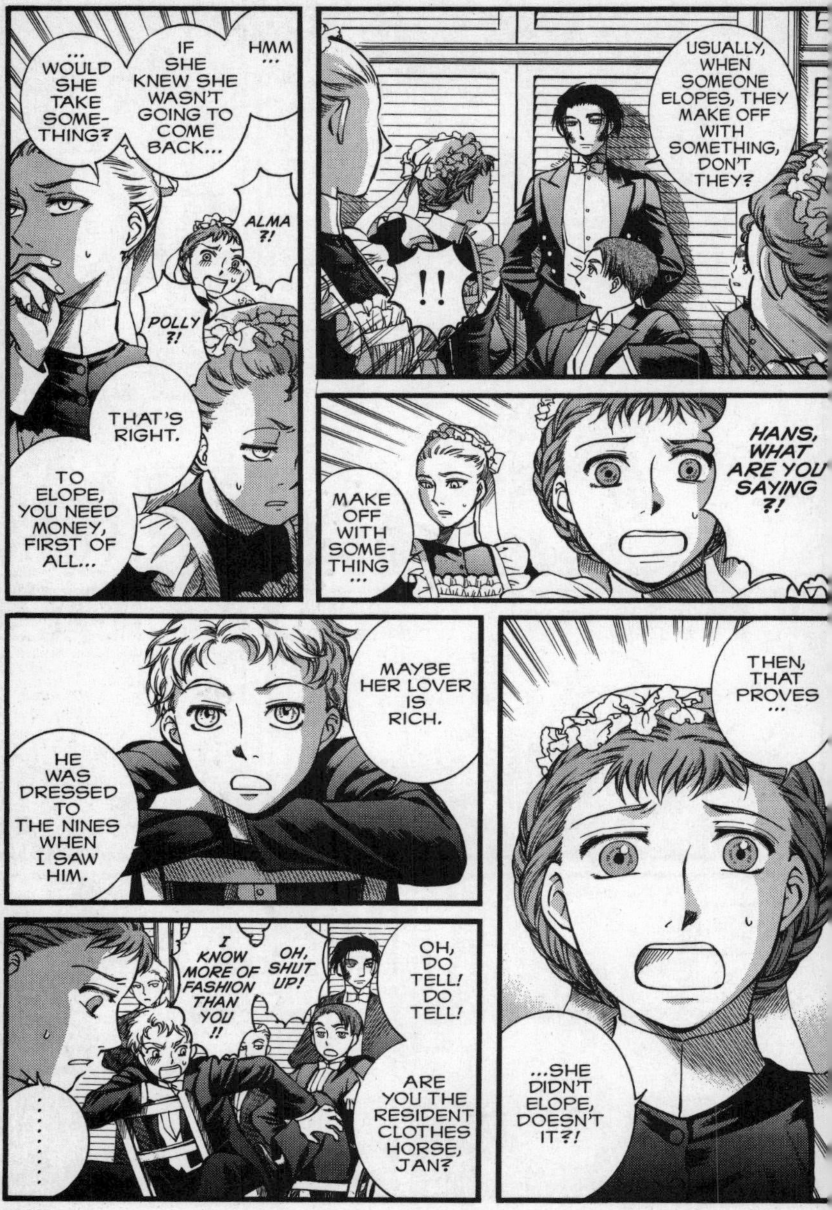
USUALLY, WHEN SOMEONE ELOPES, THEY MAKE OFF WITH SOMETHING, DON'T THEY?
!!
HANS, WHAT ARE YOU SAYING?!
MAKE OFF WITH SOME-THING...
HMM...
IF SHE KNEW SHE WASN'T GOING TO COME BACK...
...WOULD SHE TAKE SOME-THING?
ALMA?!
POLLY?!
THAT'S RIGHT.
TO ELOPE, YOU NEED MONEY, FIRST OF ALL...
THEN, THAT PROVES...
...SHE DIDN'T ELOPE, DOESN'T IT?!
MAYBE HER LOVER IS RICH.
HE WAS DRESSED TO THE NINES WHEN I SAW HIM.
OH, DO TELL! DO TELL!
ARE YOU THE RESIDENT CLOTHES HORSE, JAN?
OH, SHUT UP!
I KNOW MORE OF FASHION THAN YOU!!
......

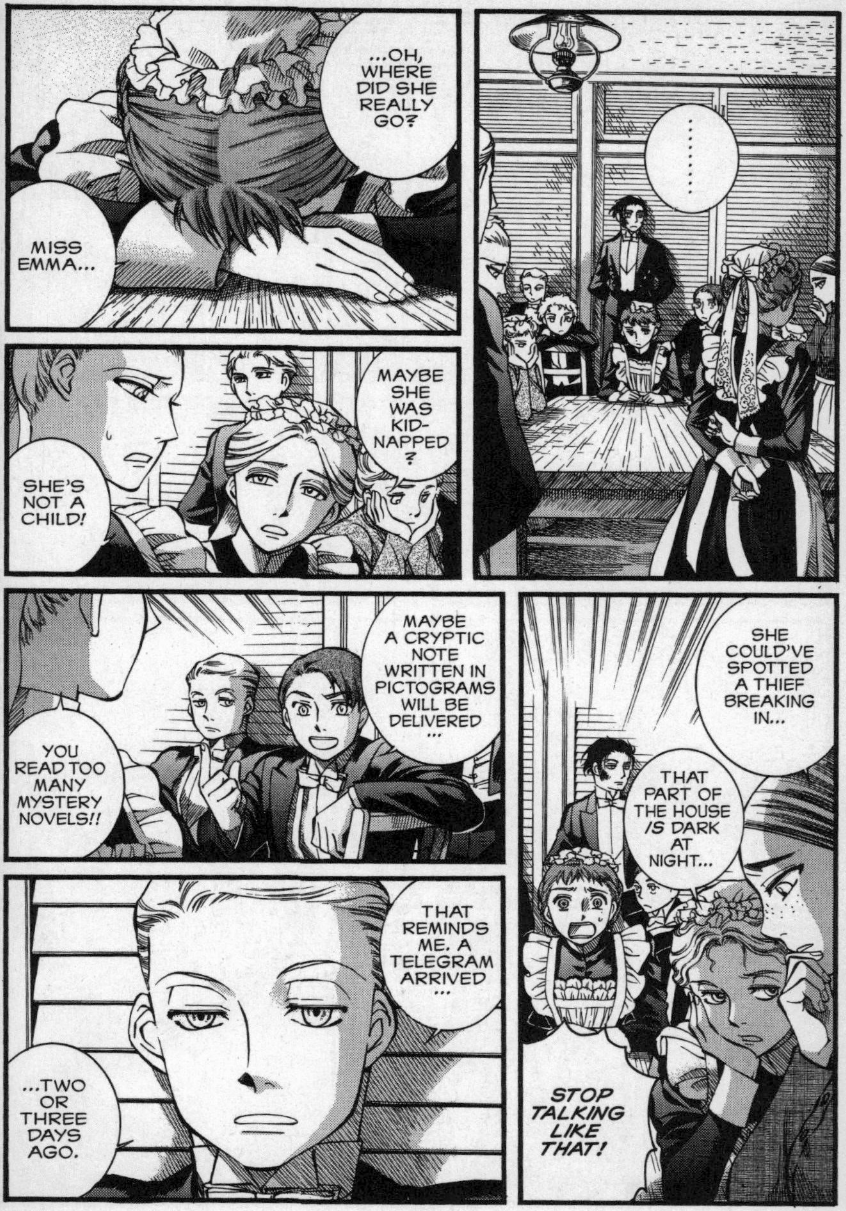
......
...OH, WHERE DID SHE REALLY GO?
MISS EMMA...
MAYBE SHE WAS KID-NAPPED?
SHE'S NOT A CHILD!
SHE COULD'VE SPOTTED A THIEF BREAKING IN...
THAT PART OF THE HOUSE *IS* DARK AT NIGHT...
STOP TALKING LIKE THAT!
MAYBE A CRYPTIC NOTE WRITTEN IN PICTOGRAMS WILL BE DELIVERED...
YOU READ TOO MANY MYSTERY NOVELS!!
THAT REMINDS ME. A TELEGRAM ARRIVED...
...TWO OR THREE DAYS AGO.

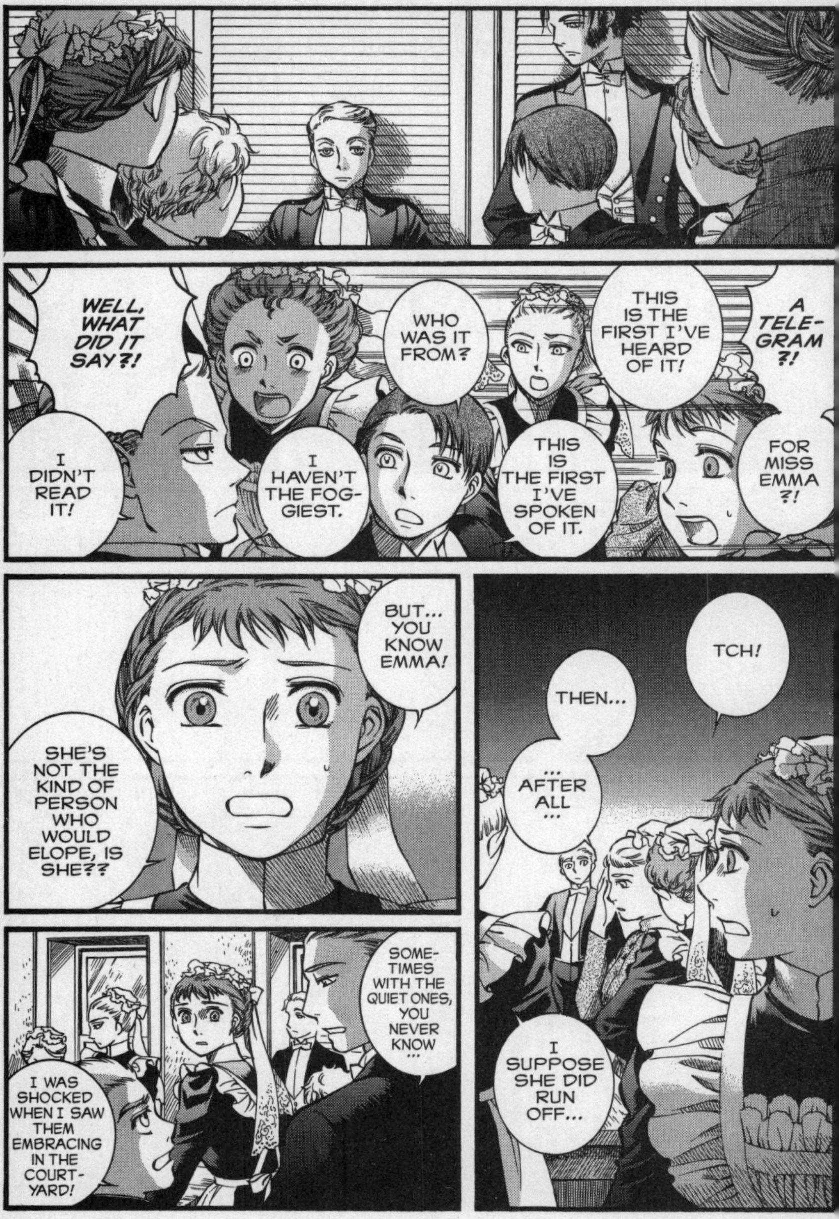
A TELEGRAM?!
FOR MISS EMMA?!
THIS IS THE FIRST I'VE HEARD OF IT!
THIS IS THE FIRST I'VE SPOKEN OF IT.
WHO WAS IT FROM?
I HAVEN'T THE FOGGIEST.
WELL, WHAT DID IT SAY?!
I DIDN'T READ IT!
BUT... YOU KNOW EMMA!
SHE'S NOT THE KIND OF PERSON WHO WOULD ELOPE, IS SHE??
SOMETIMES WITH THE QUIET ONES, YOU NEVER KNOW...
I WAS SHOCKED WHEN I SAW THEM EMBRACING IN THE COURTYARD!
TCH!
THEN...
...AFTER ALL...
I SUPPOSE SHE DID RUN OFF...

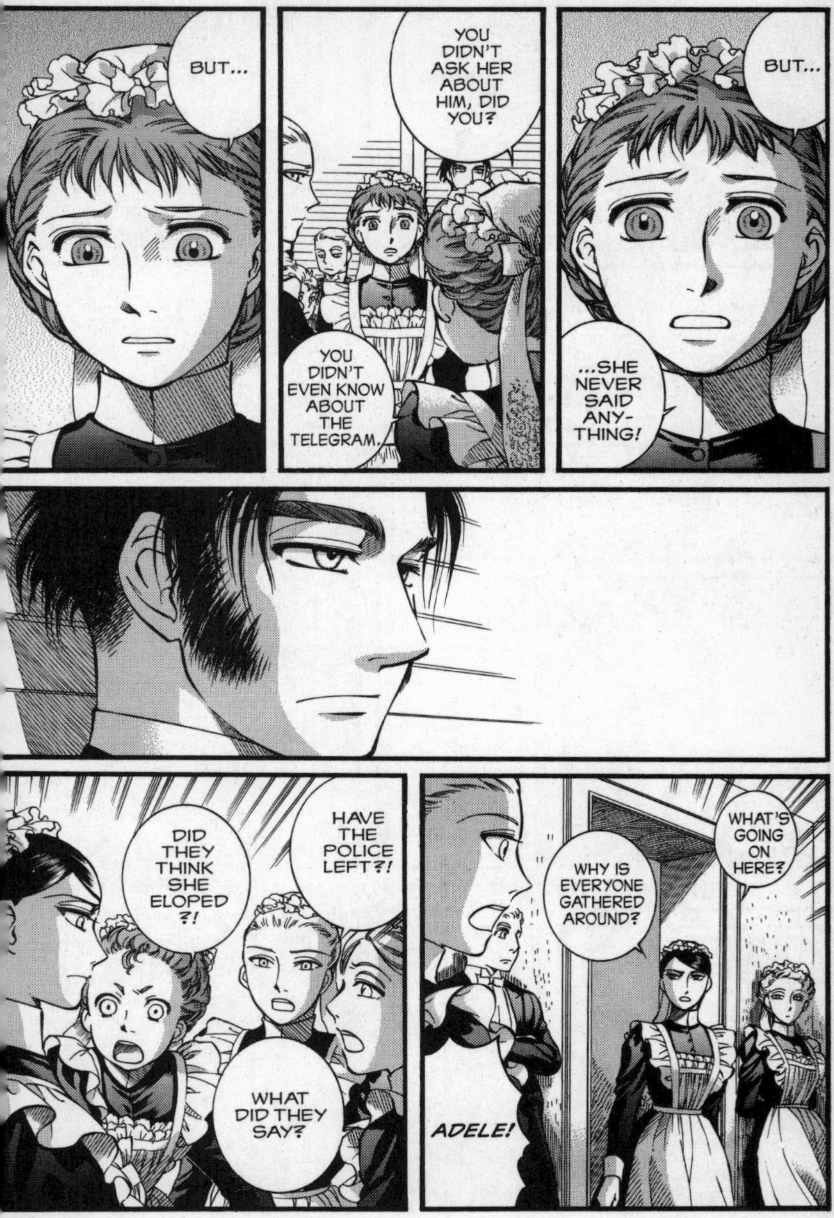
BUT...
...SHE NEVER SAID ANYTHING!
YOU DIDN'T ASK HER ABOUT HIM, DID YOU?
YOU DIDN'T EVEN KNOW ABOUT THE TELEGRAM.
BUT...
WHAT'S GOING ON HERE?
WHY IS EVERYONE GATHERED AROUND?
ADELE!
HAVE THE POLICE LEFT?!
DID THEY THINK SHE ELOPED?!
WHAT DID THEY SAY?

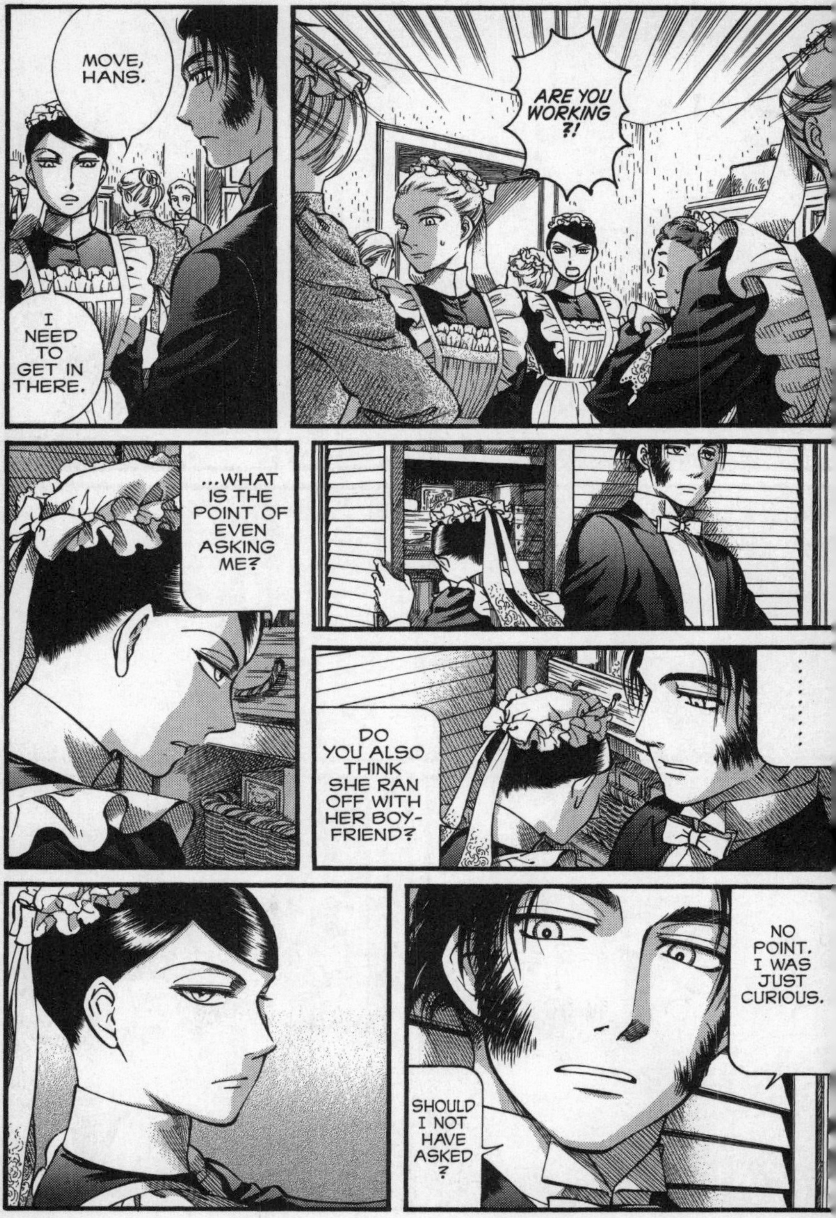
ARE YOU WORKING ?!
MOVE, HANS.
I NEED TO GET IN THERE.
......
DO YOU ALSO THINK SHE RAN OFF WITH HER BOY-FRIEND?
...WHAT IS THE POINT OF EVEN ASKING ME?
NO POINT. I WAS JUST CURIOUS.
SHOULD I NOT HAVE ASKED ?

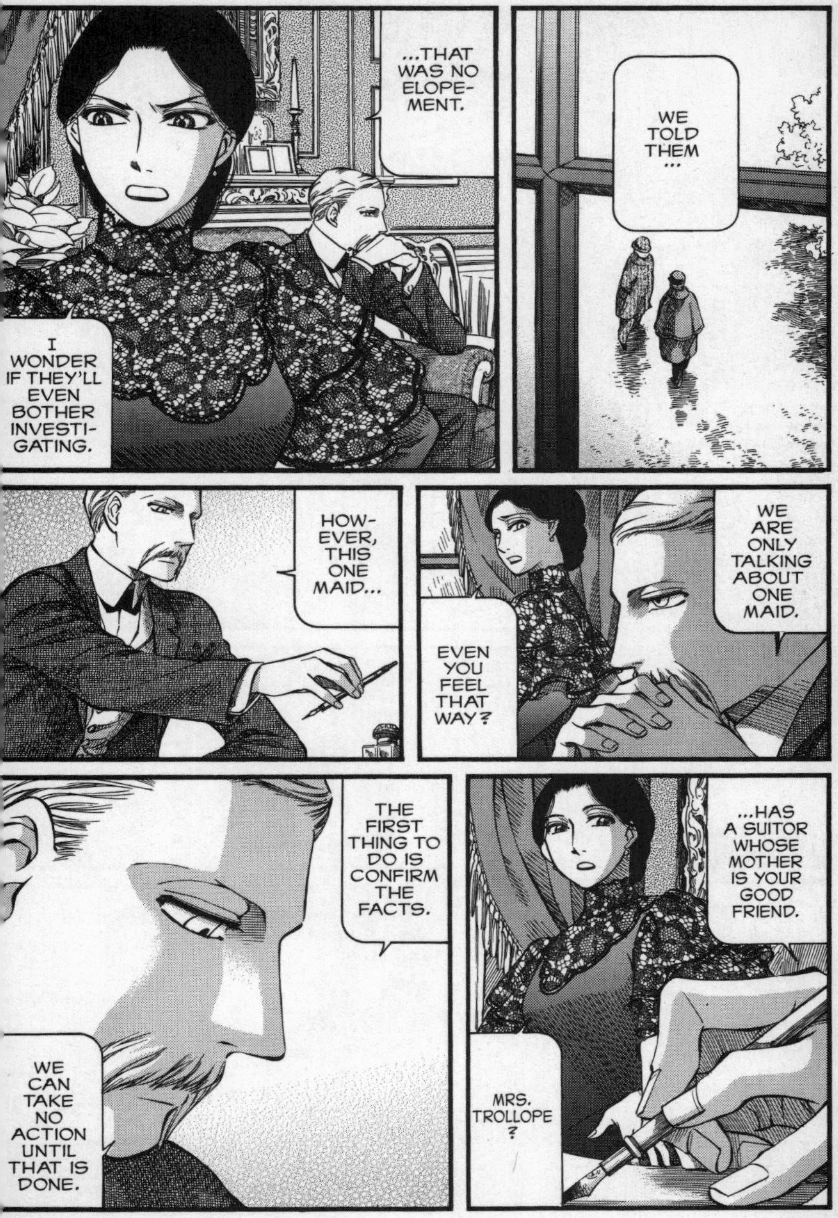
WE TOLD THEM ...
...THAT WAS NO ELOPEMENT.
I WONDER IF THEY'LL EVEN BOTHER INVESTIGATING.
WE ARE ONLY TALKING ABOUT ONE MAID.
EVEN YOU FEEL THAT WAY?
HOWEVER, THIS ONE MAID...
...HAS A SUITOR WHOSE MOTHER IS YOUR GOOD FRIEND.
MRS. TROLLOPE?
THE FIRST THING TO DO IS CONFIRM THE FACTS.
WE CAN TAKE NO ACTION UNTIL THAT IS DONE.

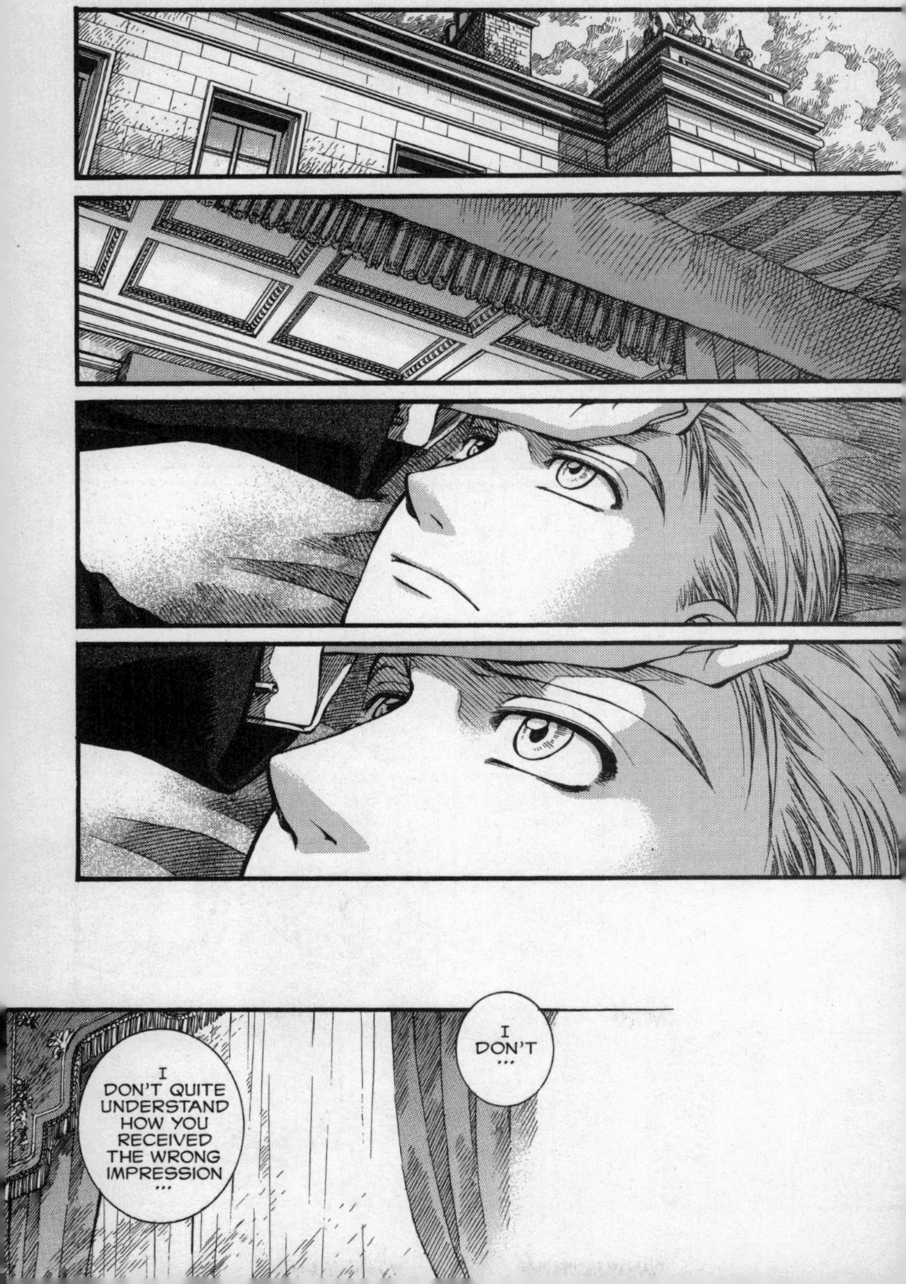
I DON'T ...
I DON'T QUITE UNDERSTAND HOW YOU RECEIVED THE WRONG IMPRESSION ...

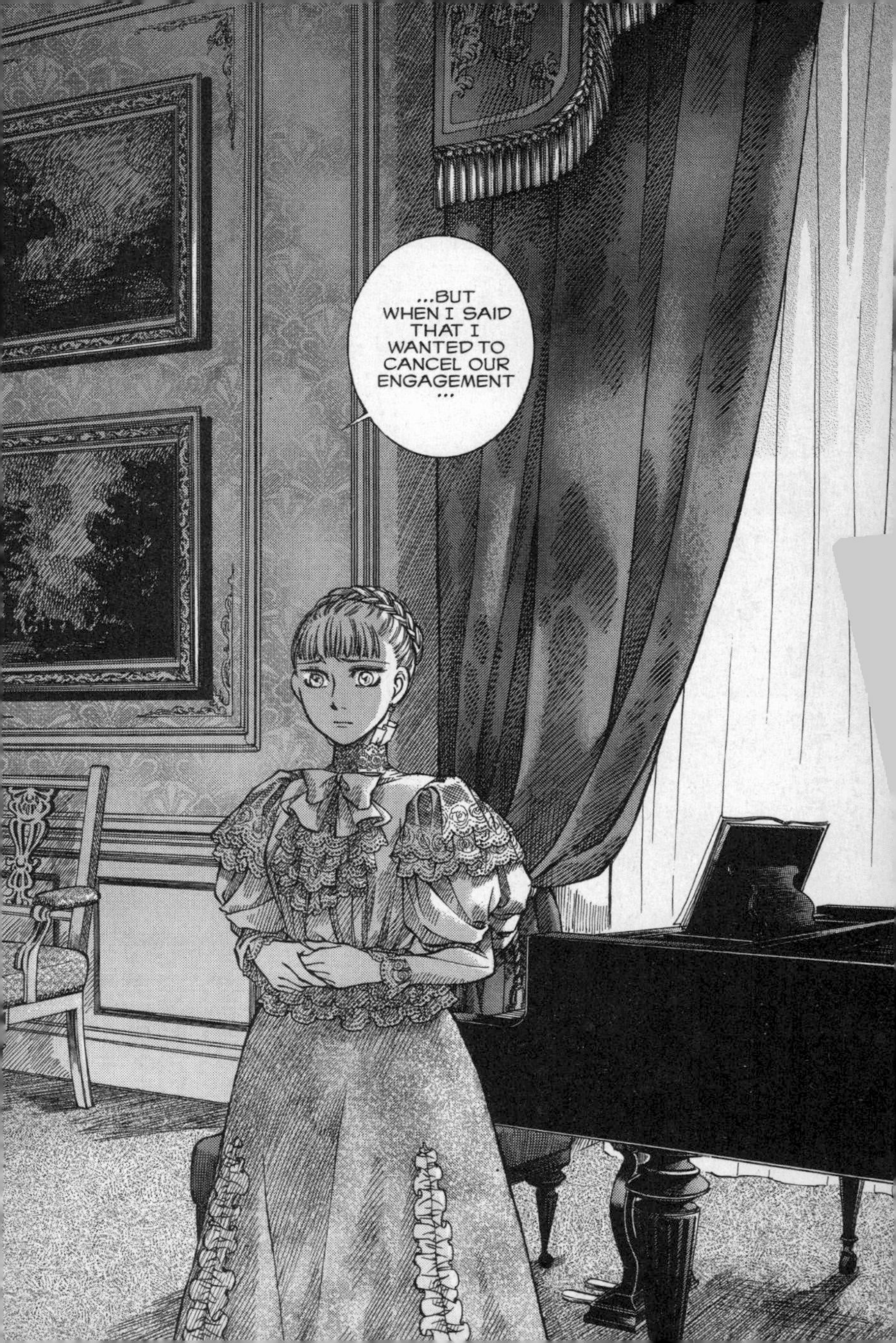
...BUT WHEN I SAID THAT I WANTED TO CANCEL OUR ENGAGEMENT ...

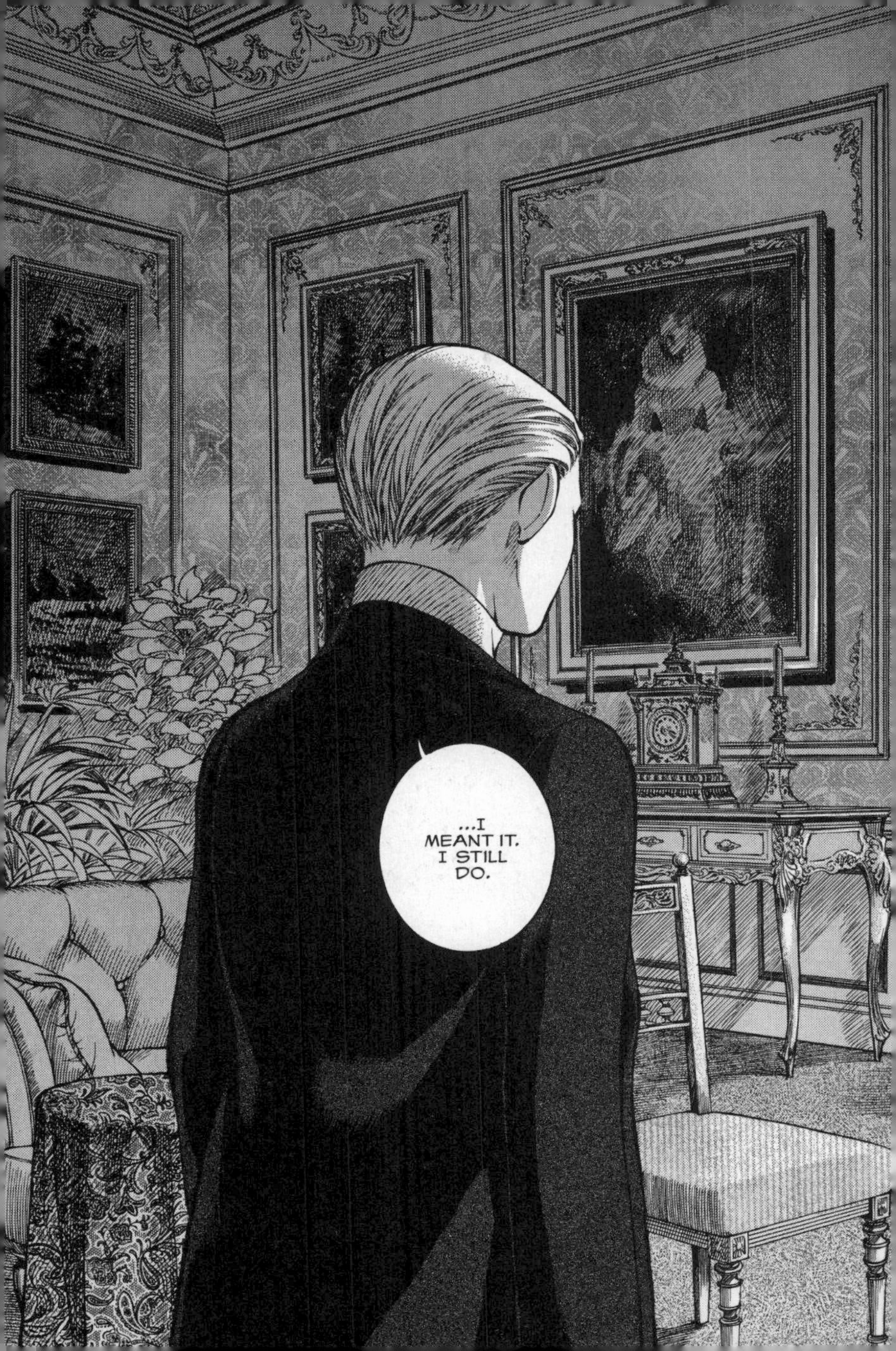
...I MEANT IT. I STILL DO.

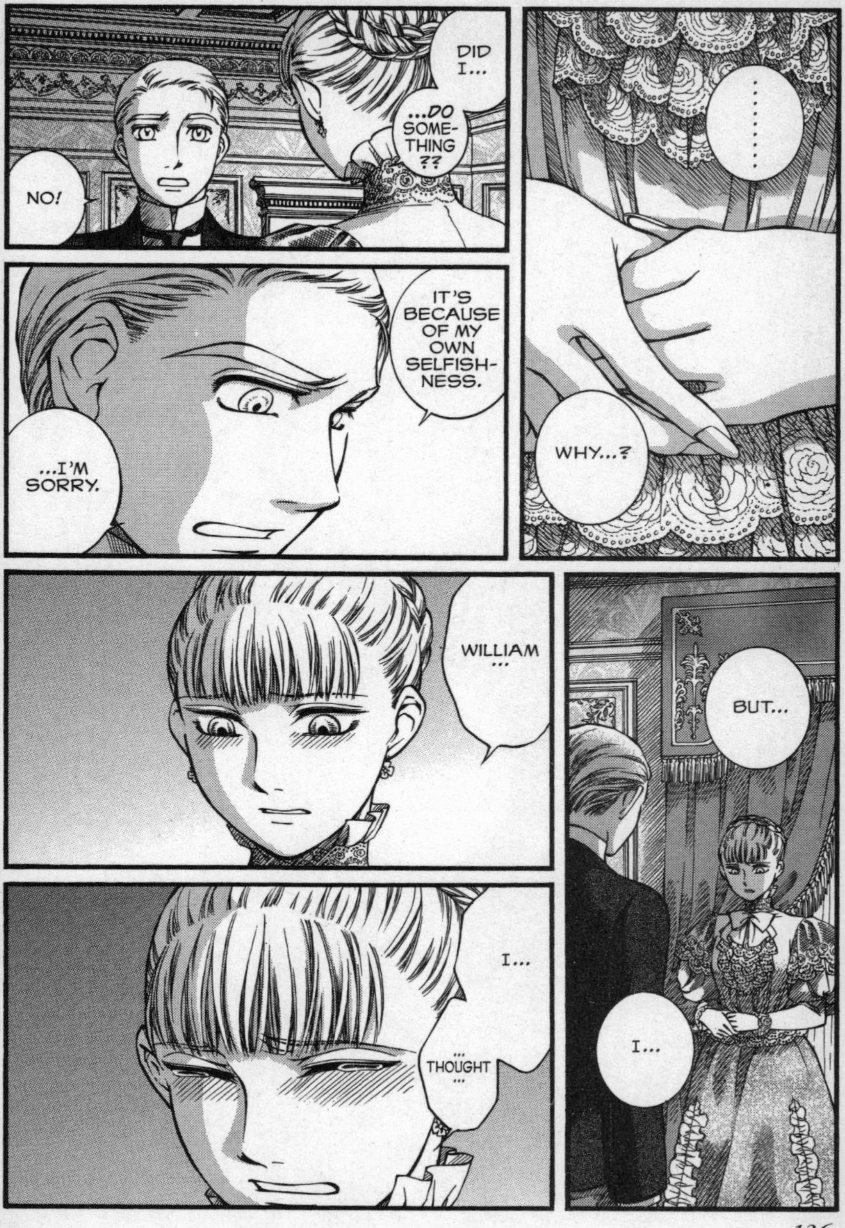
......
WHY...?
DID I...
...DO SOMETHING??
NO!
IT'S BECAUSE OF MY OWN SELFISHNESS.
...I'M SORRY.
BUT...
I...
WILLIAM...
I...
...THOUGHT...

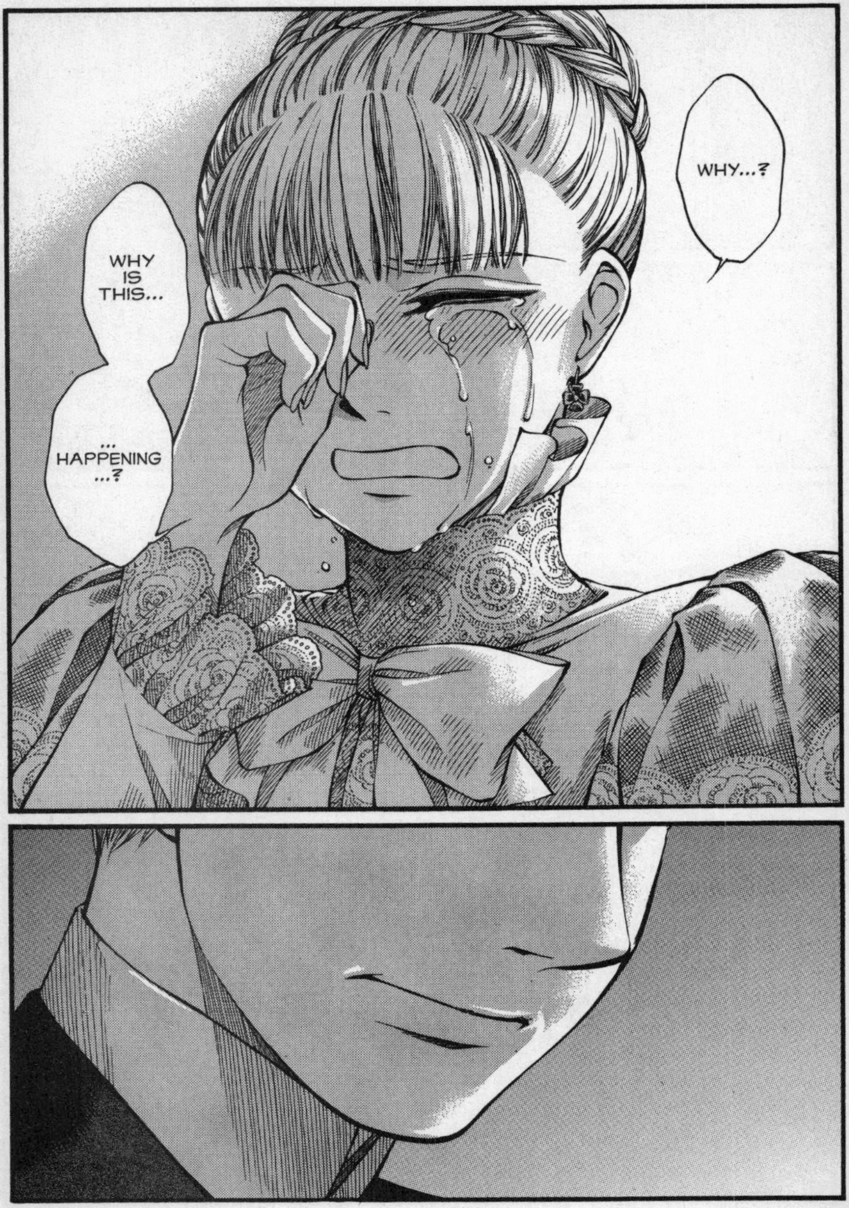
WHY...?
WHY IS THIS...
...HAPPENING...?

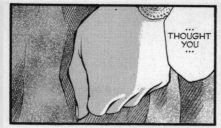
...
THOUGHT
YOU
...

WILLIAM
...

...I...

...LOVED
ME...
TOO...

....

I'M
SORRY.

....

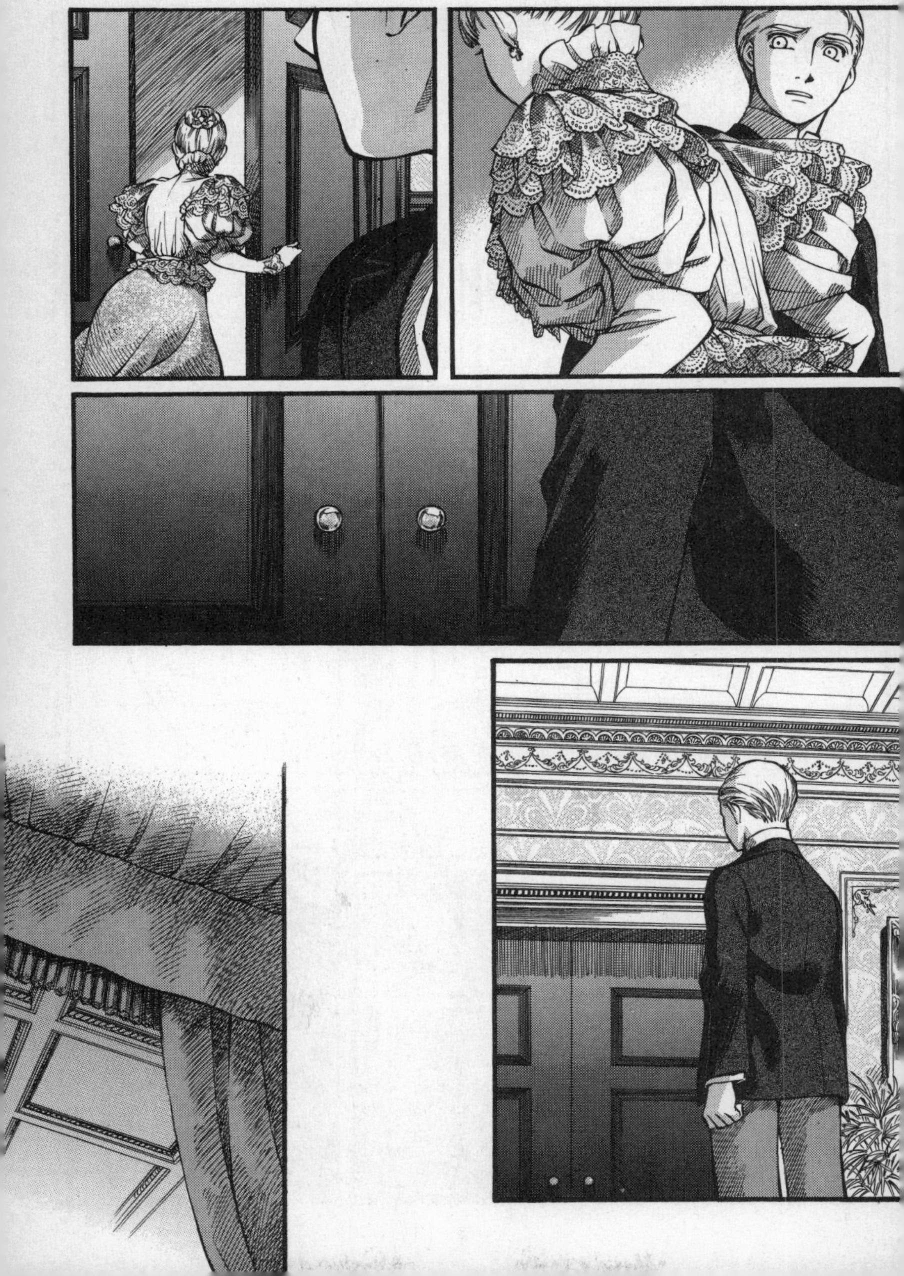

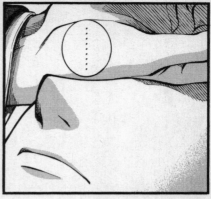

WILLIAM?

EH?

WHERE'S ELEANOR?

SHE LEFT A SHORT WHILE AGO.

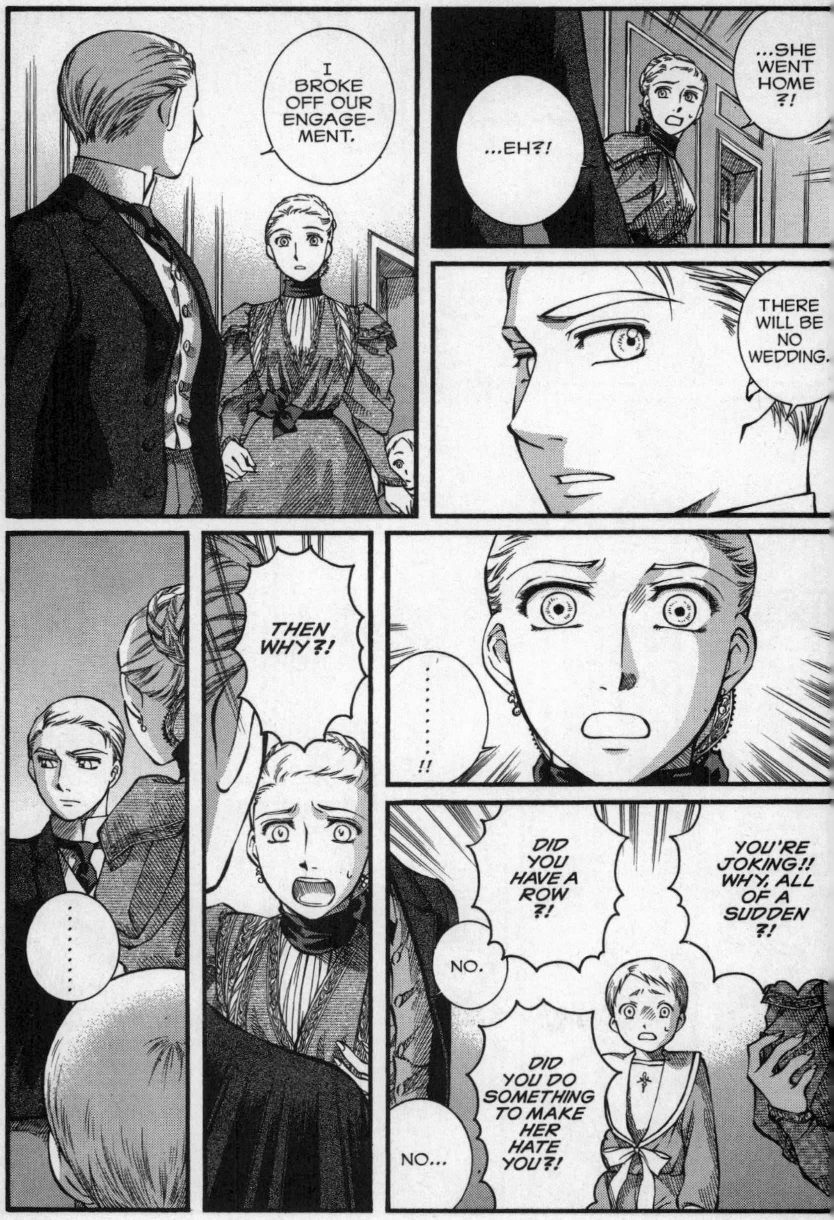
...SHE WENT HOME?!
...EH?!
THERE WILL BE NO WEDDING.
I BROKE OFF OUR ENGAGEMENT.
......!!
YOU'RE JOKING!! WHY, ALL OF A SUDDEN?!
DID YOU HAVE A ROW?!
NO.
DID YOU DO SOMETHING TO MAKE HER HATE YOU?!
NO...
THEN WHY?!
......

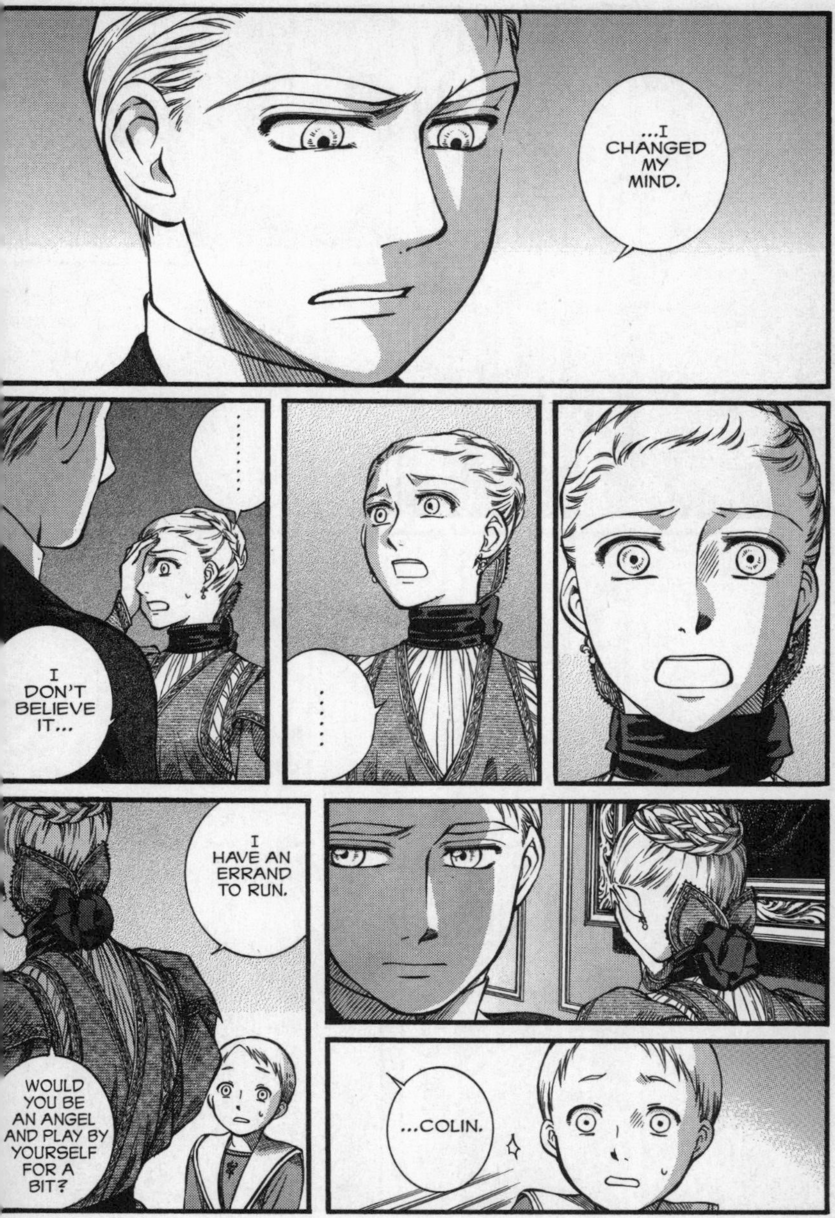
...I CHANGED MY MIND.
......
......
I DON'T BELIEVE IT...
...COLIN.
I HAVE AN ERRAND TO RUN.
WOULD YOU BE AN ANGEL AND PLAY BY YOURSELF FOR A BIT?

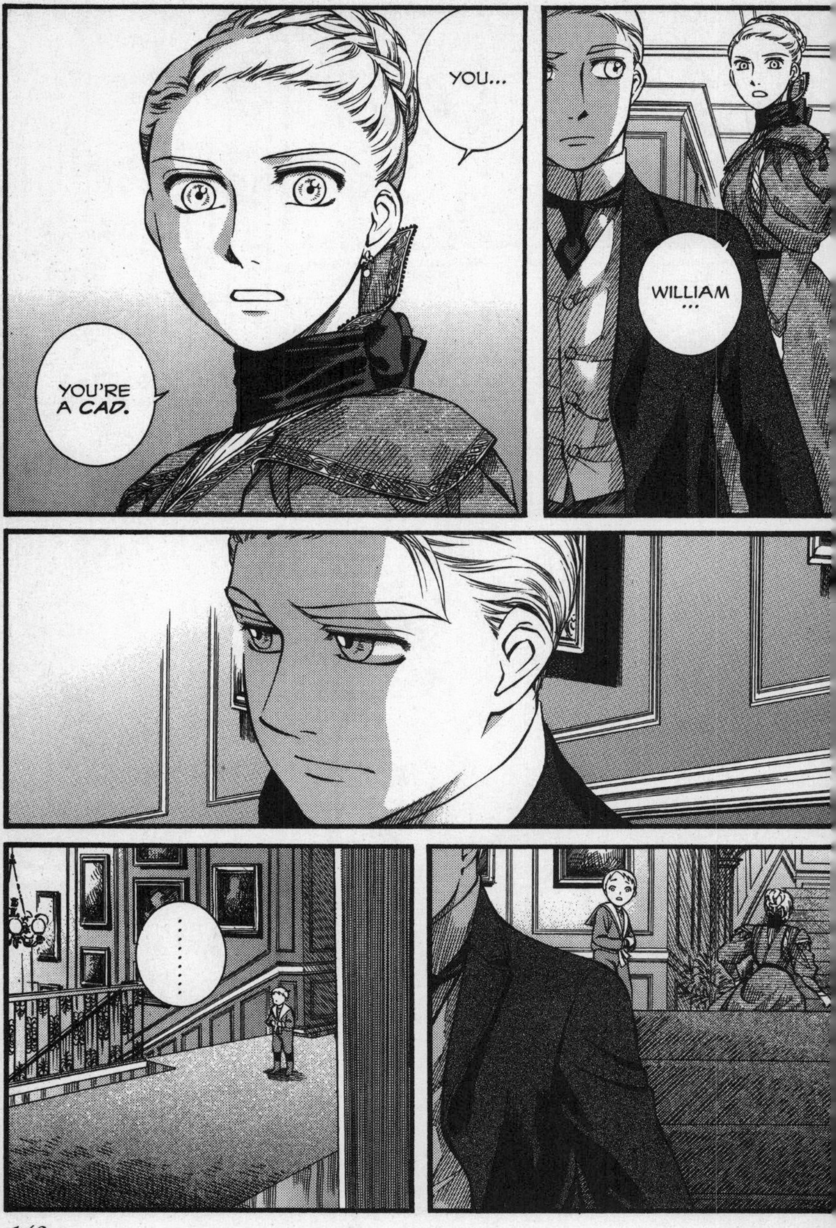
WILLIAM ...
YOU...
YOU'RE A *CAD.*
......

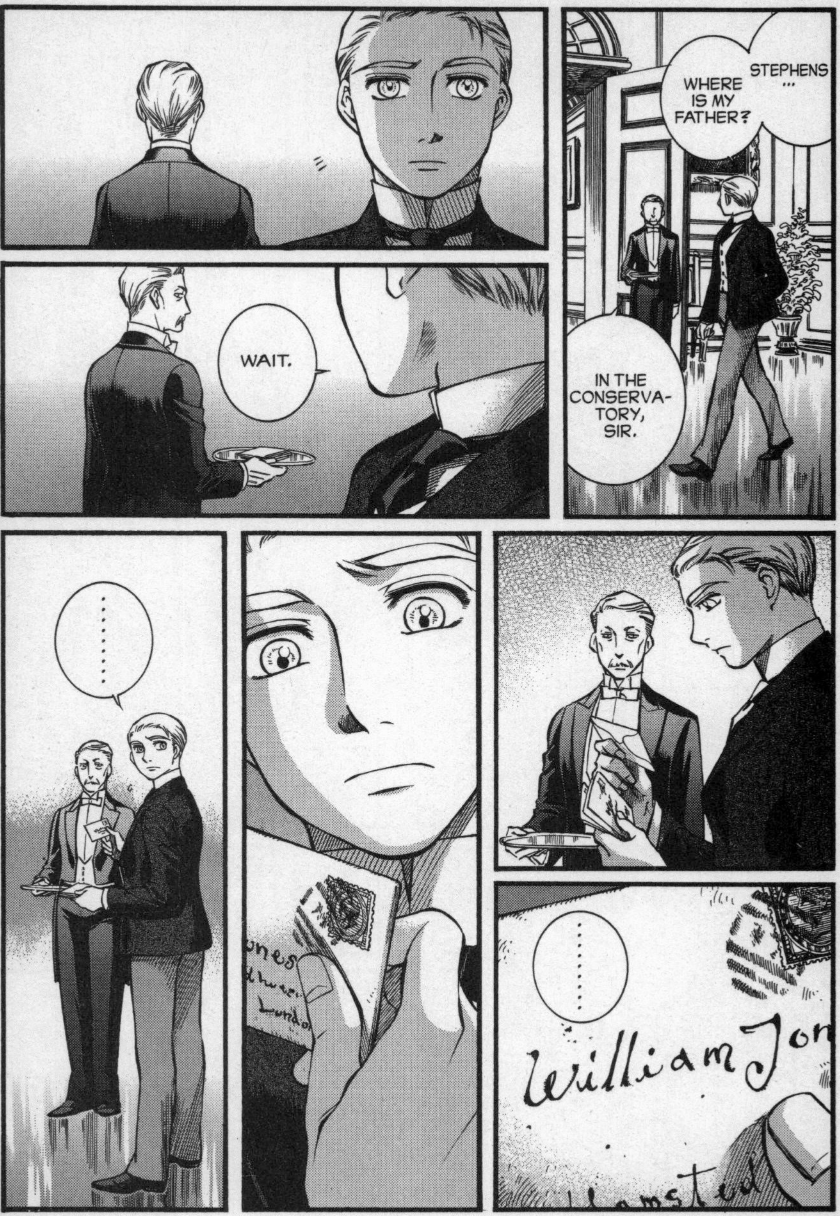
STEPHENS ...
WHERE IS MY FATHER?
IN THE CONSERVATORY, SIR.
WAIT.
......
William Jon
......

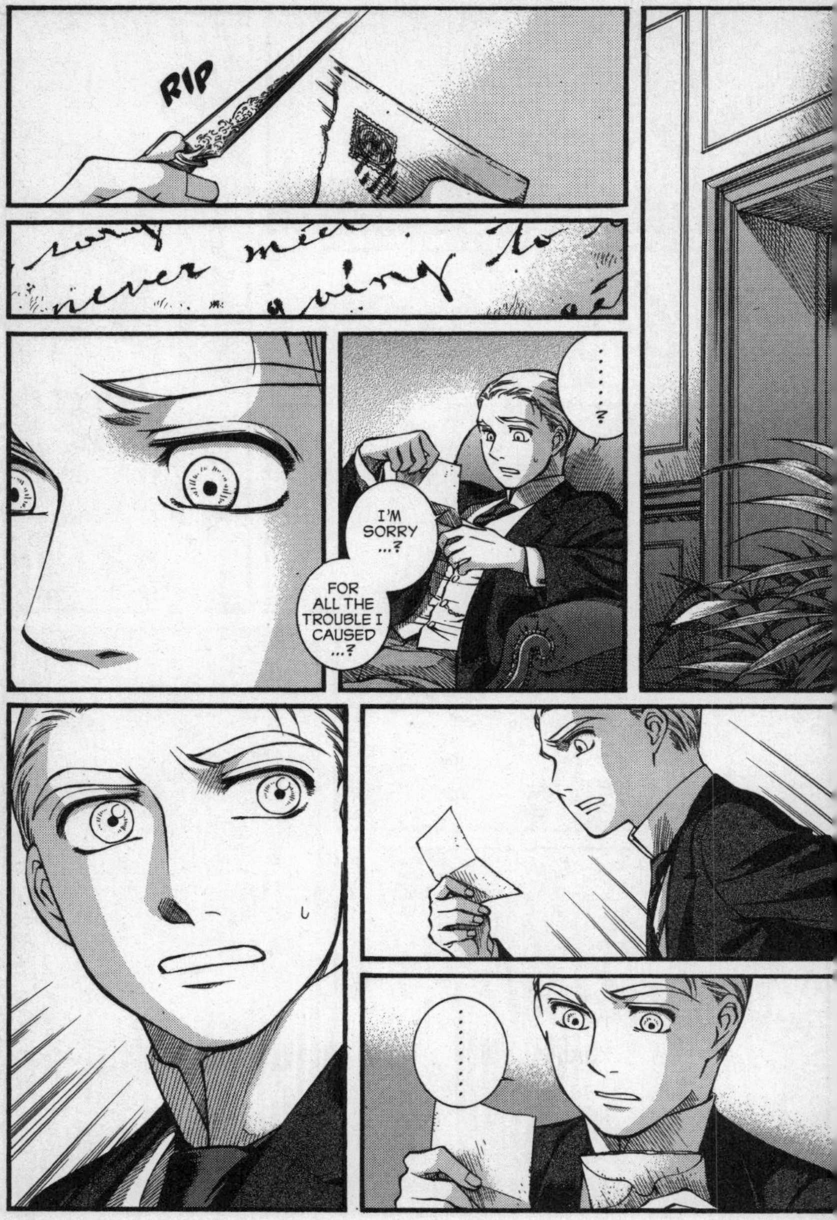
RIP
......?
I'M SORRY ...?
FOR ALL THE TROUBLE I CAUSED ...?
......

I'm
sorry...

...for
all
the...

...
trouble
I
caused.

YOU
CALLED,
SIR?

We will
not meet
again...

...so you
no longer
need
worry
about
me.

I WANT
TO SEND
A TELE-
GRAM!!

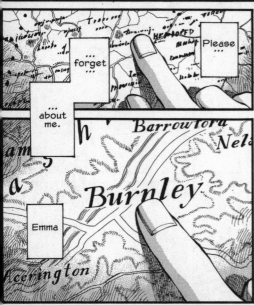

...
forget
...

Please
...

...
about
me.

Emma

I am
going
...

...to
America.

**Chapter Forty Two:
The End**

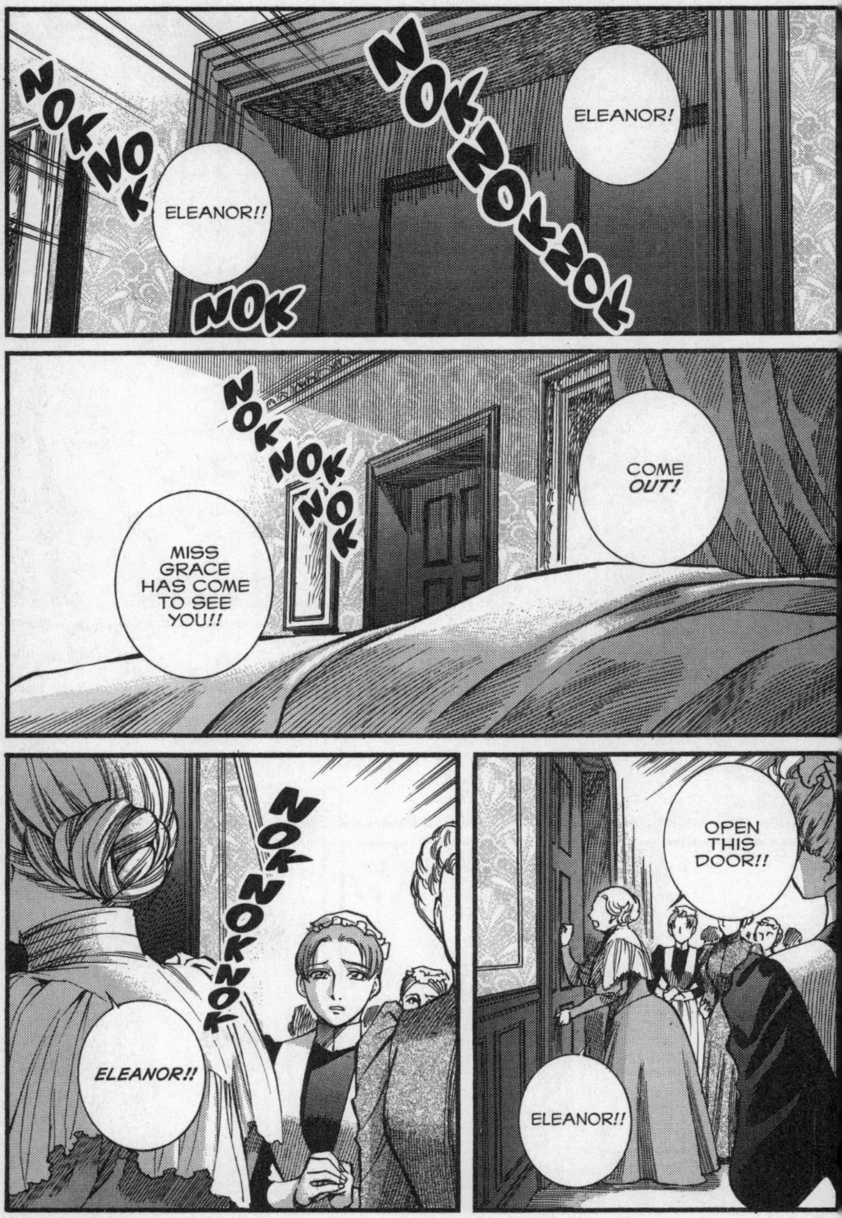
ELEANOR!
NOKNOKNOK
ELEANOR!!
NOKNOK
NOK
COME OUT!
NOKNOKNOK
MISS GRACE HAS COME TO SEE YOU!!
OPEN THIS DOOR!!
ELEANOR!!
NOKNOKNOK
ELEANOR!!

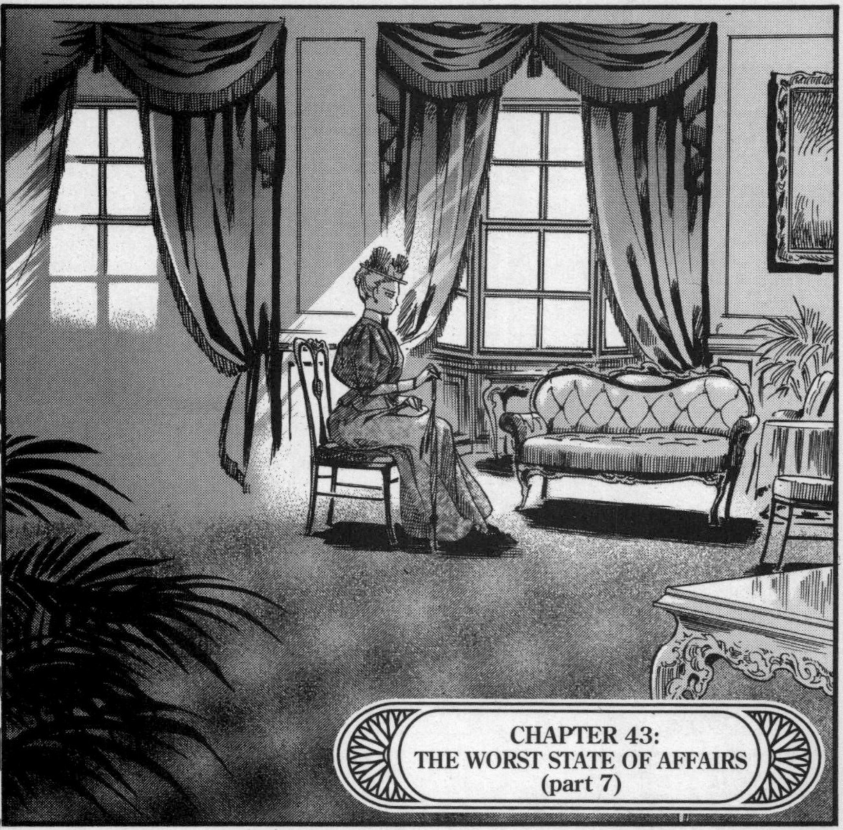
CHAPTER 43:
THE WORST STATE OF AFFAIRS
(part 7)

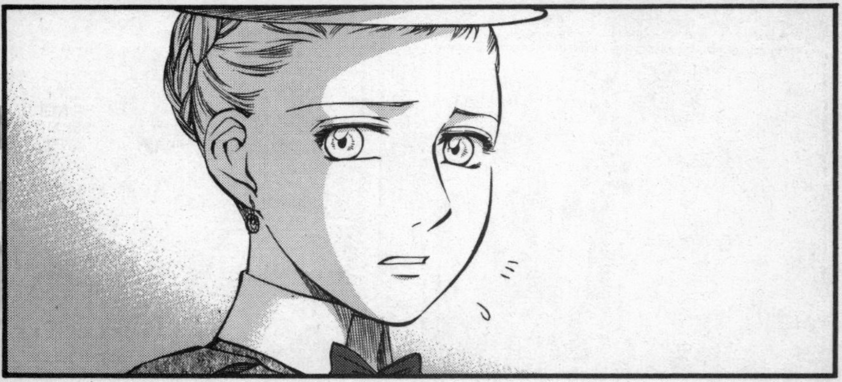

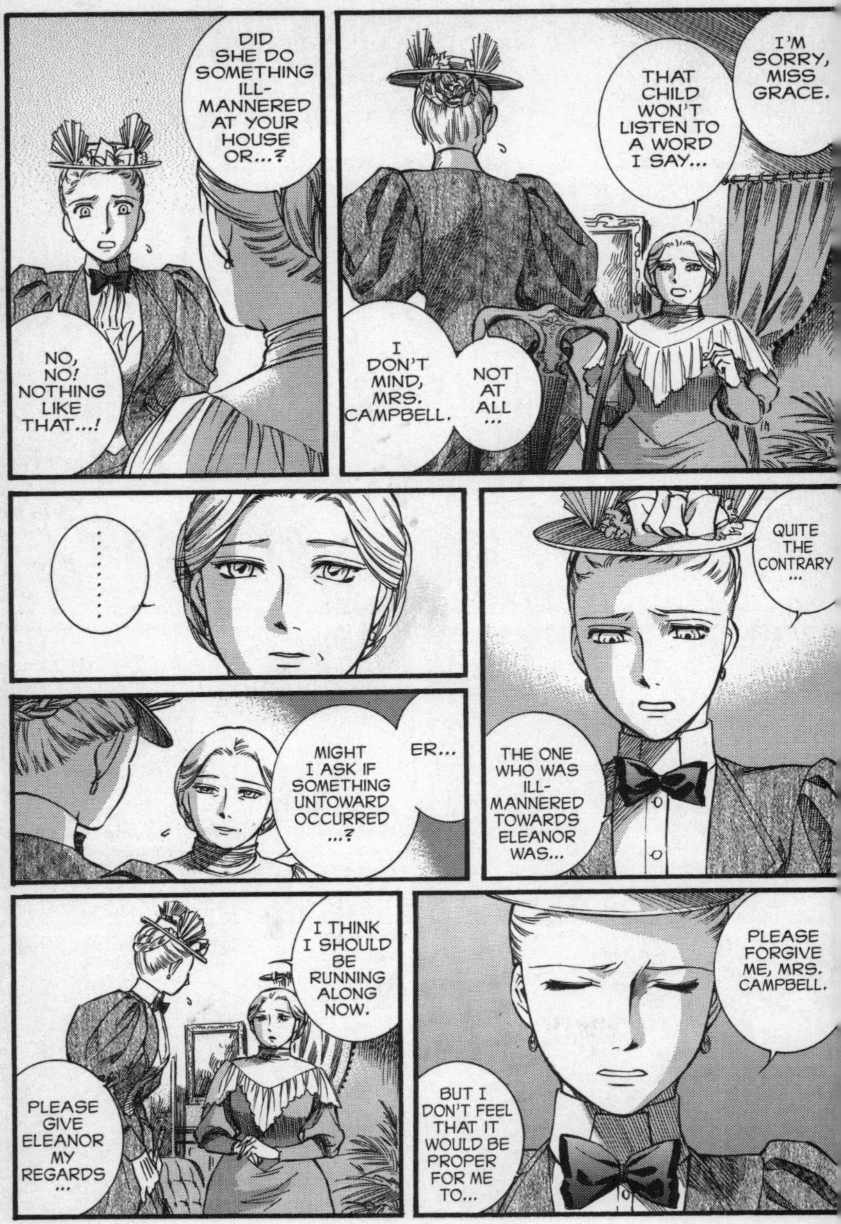
I'M SORRY, MISS GRACE.
THAT CHILD WON'T LISTEN TO A WORD I SAY...
NOT AT ALL...
I DON'T MIND, MRS. CAMPBELL.
DID SHE DO SOMETHING ILL-MANNERED AT YOUR HOUSE OR...?
NO, NO! NOTHING LIKE THAT...!
QUITE THE CONTRARY...
THE ONE WHO WAS ILL-MANNERED TOWARDS ELEANOR WAS...
......
ER...
MIGHT I ASK IF SOMETHING UNTOWARD OCCURRED...?
PLEASE FORGIVE ME, MRS. CAMPBELL.
BUT I DON'T FEEL THAT IT WOULD BE PROPER FOR ME TO...
I THINK I SHOULD BE RUNNING ALONG NOW.
PLEASE GIVE ELEANOR MY REGARDS...

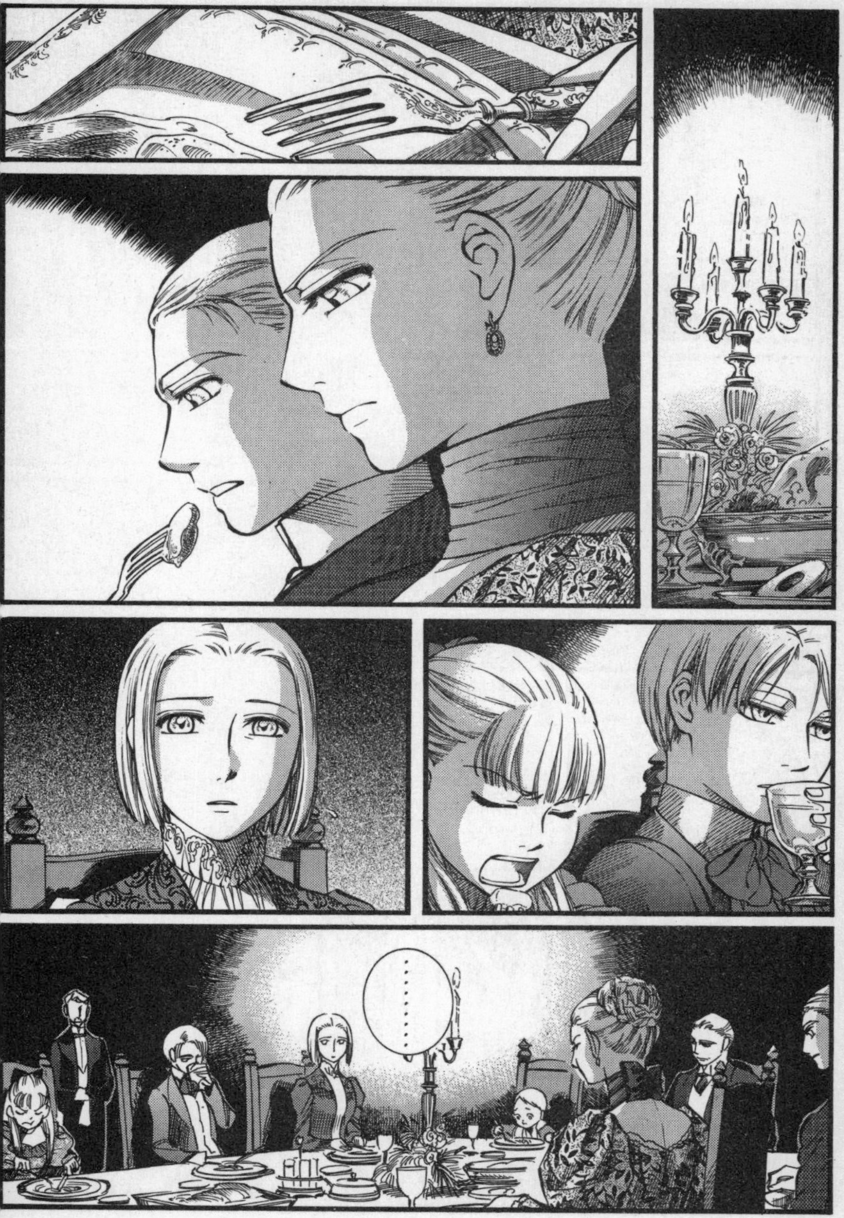
......

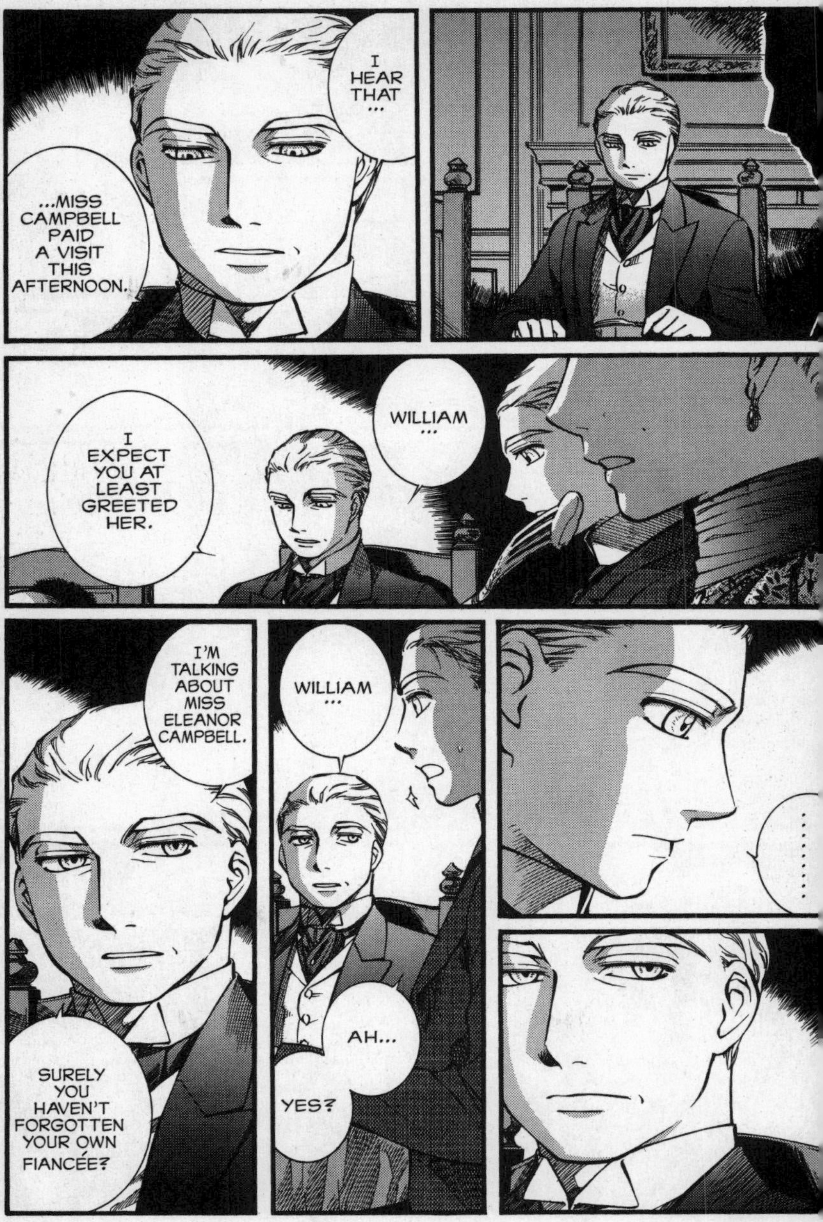
I HEAR THAT...
...MISS CAMPBELL PAID A VISIT THIS AFTERNOON.
WILLIAM...
I EXPECT YOU AT LEAST GREETED HER.
......
WILLIAM...
AH...
YES?
I'M TALKING ABOUT MISS ELEANOR CAMPBELL.
SURELY YOU HAVEN'T FORGOTTEN YOUR OWN FIANCÉE?

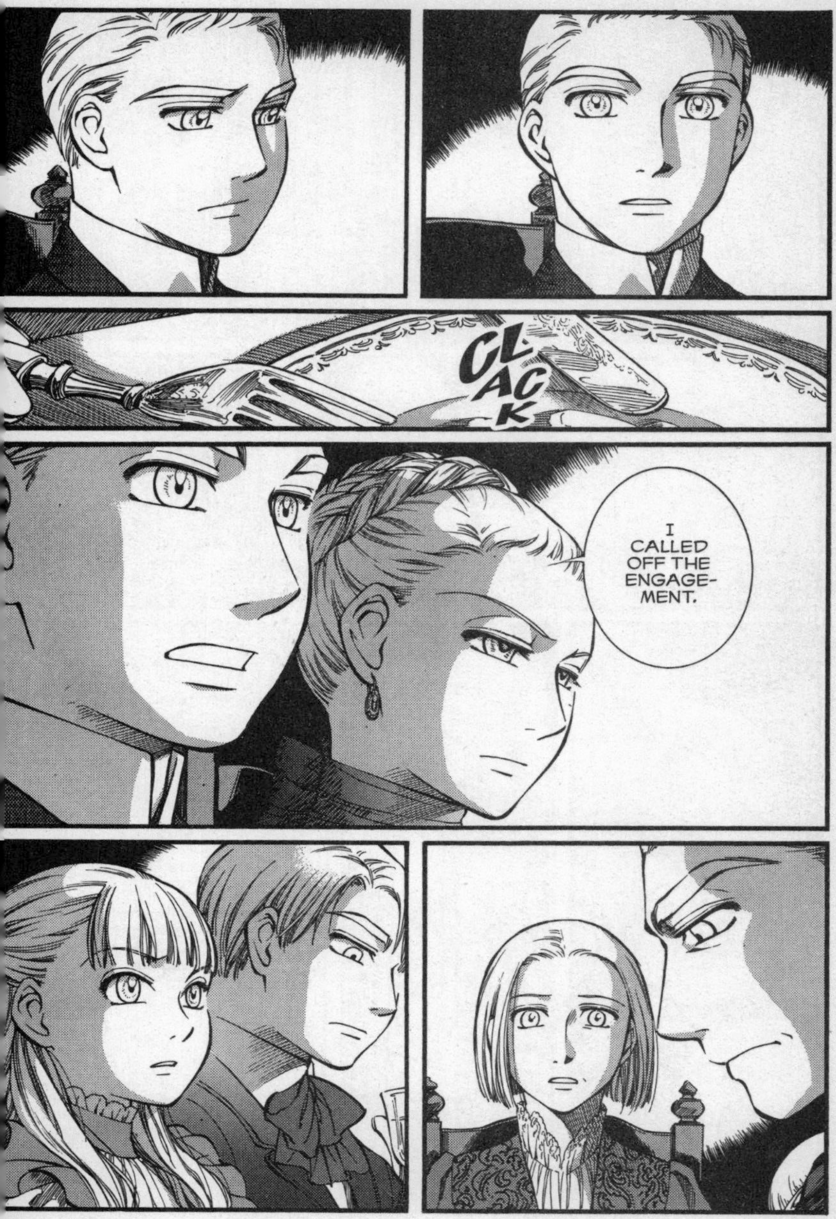
CLACK
I CALLED OFF THE ENGAGE-MENT.

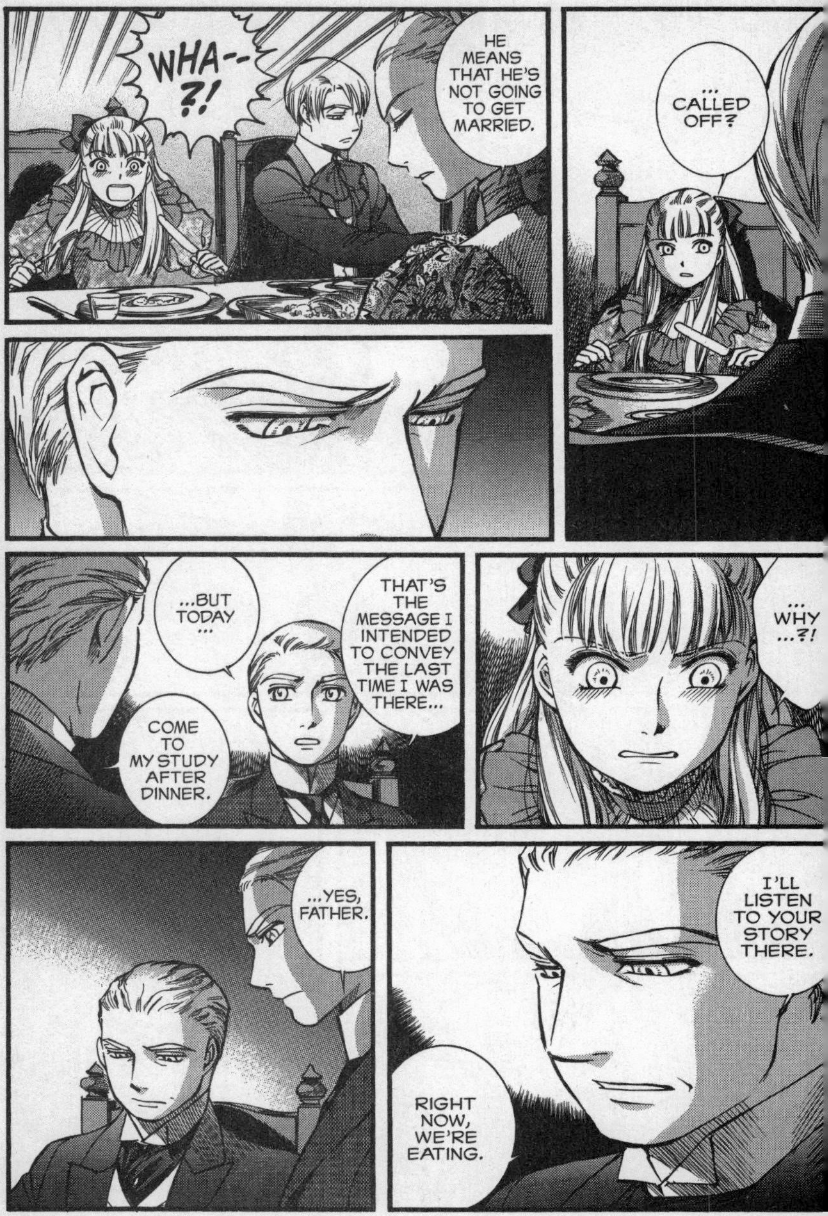
...
CALLED
OFF?
HE MEANS THAT HE'S NOT GOING TO GET MARRIED.
WHA--?!
... WHY ...?!
THAT'S THE MESSAGE I INTENDED TO CONVEY THE LAST TIME I WAS THERE...
...BUT TODAY ...
COME TO MY STUDY AFTER DINNER.
I'LL LISTEN TO YOUR STORY THERE.
RIGHT NOW, WE'RE EATING.
...YES, FATHER.

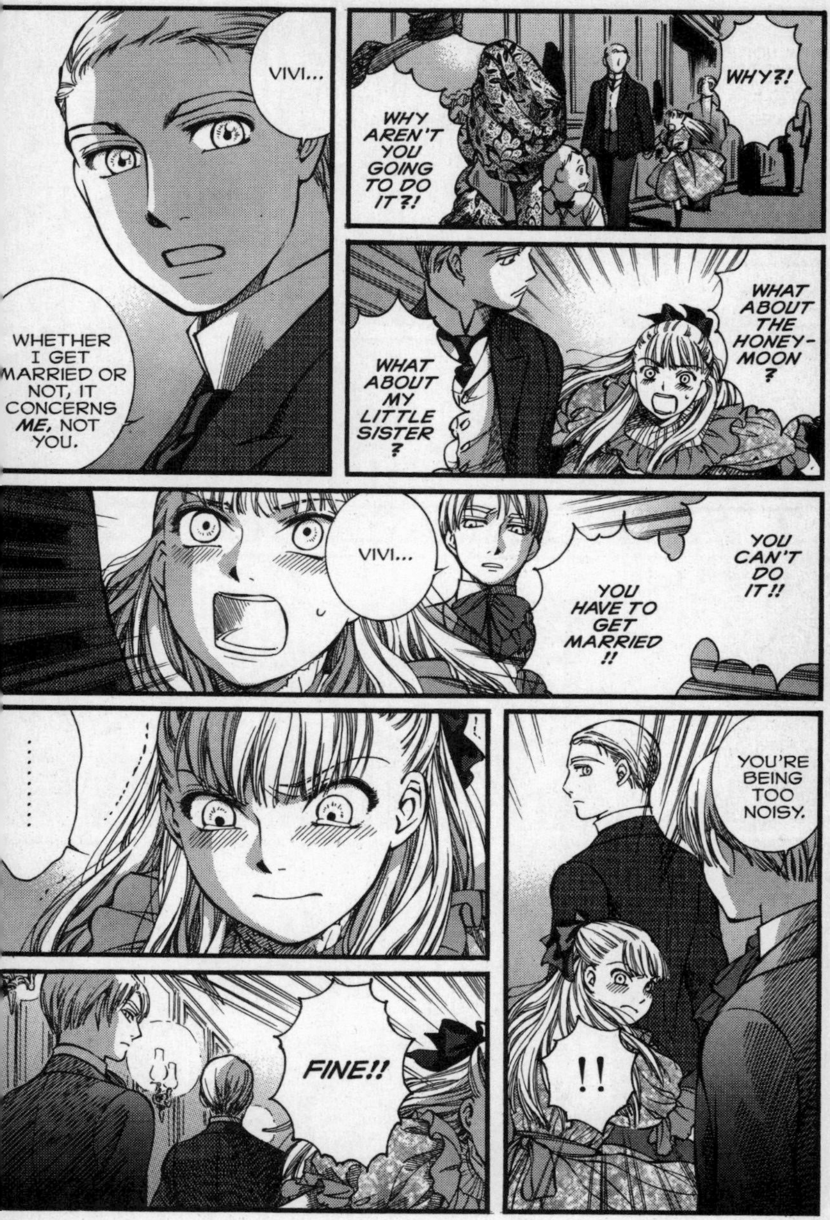
WHY?!
WHY AREN'T YOU GOING TO DO IT?!
WHAT ABOUT THE HONEY-MOON?
WHAT ABOUT MY LITTLE SISTER?
VIVI...
WHETHER I GET MARRIED OR NOT, IT CONCERNS *ME,* NOT YOU.
YOU CAN'T DO IT!!
YOU HAVE TO GET MARRIED!!
VIVI...
YOU'RE BEING TOO NOISY.
!!
......
FINE!!

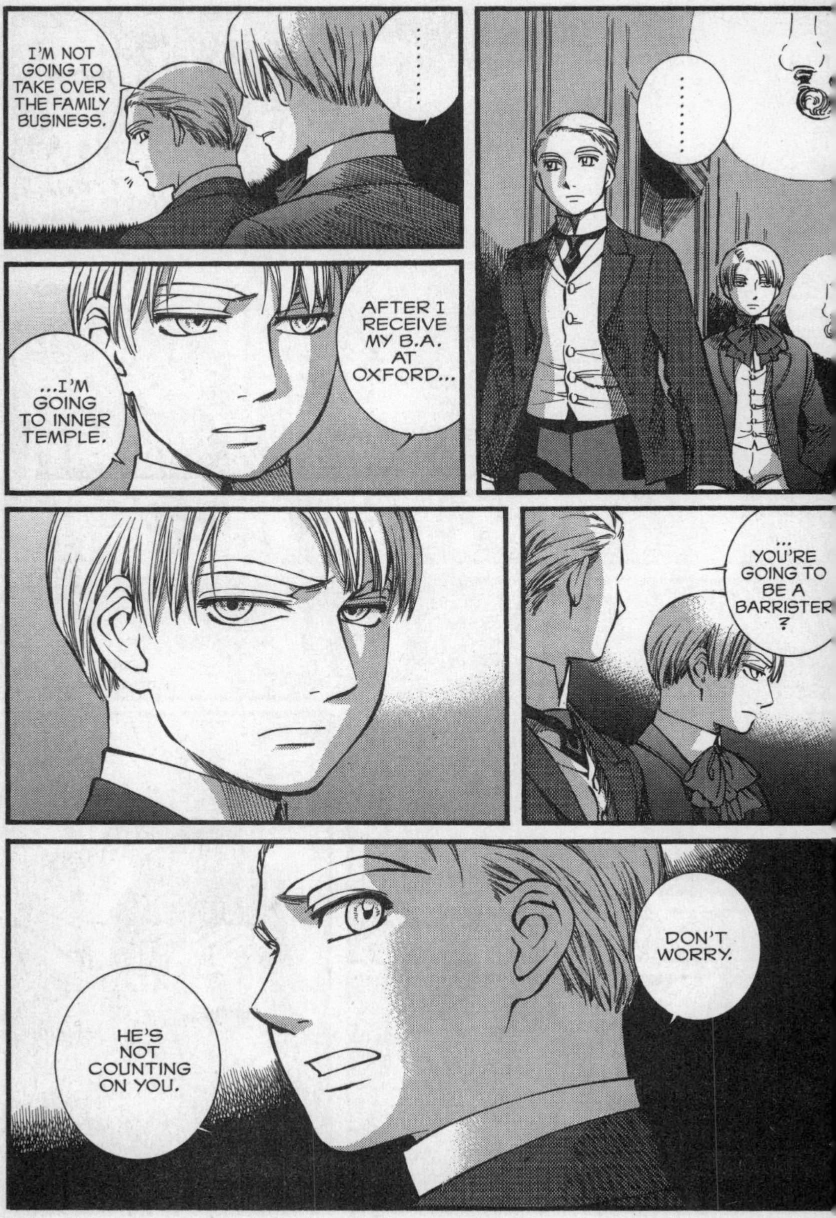
……
……
I'M NOT GOING TO TAKE OVER THE FAMILY BUSINESS.
AFTER I RECEIVE MY B.A. AT OXFORD...
...I'M GOING TO INNER TEMPLE.
...YOU'RE GOING TO BE A BARRISTER?
DON'T WORRY.
HE'S NOT COUNTING ON YOU.

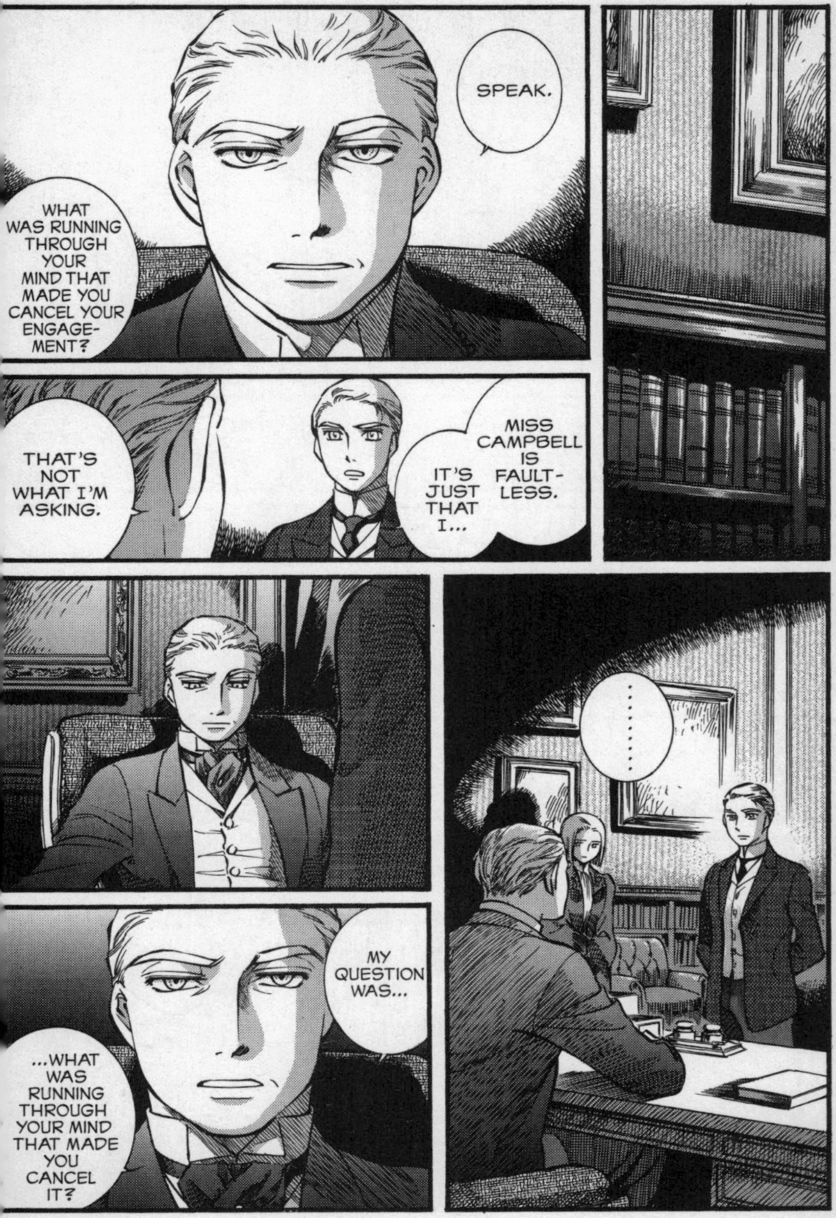
SPEAK.
WHAT WAS RUNNING THROUGH YOUR MIND THAT MADE YOU CANCEL YOUR ENGAGE-MENT?
MISS CAMPBELL IS FAULT-LESS. IT'S JUST THAT I...
THAT'S NOT WHAT I'M ASKING.
......
MY QUESTION WAS...
...WHAT WAS RUNNING THROUGH YOUR MIND THAT MADE YOU CANCEL IT?

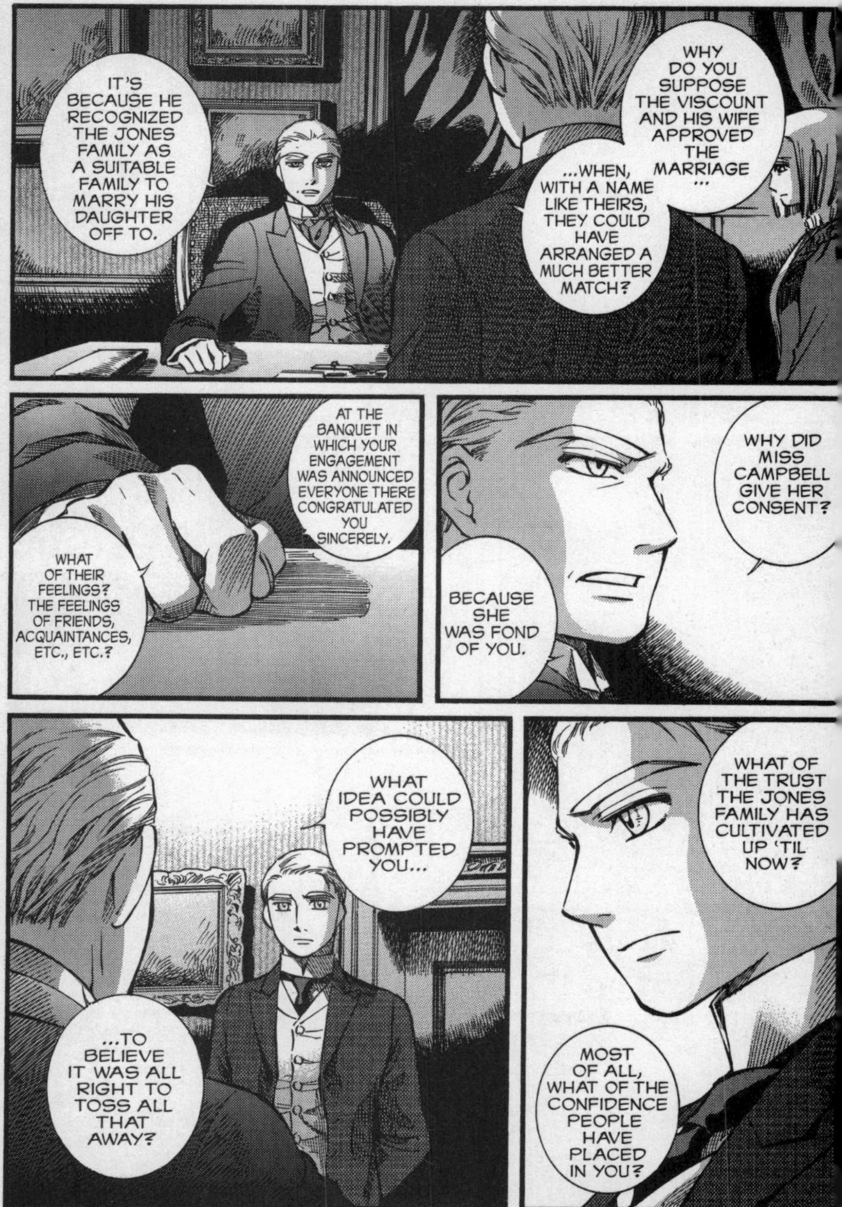
WHY DO YOU SUPPOSE THE VISCOUNT AND HIS WIFE APPROVED THE MARRIAGE...
...WHEN, WITH A NAME LIKE THEIRS, THEY COULD HAVE ARRANGED A MUCH BETTER MATCH?
IT'S BECAUSE HE RECOGNIZED THE JONES FAMILY AS A SUITABLE FAMILY TO MARRY HIS DAUGHTER OFF TO.
WHY DID MISS CAMPBELL GIVE HER CONSENT?
BECAUSE SHE WAS FOND OF YOU.
AT THE BANQUET IN WHICH YOUR ENGAGEMENT WAS ANNOUNCED EVERYONE THERE CONGRATULATED YOU SINCERELY.
WHAT OF THEIR FEELINGS? THE FEELINGS OF FRIENDS, ACQUAINTANCES, ETC., ETC.?
WHAT OF THE TRUST THE JONES FAMILY HAS CULTIVATED UP 'TIL NOW?
MOST OF ALL, WHAT OF THE CONFIDENCE PEOPLE HAVE PLACED IN YOU?
WHAT IDEA COULD POSSIBLY HAVE PROMPTED YOU...
...TO BELIEVE IT WAS ALL RIGHT TO TOSS ALL THAT AWAY?

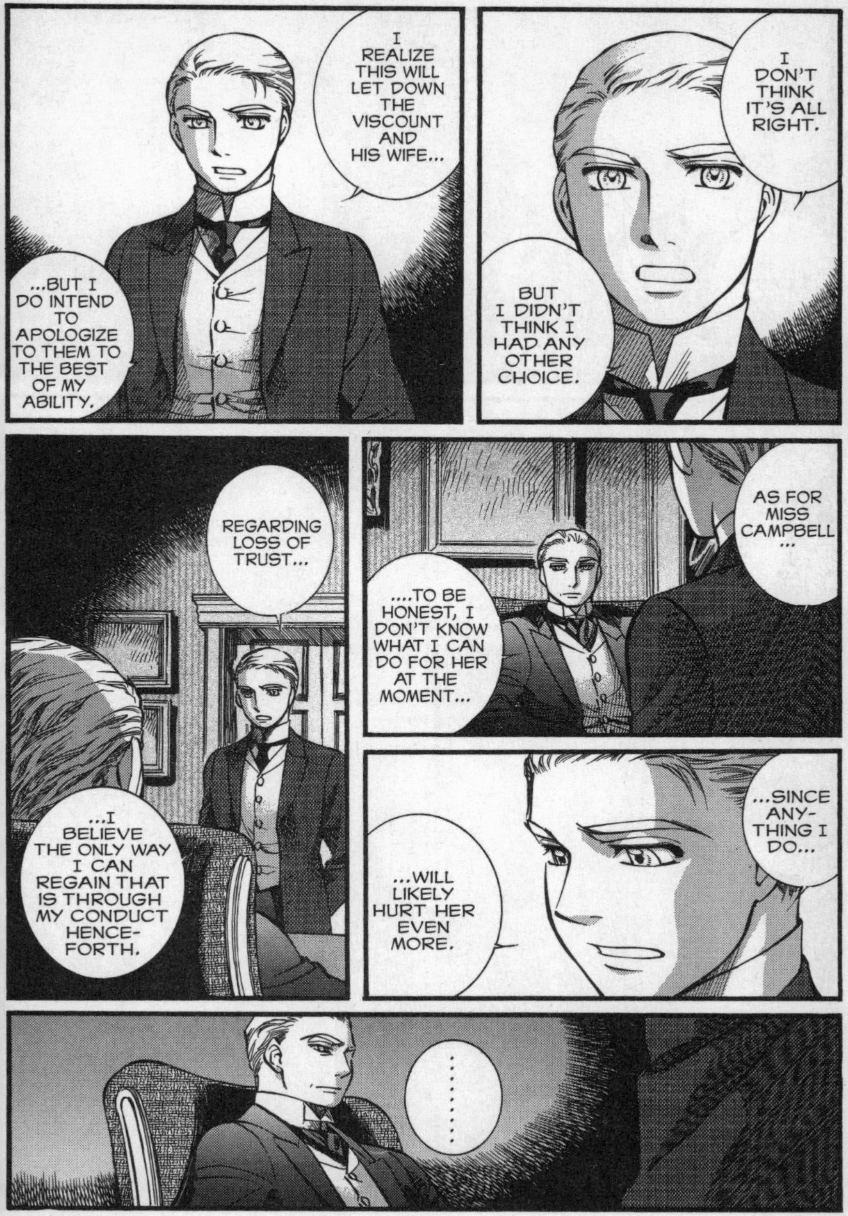
I DON'T THINK IT'S ALL RIGHT.
BUT I DIDN'T THINK I HAD ANY OTHER CHOICE.
I REALIZE THIS WILL LET DOWN THE VISCOUNT AND HIS WIFE...
...BUT I DO INTEND TO APOLOGIZE TO THEM TO THE BEST OF MY ABILITY.
AS FOR MISS CAMPBELL...
....TO BE HONEST, I DON'T KNOW WHAT I CAN DO FOR HER AT THE MOMENT...
...SINCE ANY-THING I DO...
...WILL LIKELY HURT HER EVEN MORE.
REGARDING LOSS OF TRUST...
...I BELIEVE THE ONLY WAY I CAN REGAIN THAT IS THROUGH MY CONDUCT HENCE-FORTH.
....

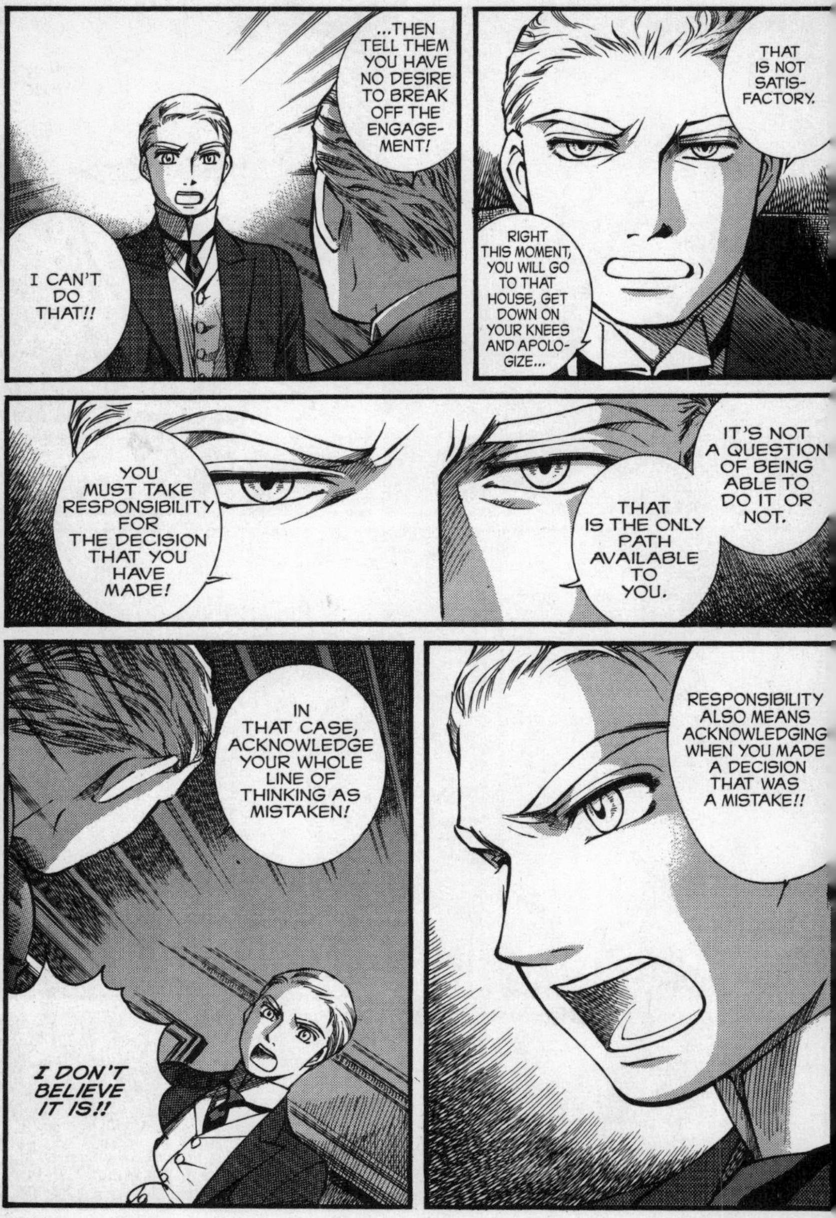
THAT IS NOT SATIS-FACTORY.
RIGHT THIS MOMENT, YOU WILL GO TO THAT HOUSE, GET DOWN ON YOUR KNEES AND APOLO-GIZE...
...THEN TELL THEM YOU HAVE NO DESIRE TO BREAK OFF THE ENGAGE-MENT!
I CAN'T DO THAT!!
IT'S NOT A QUESTION OF BEING ABLE TO DO IT OR NOT.
THAT IS THE ONLY PATH AVAILABLE TO YOU.
YOU MUST TAKE RESPONSIBILITY FOR THE DECISION THAT YOU HAVE MADE!
RESPONSIBILITY ALSO MEANS ACKNOWLEDGING WHEN YOU MADE A DECISION THAT WAS A MISTAKE!!
I DON'T BELIEVE IT IS!!
IN THAT CASE, ACKNOWLEDGE YOUR WHOLE LINE OF THINKING AS MISTAKEN!

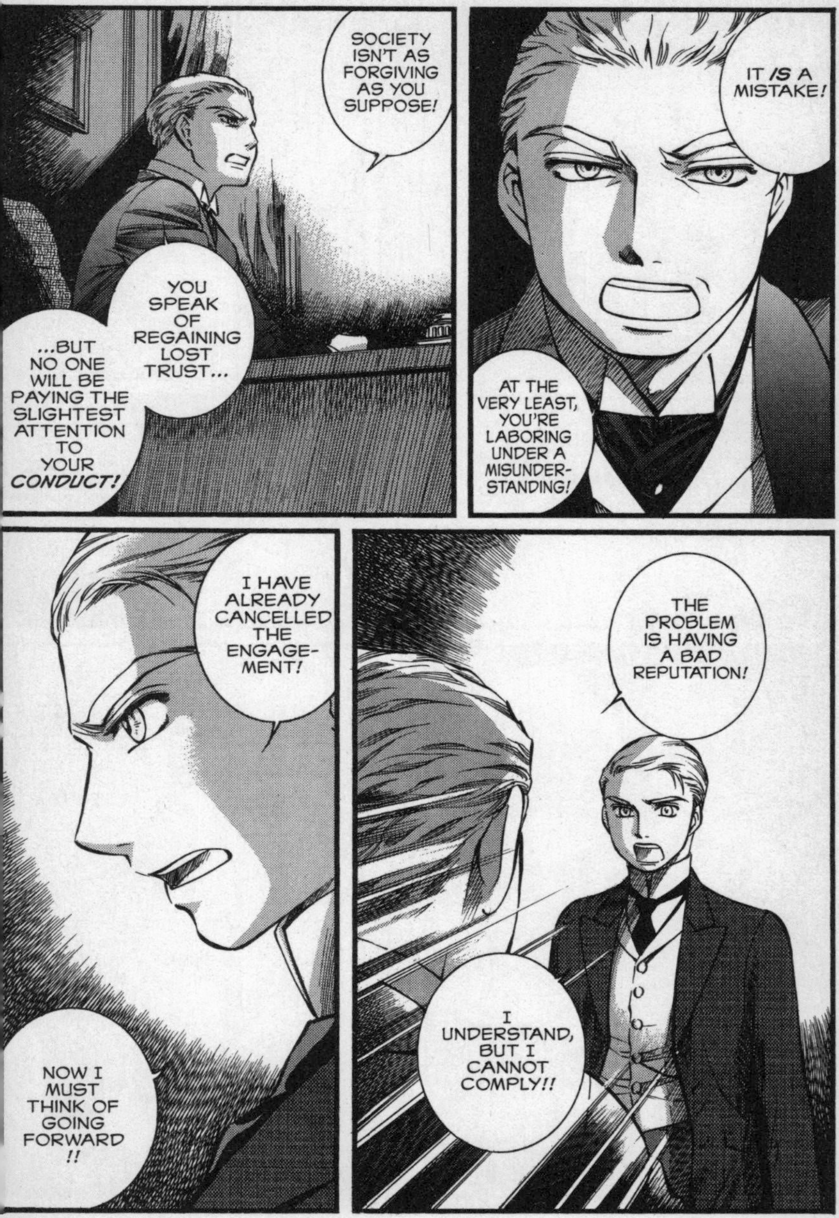
IT *IS* A MISTAKE!
AT THE VERY LEAST, YOU'RE LABORING UNDER A MISUNDERSTANDING!
SOCIETY ISN'T AS FORGIVING AS YOU SUPPOSE!
YOU SPEAK OF REGAINING LOST TRUST...
...BUT NO ONE WILL BE PAYING THE SLIGHTEST ATTENTION TO YOUR *CONDUCT!*
THE PROBLEM IS HAVING A BAD REPUTATION!
I UNDERSTAND, BUT I CANNOT COMPLY!!
I HAVE ALREADY CANCELLED THE ENGAGEMENT!
NOW I MUST THINK OF GOING FORWARD!!

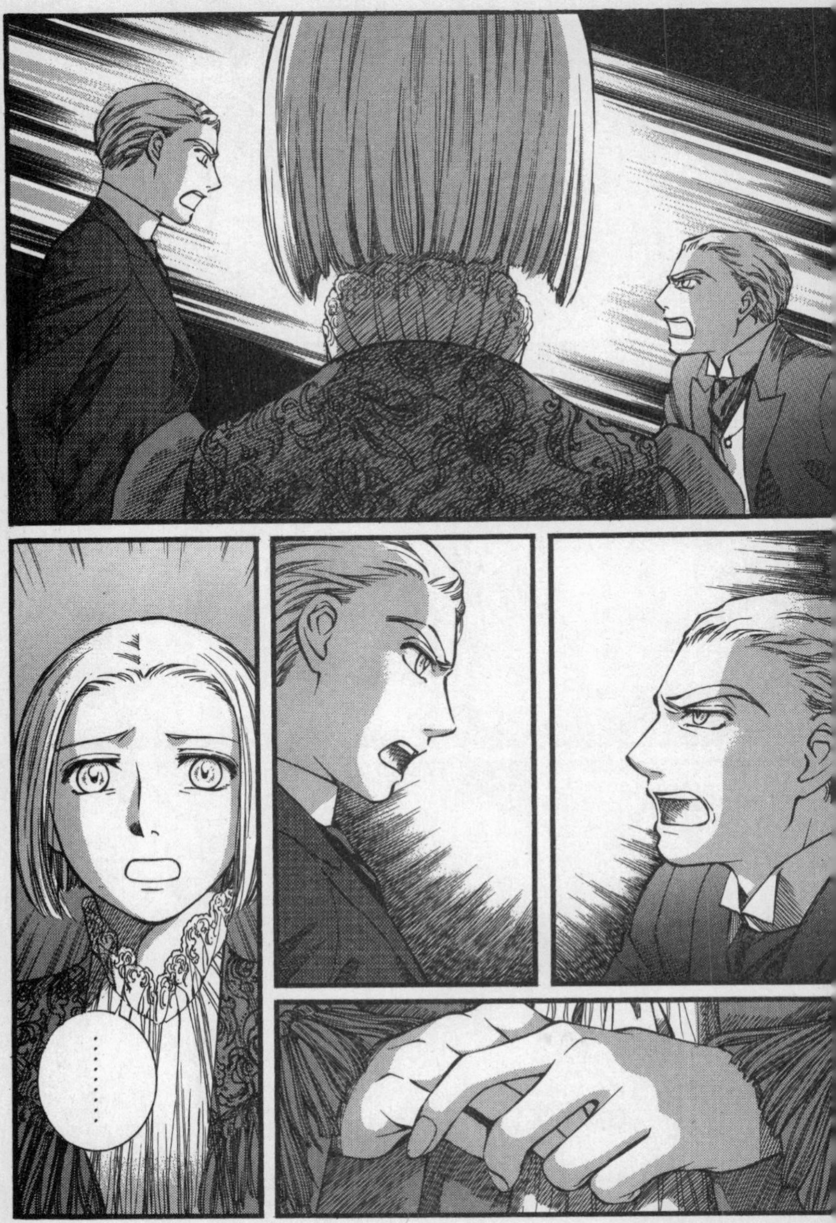
......

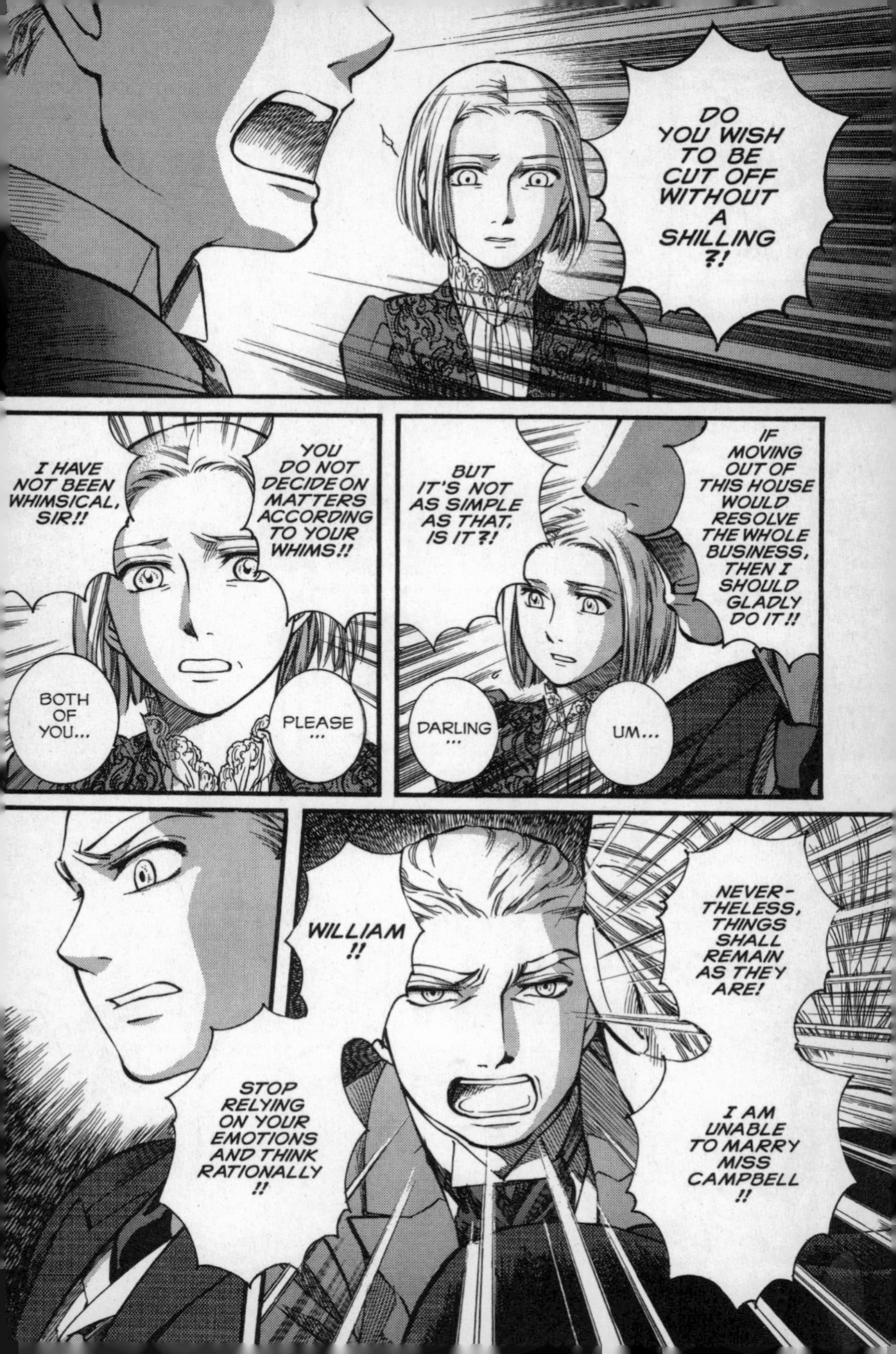
DO YOU WISH TO BE CUT OFF WITHOUT A SHILLING ?!
IF MOVING OUT OF THIS HOUSE WOULD RESOLVE THE WHOLE BUSINESS, THEN I SHOULD GLADLY DO IT!!
BUT IT'S NOT AS SIMPLE AS THAT, IS IT?!
UM...
DARLING ...
YOU DO NOT DECIDE ON MATTERS ACCORDING TO YOUR WHIMS!!
I HAVE NOT BEEN WHIMSICAL, SIR!!
PLEASE ...
BOTH OF YOU...
NEVER-THELESS, THINGS SHALL REMAIN AS THEY ARE!
I AM UNABLE TO MARRY MISS CAMPBELL !!
STOP RELYING ON YOUR EMOTIONS AND THINK RATIONALLY !!
WILLIAM !!

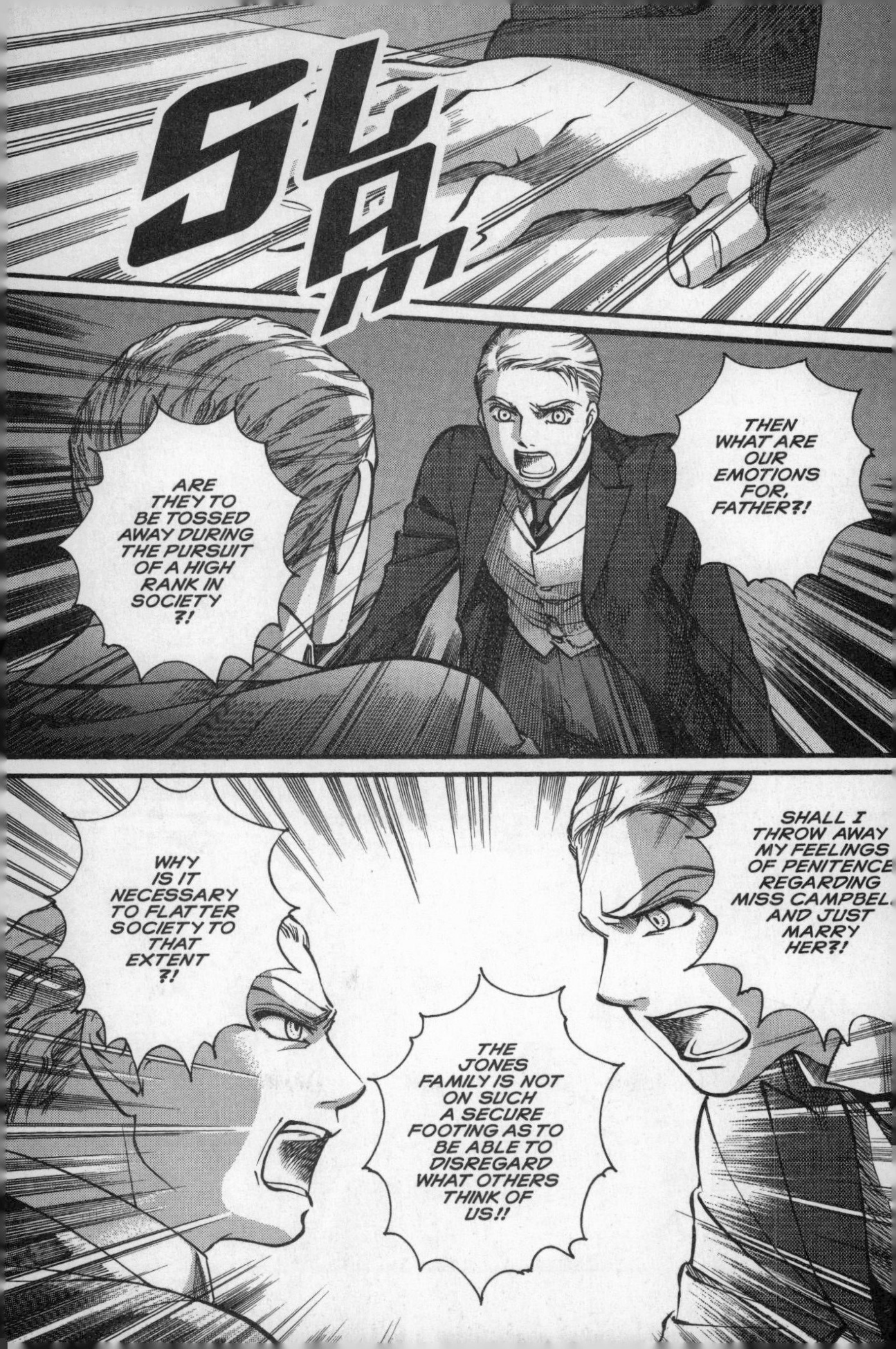
SLAM
THEN WHAT ARE OUR EMOTIONS FOR, FATHER?!
ARE THEY TO BE TOSSED AWAY DURING THE PURSUIT OF A HIGH RANK IN SOCIETY?!
SHALL I THROW AWAY MY FEELINGS OF PENITENCE REGARDING MISS CAMPBEL AND JUST MARRY HER?!
THE JONES FAMILY IS NOT ON SUCH A SECURE FOOTING AS TO BE ABLE TO DISREGARD WHAT OTHERS THINK OF US!!
WHY IS IT NECESSARY TO FLATTER SOCIETY TO THAT EXTENT?!

I'M SORRY.

165

......

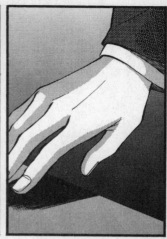

IF YOU ARE DONE AS WELL, FATHER...

...THEN I SHALL...

THAT'S ALL...

...I HAVE TO SAY.

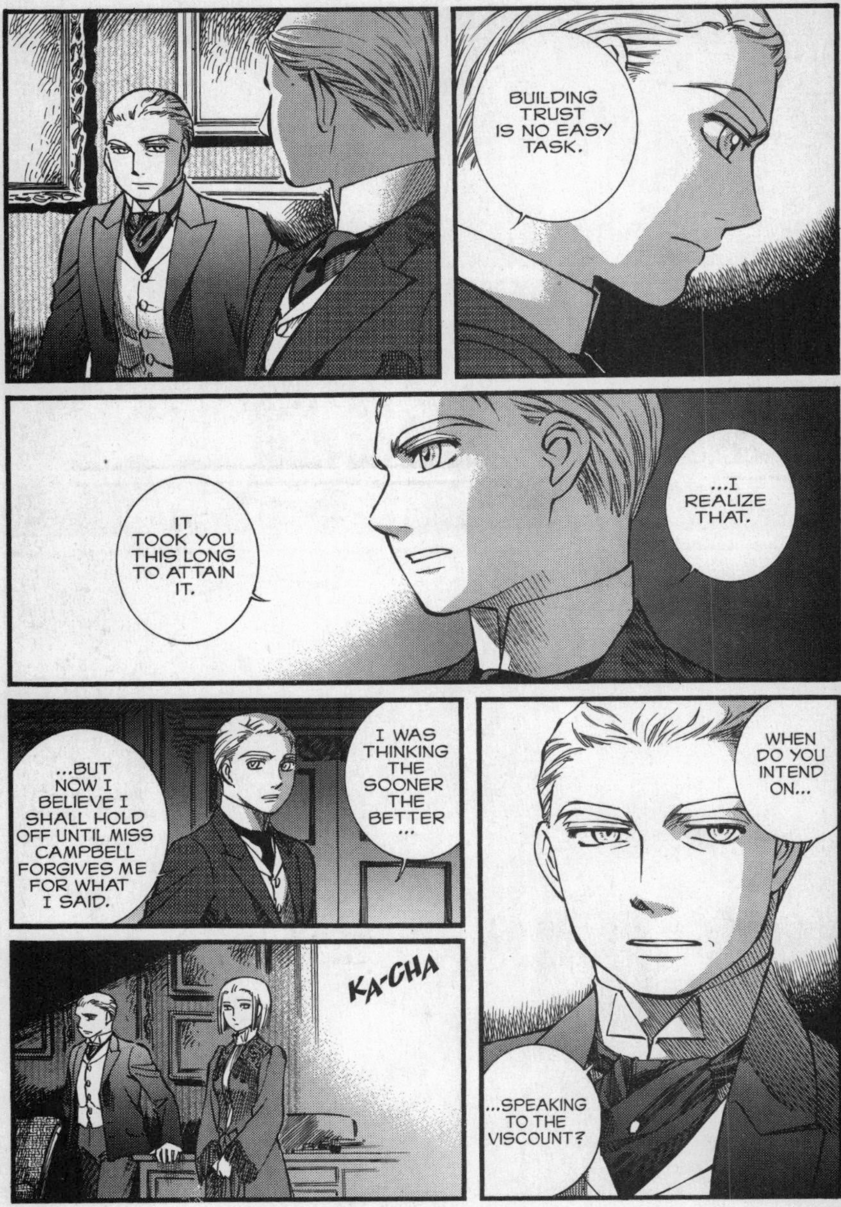
BUILDING TRUST IS NO EASY TASK.
...I REALIZE THAT.
IT TOOK YOU THIS LONG TO ATTAIN IT.
WHEN DO YOU INTEND ON...
...SPEAKING TO THE VISCOUNT?
I WAS THINKING THE SOONER THE BETTER ...
...BUT NOW I BELIEVE I SHALL HOLD OFF UNTIL MISS CAMPBELL FORGIVES ME FOR WHAT I SAID.
KA-CHA

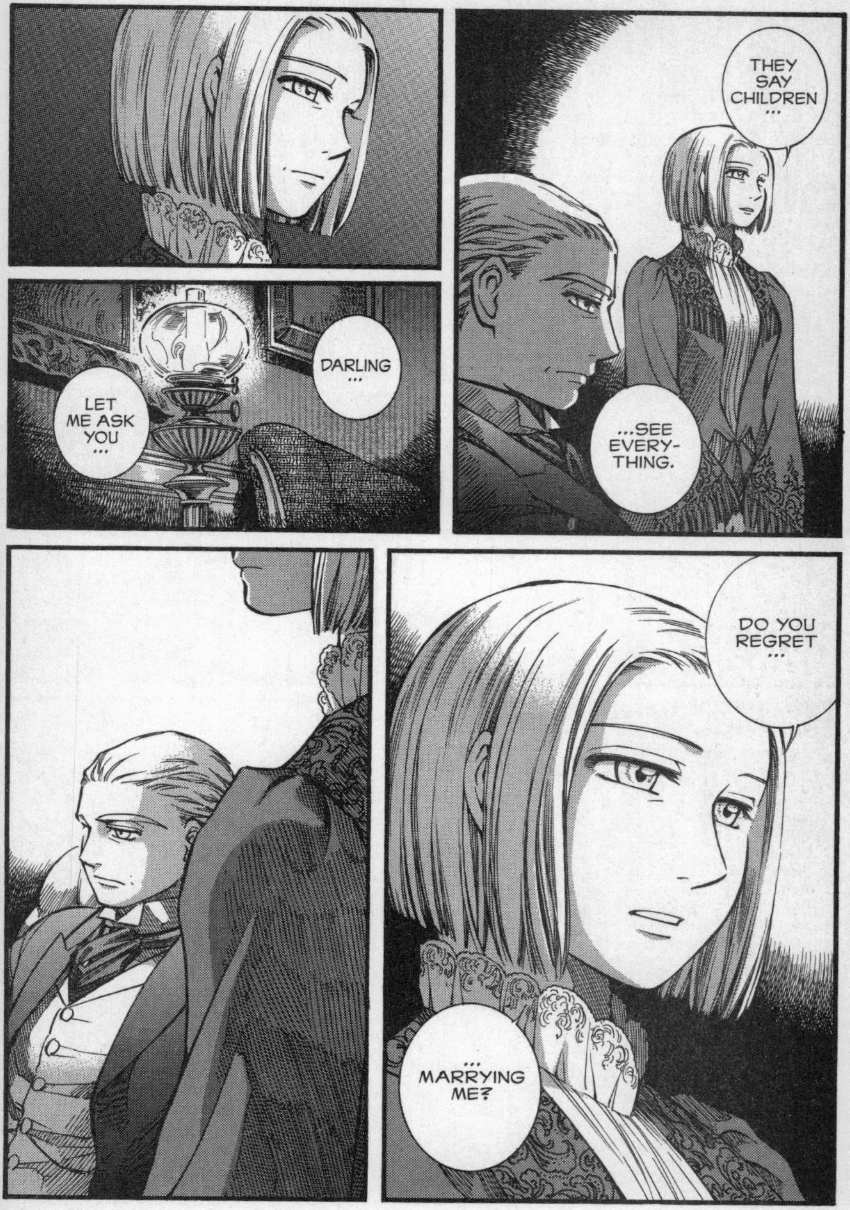
THEY SAY CHILDREN ...
...SEE EVERYTHING.
DARLING ...
LET ME ASK YOU ...
DO YOU REGRET ...
... MARRYING ME?

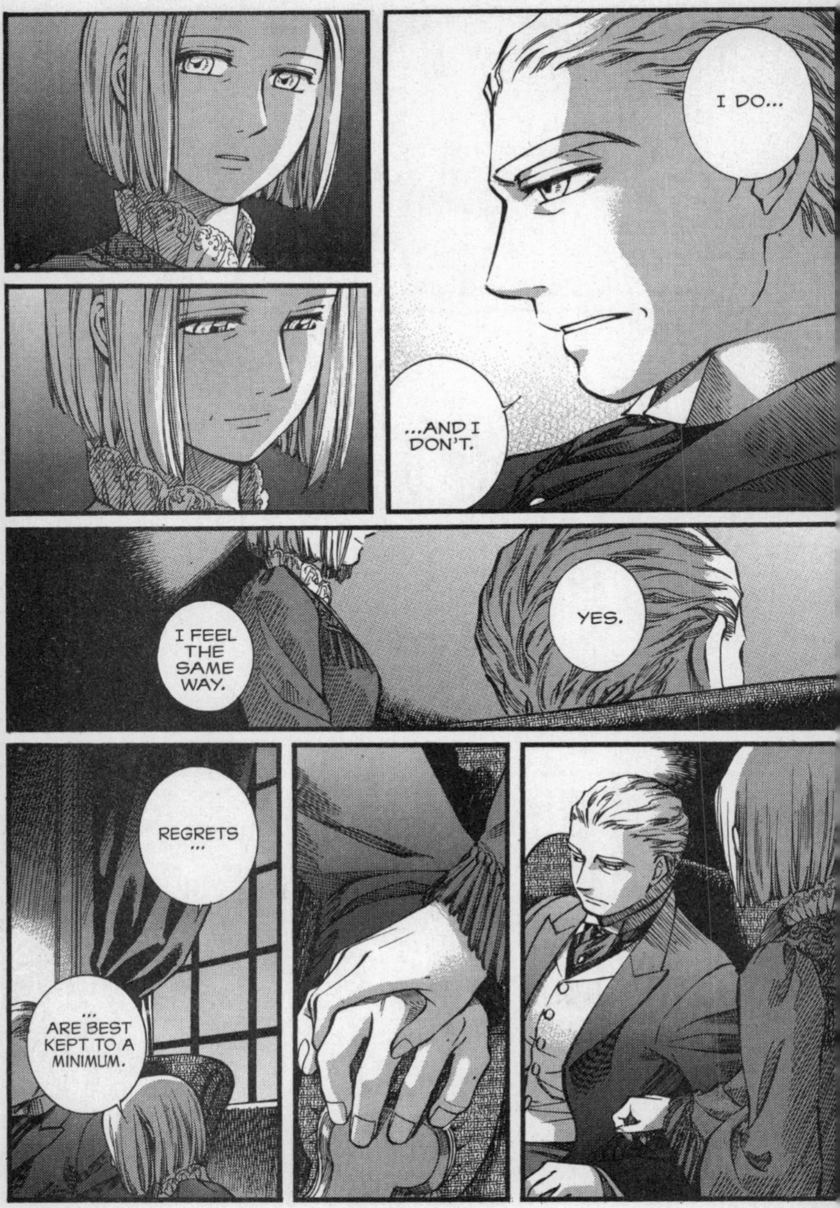
I DO...
...AND I DON'T.
YES.
I FEEL THE SAME WAY.
REGRETS...
...ARE BEST KEPT TO A MINIMUM.

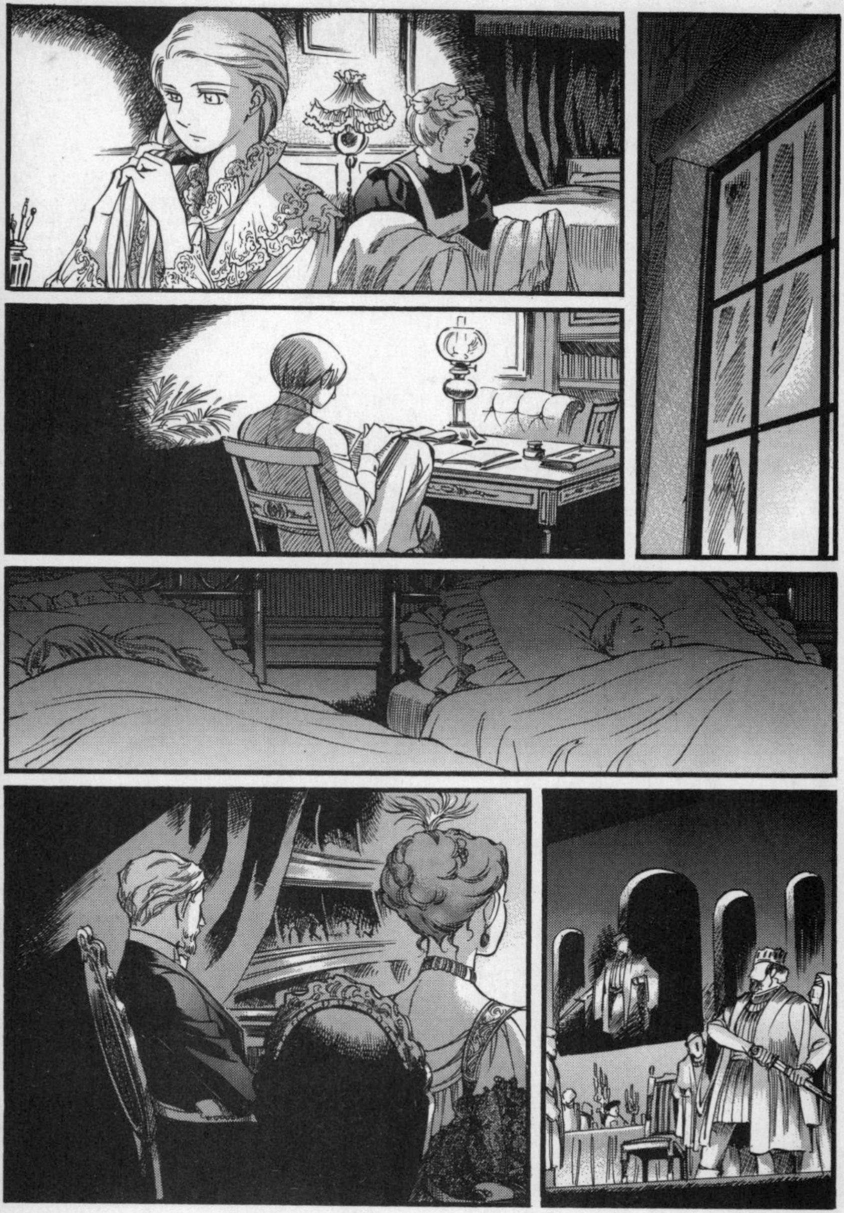

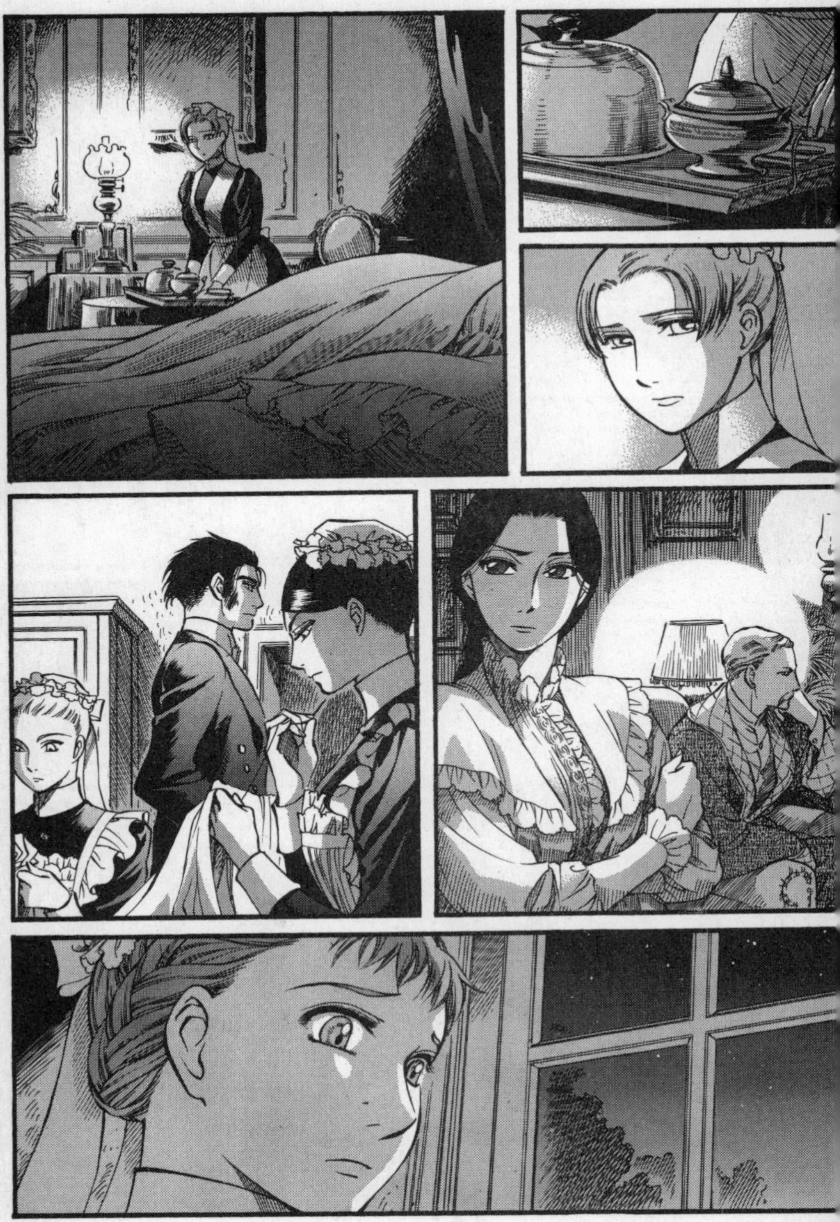

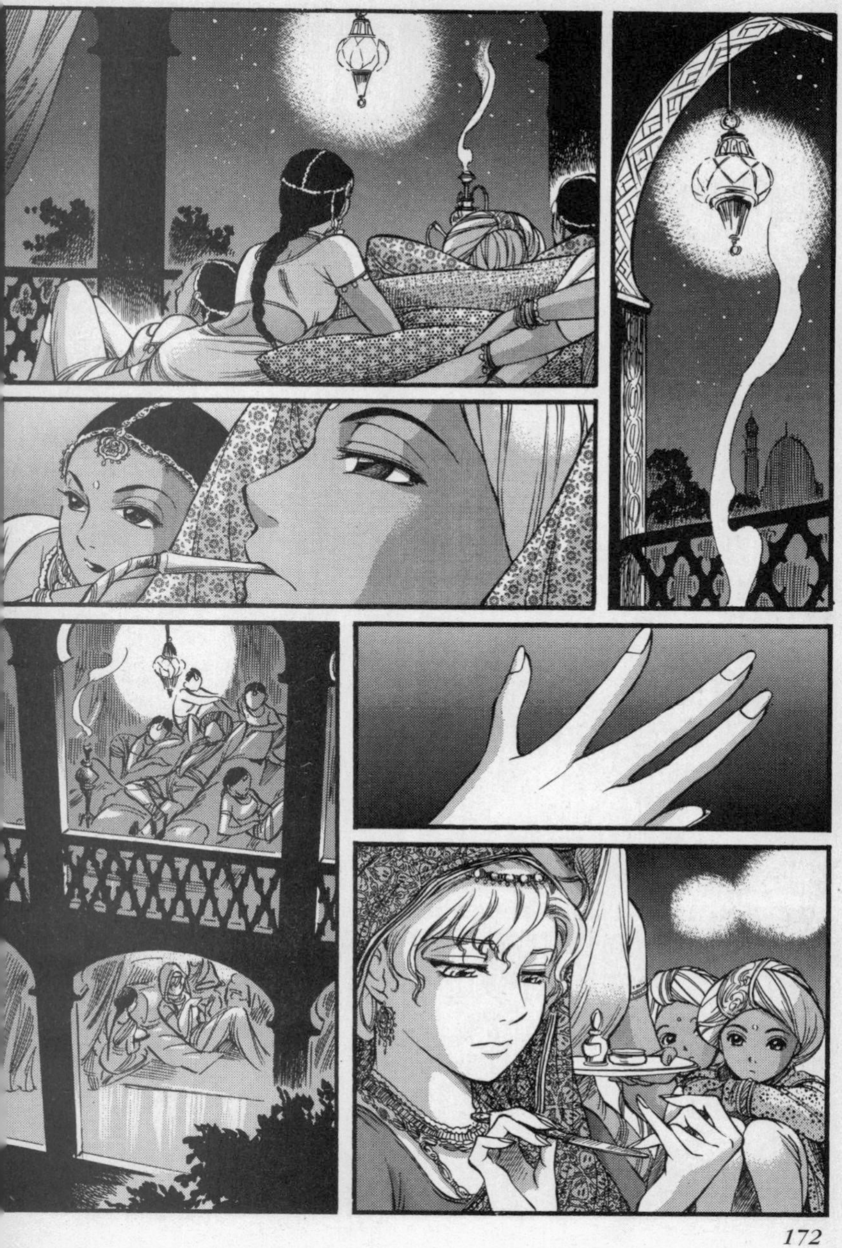

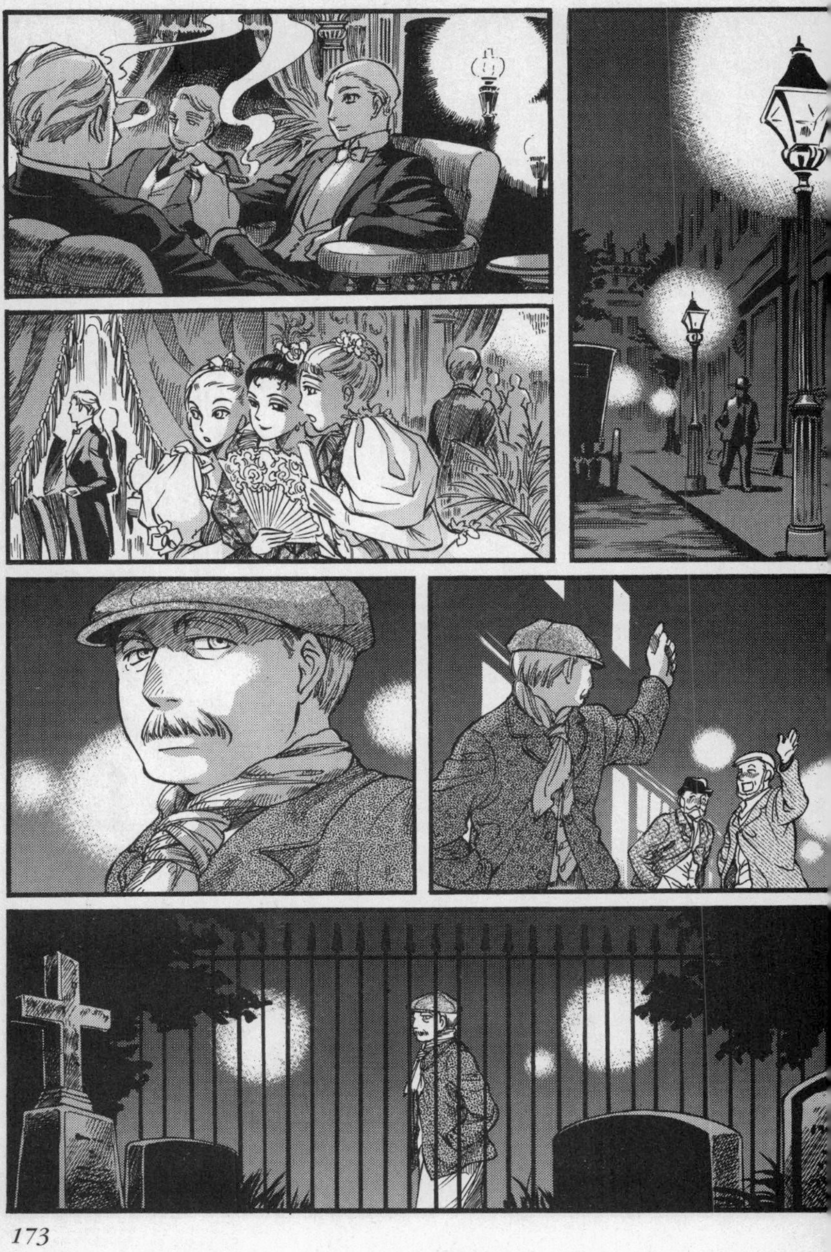

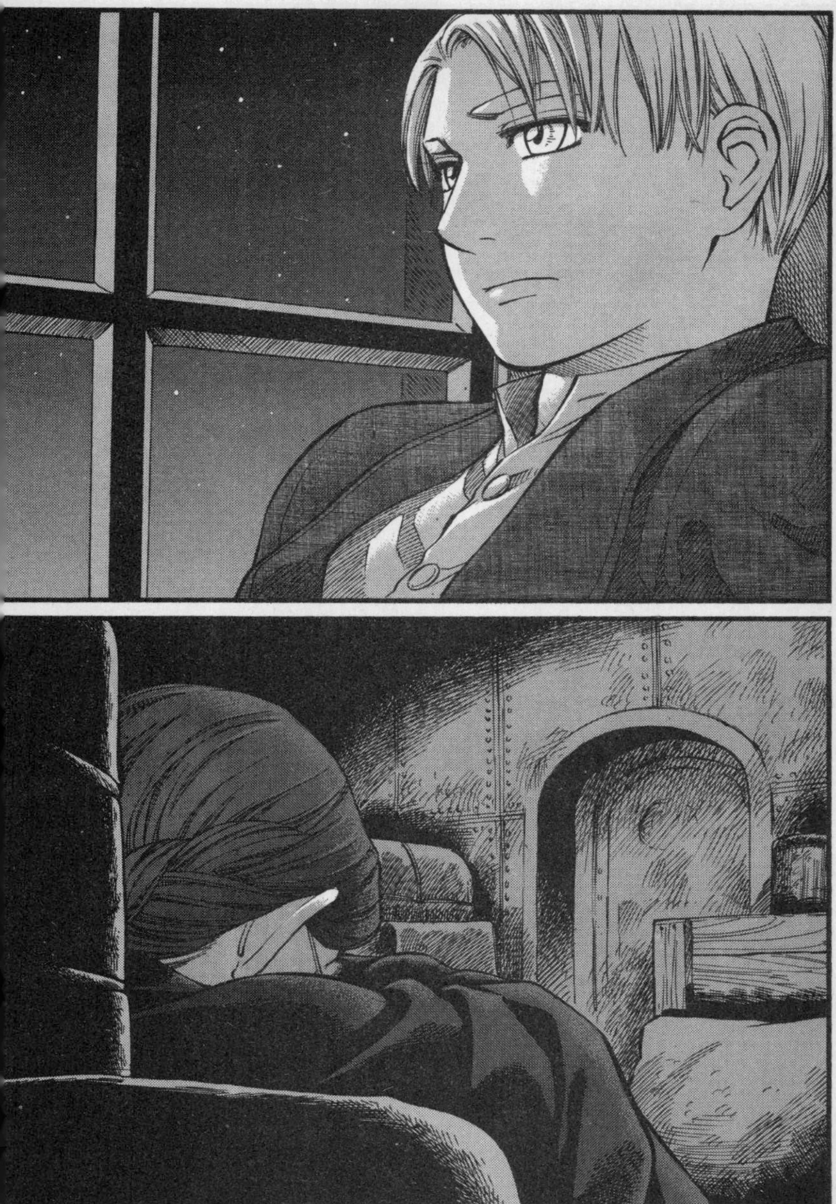

Chapter Forty Three:
The End

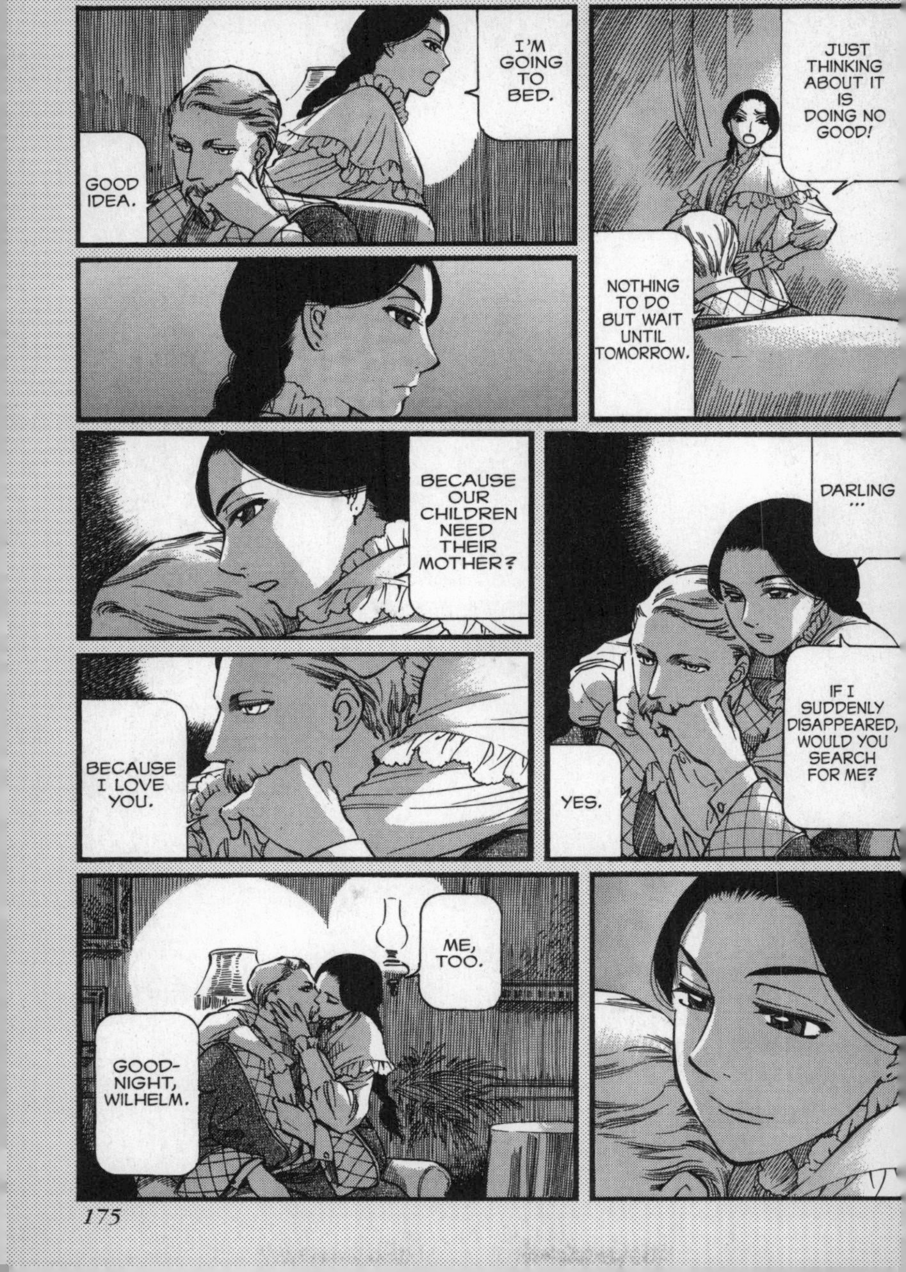
JUST THINKING ABOUT IT IS DOING NO GOOD!
NOTHING TO DO BUT WAIT UNTIL TOMORROW.
I'M GOING TO BED.
GOOD IDEA.
DARLING...
IF I SUDDENLY DISAPPEARED, WOULD YOU SEARCH FOR ME?
YES.
BECAUSE OUR CHILDREN NEED THEIR MOTHER?
BECAUSE I LOVE YOU.
ME, TOO.
GOOD-NIGHT, WILHELM.

SILLY AFTERWORD MANGA

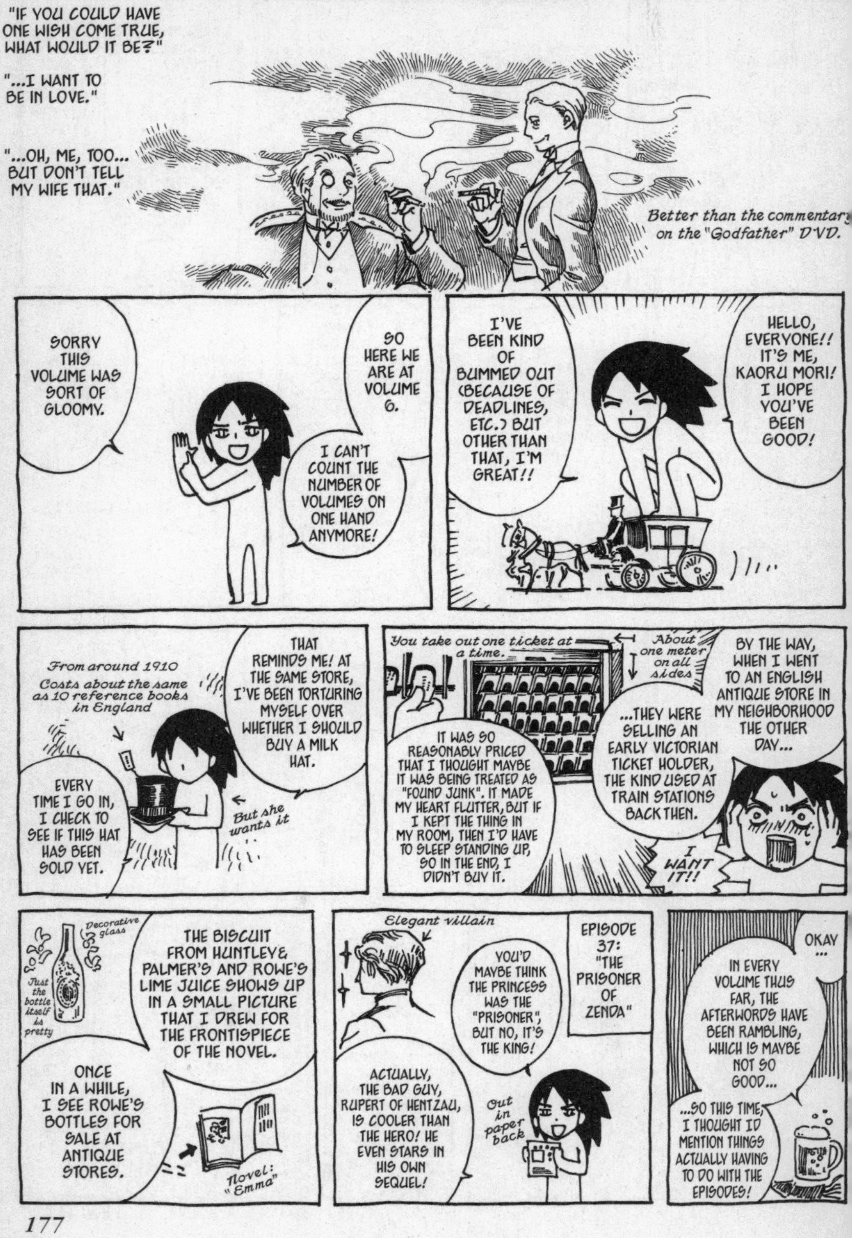
"IF YOU COULD HAVE ONE WISH COME TRUE, WHAT WOULD IT BE?"
"...I WANT TO BE IN LOVE."
"...OH, ME, TOO... BUT DON'T TELL MY WIFE THAT."
Better than the commentary on the "Godfather" DVD.
HELLO, EVERYONE!! IT'S ME, KAORU MORI! I HOPE YOU'VE BEEN GOOD!
I'VE BEEN KIND OF BUMMED OUT (BECAUSE OF DEADLINES, ETC.) BUT OTHER THAN THAT, I'M GREAT!!
SO HERE WE ARE AT VOLUME 6.
I CAN'T COUNT THE NUMBER OF VOLUMES ON ONE HAND ANYMORE!
SORRY THIS VOLUME WAS SORT OF GLOOMY.
BY THE WAY, WHEN I WENT TO AN ENGLISH ANTIQUE STORE IN MY NEIGHBORHOOD THE OTHER DAY...
...THEY WERE SELLING AN EARLY VICTORIAN TICKET HOLDER, THE KIND USED AT TRAIN STATIONS BACK THEN.
About one meter on all sides
You take out one ticket at a time.
I WANT IT!!
IT WAS SO REASONABLY PRICED THAT I THOUGHT MAYBE IT WAS BEING TREATED AS "FOUND JUNK". IT MADE MY HEART FLUTTER, BUT IF I KEPT THE THING IN MY ROOM, THEN I'D HAVE TO SLEEP STANDING UP, SO IN THE END, I DIDN'T BUY IT.
THAT REMINDS ME! AT THE SAME STORE, I'VE BEEN TORTURING MYSELF OVER WHETHER I SHOULD BUY A MILK HAT.
From around 1910
Costs about the same as 10 reference books in England
But she wants it
EVERY TIME I GO IN, I CHECK TO SEE IF THIS HAT HAS BEEN SOLD YET.
OKAY...
IN EVERY VOLUME THUS FAR, THE AFTERWORDS HAVE BEEN RAMBLING, WHICH IS MAYBE NOT SO GOOD...
...SO THIS TIME, I THOUGHT I'D MENTION THINGS ACTUALLY HAVING TO DO WITH THE EPISODES!
EPISODE 37: "THE PRISONER OF ZENDA"
YOU'D MAYBE THINK THE PRINCESS WAS THE "PRISONER", BUT NO, IT'S THE KING!
Elegant villain
ACTUALLY, THE BAD GUY, RUPERT OF HENTZAU, IS COOLER THAN THE HERO! HE EVEN STARS IN HIS OWN SEQUEL!
Out in paper back
THE BISCUIT FROM HUNTLEY& PALMER'S AND ROWE'S LIME JUICE SHOWS UP IN A SMALL PICTURE THAT I DREW FOR THE FRONTISPIECE OF THE NOVEL.
Decorative glass
Just the bottle itself is pretty
ONCE IN A WHILE, I SEE ROWE'S BOTTLES FOR SALE AT ANTIQUE STORES.
Novel: "Emma"

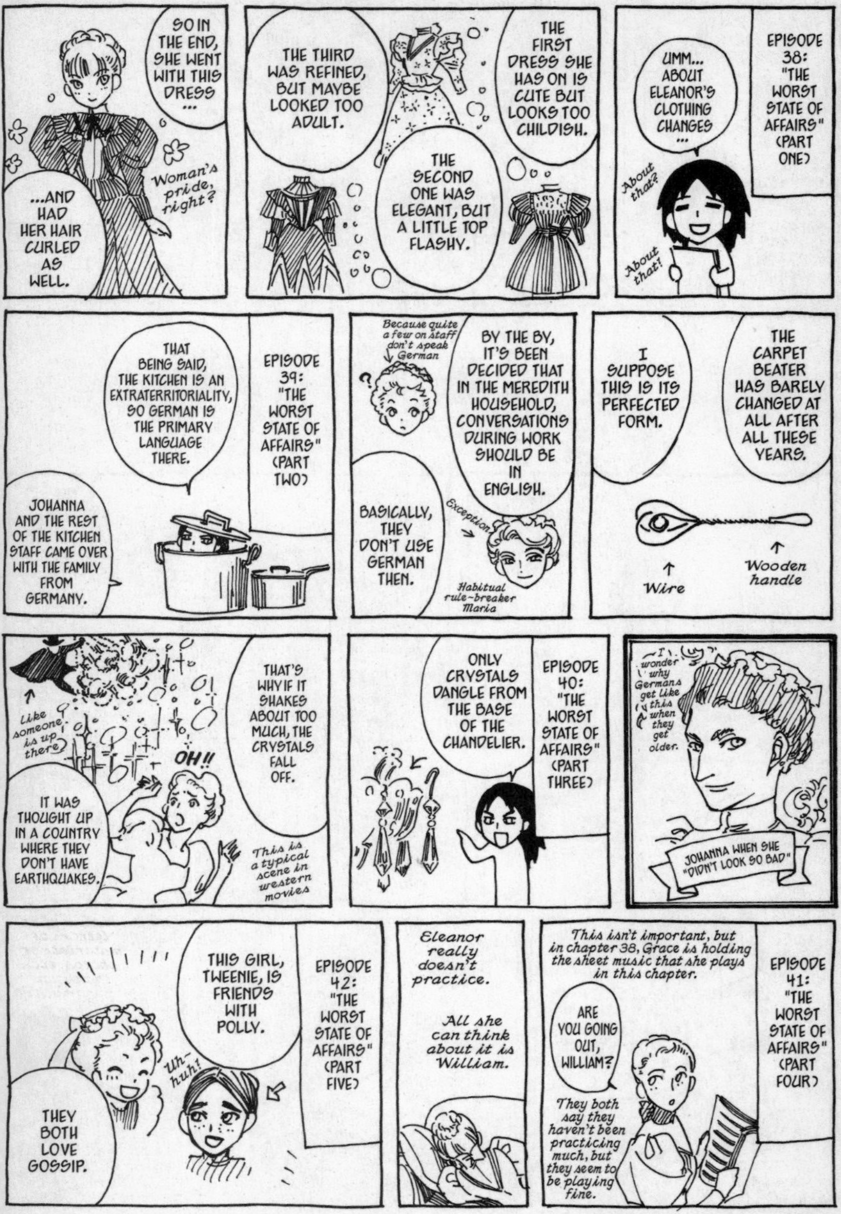
EPISODE 38: "THE WORST STATE OF AFFAIRS" (PART ONE)
UMM... ABOUT ELEANOR'S CLOTHING CHANGES ...
About that?
About that?
THE FIRST DRESS SHE HAS ON IS CUTE BUT LOOKS TOO CHILDISH.
THE SECOND ONE WAS ELEGANT, BUT A LITTLE TOP FLASHY.
THE THIRD WAS REFINED, BUT MAYBE LOOKED TOO ADULT.
SO IN THE END, SHE WENT WITH THIS DRESS ...
Woman's pride, right?
...AND HAD HER HAIR CURLED AS WELL.
THE CARPET BEATER HAS BARELY CHANGED AT ALL AFTER ALL THESE YEARS.
I SUPPOSE THIS IS ITS PERFECTED FORM.
Wooden handle
Wire
BY THE BY, IT'S BEEN DECIDED THAT IN THE MEREDITH HOUSEHOLD, CONVERSATIONS DURING WORK SHOULD BE IN ENGLISH.
Because quite a few on staff don't speak German
Exception
BASICALLY, THEY DON'T USE GERMAN THEN.
Habitual rule-breaker Maria
EPISODE 39: "THE WORST STATE OF AFFAIRS" (PART TWO)
THAT BEING SAID, THE KITCHEN IS AN EXTRATERRITORIALITY, SO GERMAN IS THE PRIMARY LANGUAGE THERE.
JOHANNA AND THE REST OF THE KITCHEN STAFF CAME OVER WITH THE FAMILY FROM GERMANY.
I wonder why Germans get like this when they get older.
JOHANNA WHEN SHE "DIDN'T LOOK SO BAD"
EPISODE 40: "THE WORST STATE OF AFFAIRS" (PART THREE)
ONLY CRYSTALS DANGLE FROM THE BASE OF THE CHANDELIER.
THAT'S WHY IF IT SHAKES ABOUT TOO MUCH, THE CRYSTALS FALL OFF.
Like someone is up there
OH!!
IT WAS THOUGHT UP IN A COUNTRY WHERE THEY DON'T HAVE EARTHQUAKES.
This is a typical scene in western movies
EPISODE 41: "THE WORST STATE OF AFFAIRS" (PART FOUR)
This isn't important, but in chapter 38, Grace is holding the sheet music that she plays in this chapter.
ARE YOU GOING OUT, WILLIAM?
They both say they haven't been practicing much, but they seem to be playing fine.
Eleanor really doesn't practice.
All she can think about it is William.
EPISODE 42: "THE WORST STATE OF AFFAIRS" (PART FIVE)
THIS GIRL, TWEENIE, IS FRIENDS WITH POLLY.
Uh-huh!
THEY BOTH LOVE GOSSIP.

Are they studying for a test?

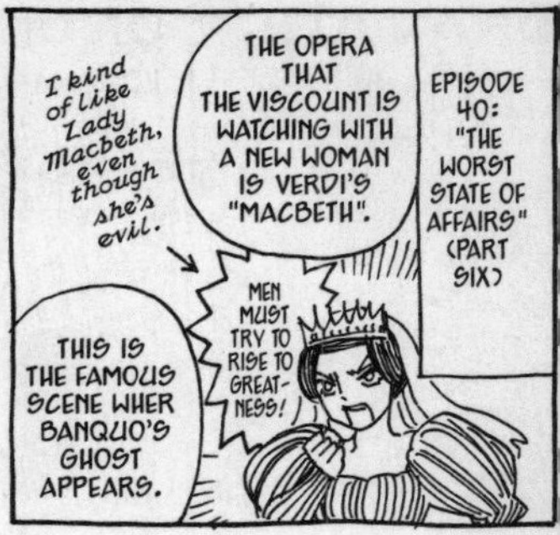
EPISODE 40: "THE WORST STATE OF AFFAIRS" (PART SIX)
THE OPERA THAT THE VISCOUNT IS WATCHING WITH A NEW WOMAN IS VERDI'S "MACBETH".
I kind of like Lady Macbeth, even though she's evil.
MEN MUST TRY TO RISE TO GREAT-NESS!
THIS IS THE FAMOUS SCENE WHER BANQUO'S GHOST APPEARS.
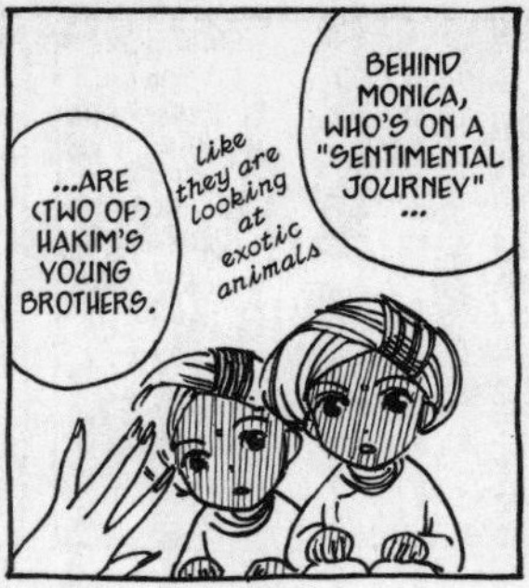
BEHIND MONICA, WHO'S ON A "SENTIMENTAL JOURNEY" ...
Like they are looking at exotic animals
...ARE (TWO OF) HAKIM'S YOUNG BROTHERS.
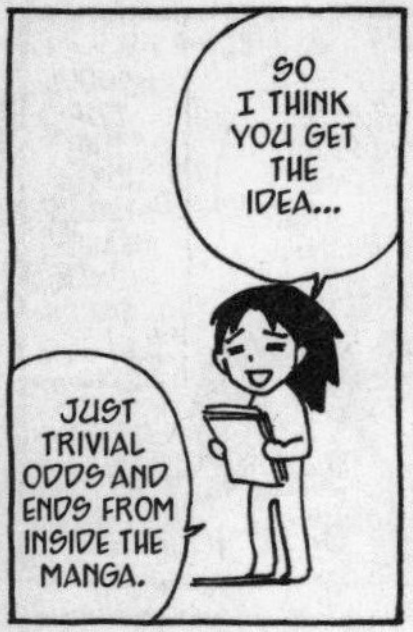
SO I THINK YOU GET THE IDEA...
JUST TRIVIAL ODDS AND ENDS FROM INSIDE THE MANGA.
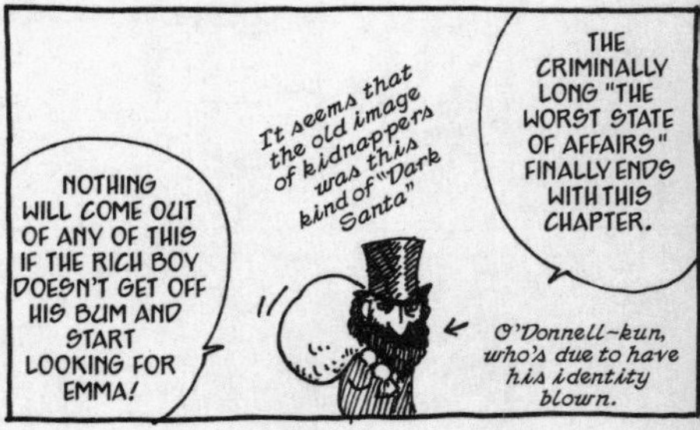
THE CRIMINALLY LONG "THE WORST STATE OF AFFAIRS" FINALLY ENDS WITH THIS CHAPTER.
It seems that the old image of kidnappers was this kind of "Dark Santa"
NOTHING WILL COME OUT OF ANY OF THIS IF THE RICH BOY DOESN'T GET OFF HIS BUM AND START LOOKING FOR EMMA!
O'Donnell-kun, who's due to have his identity blown.
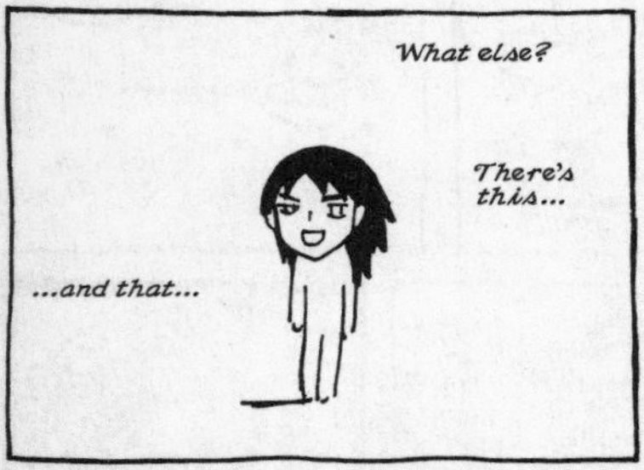
What else?
There's this...
...and that...
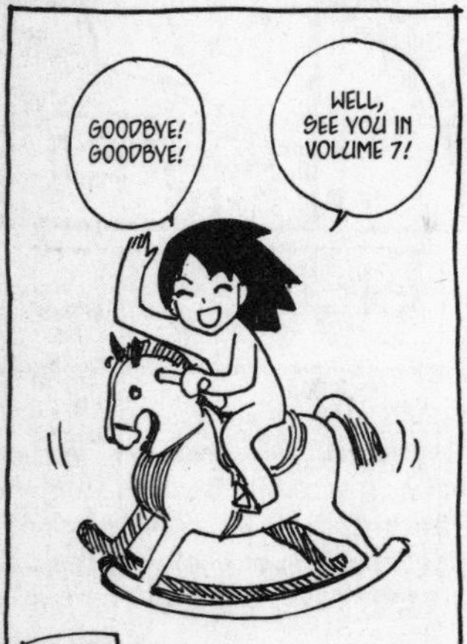
WELL, SEE YOU IN VOLUME 7!
GOODBYE! GOODBYE!
THE END

To everyone who's sent me letters or materials or photos, etc., thank you very much.

It looks like I'm not going to be able to reply, but I really appreciate everything.

HE SAGA OF EMMA AND WILLIAM COMES TO ITS DRAMATIC CONCLUSION! ON SALE IN MARCH.

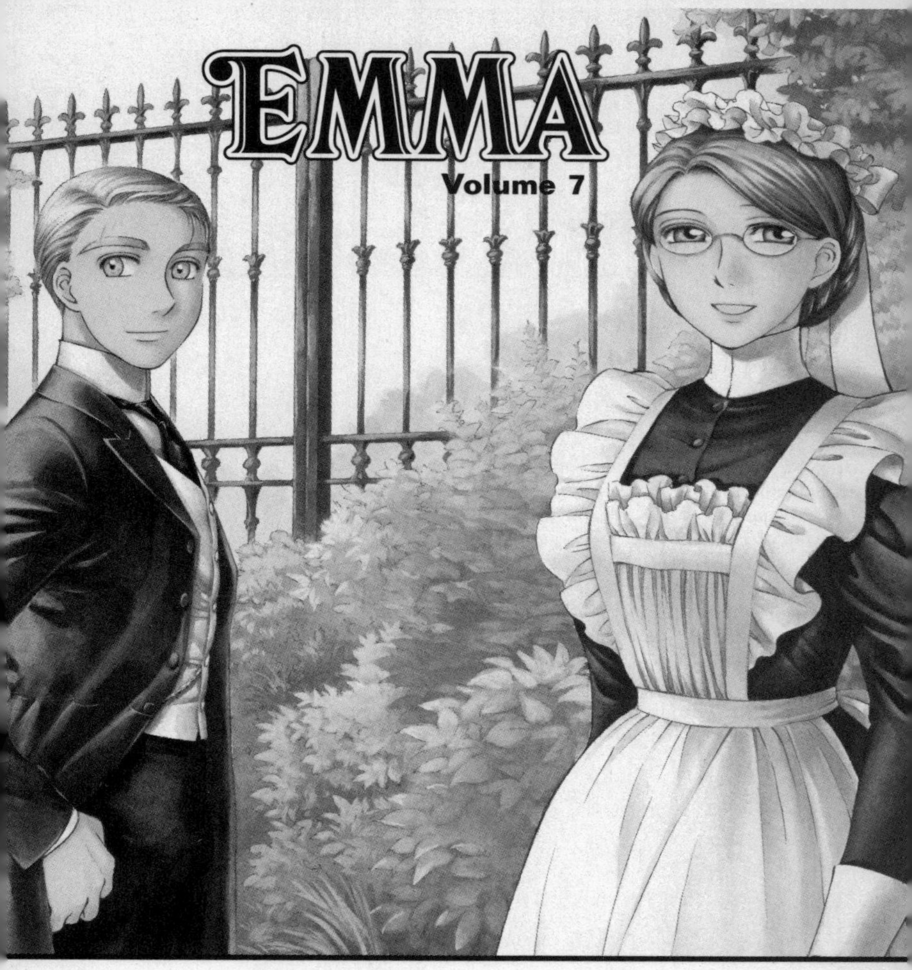
EMMA
Volume 7

By Kaoru Mori. Emma's been shipped off to America and William and Hakim set sail across the Atlantic in pursuit. Back in England, Mrs. Meredith has plans for their return that could elevate Emma's social standing. Meanwhile, the Jones family must deal with the consequences of the societal blackballing they have received, courtesy of the Viscount.

EMMA

ART GALLERY

Due to space limitations, we are not always able to feature all of the additional art that appears in the original Japanese editions of *Emma*. In the following pages, we present the art which Kaoru Mori created as the frontispieces for the first 6 volumes of the series. Each piece features a study of either urban London or the surrounding English countryside in the late nineteenth century, all rendered with the artist's characteristically exquisite detail. We hope you enjoy them.

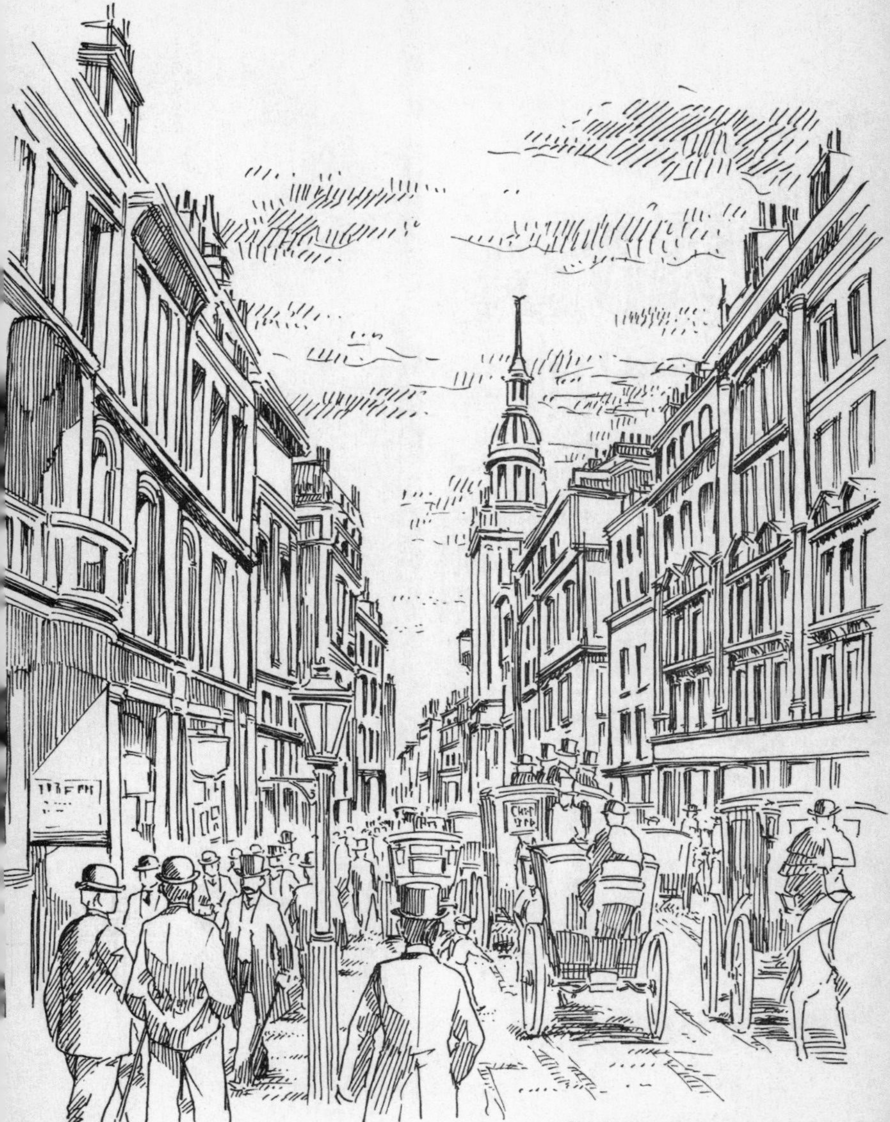

CHEAPSIDE. LONDON 1896

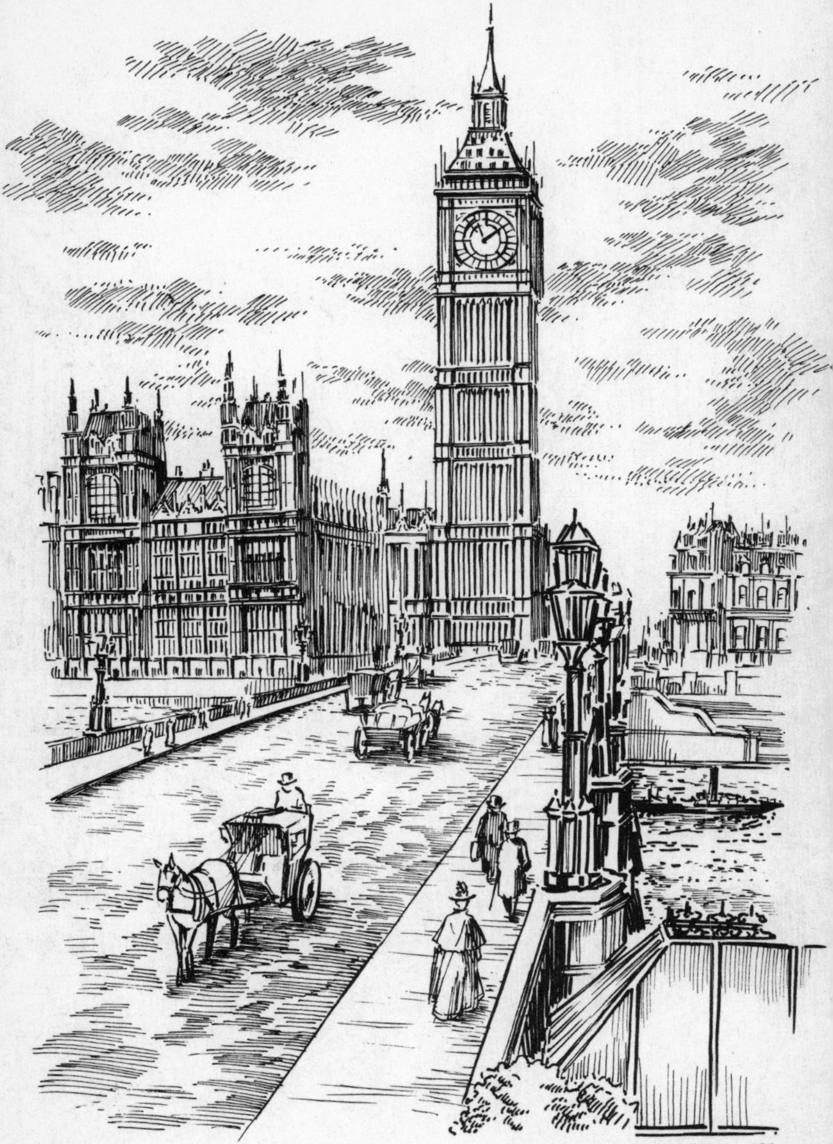

WESTMINSTER BRIDGE 1896

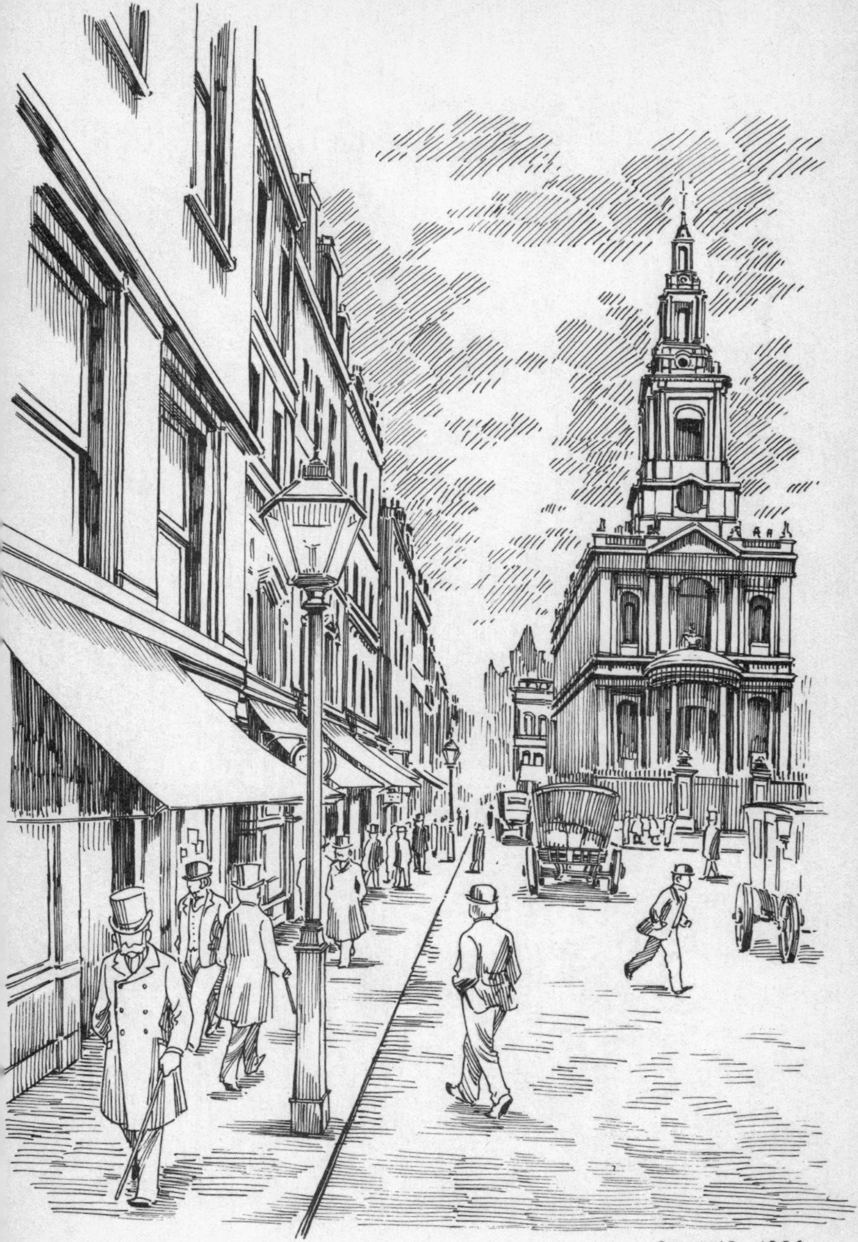
STRAND 1896

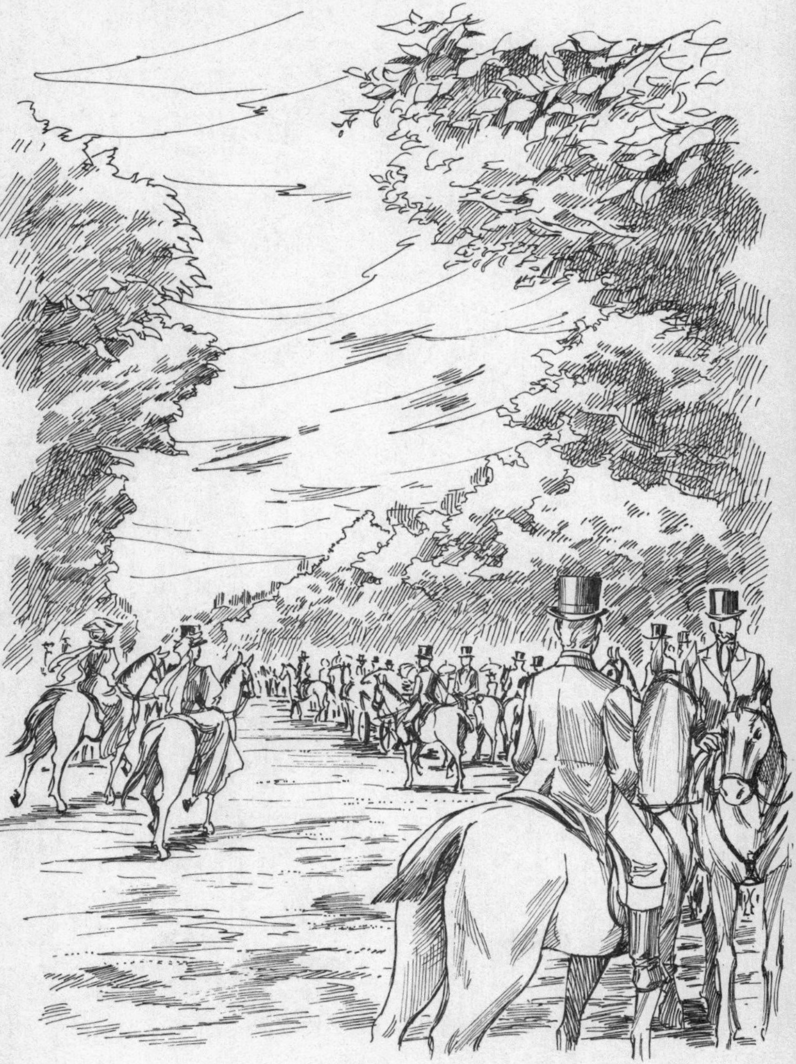
ROTTEN ROW 1897

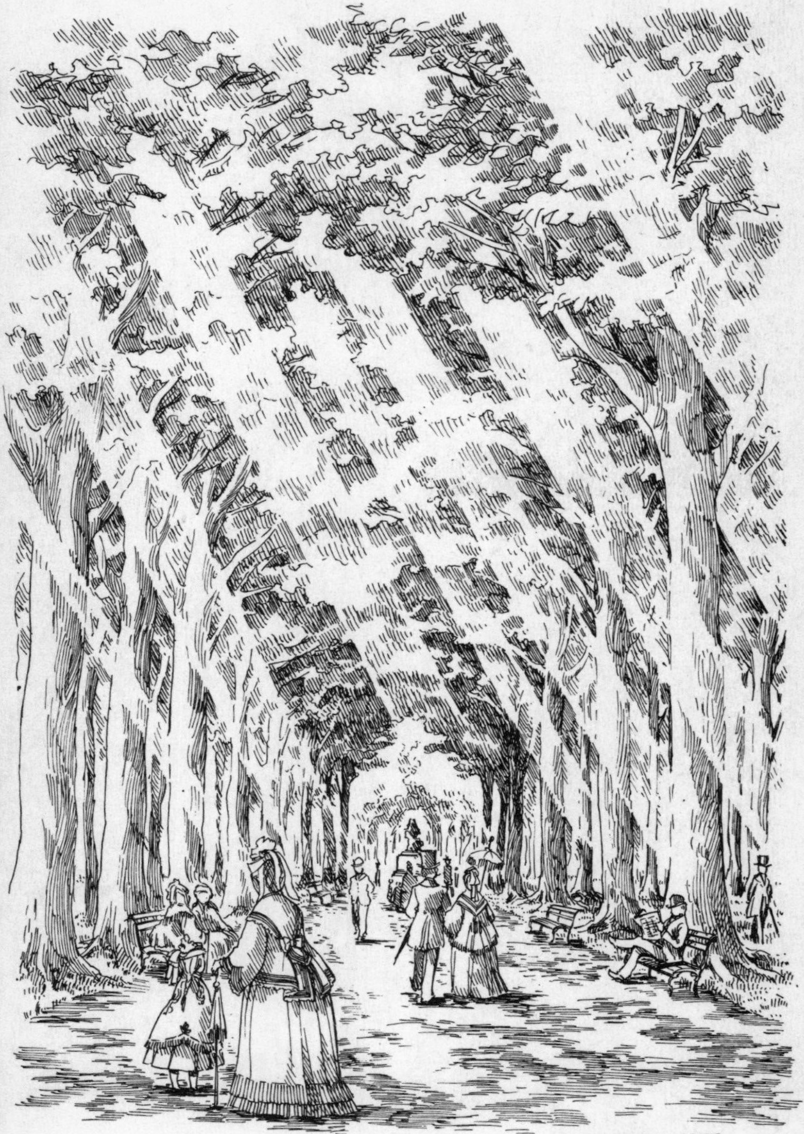

HYDE PARK 1872

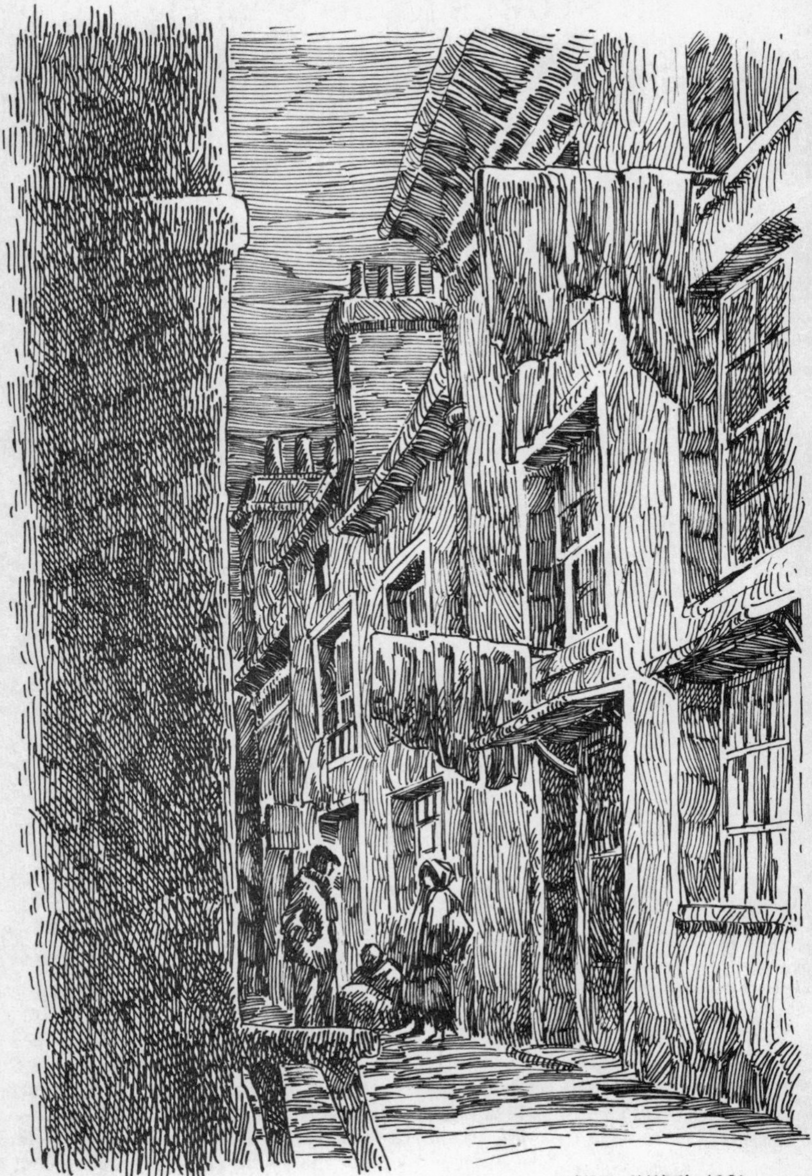

WHITE CHAPEL 1895

CLASS IS NOW IN SESSION!
IN STORES EVERYWHERE!

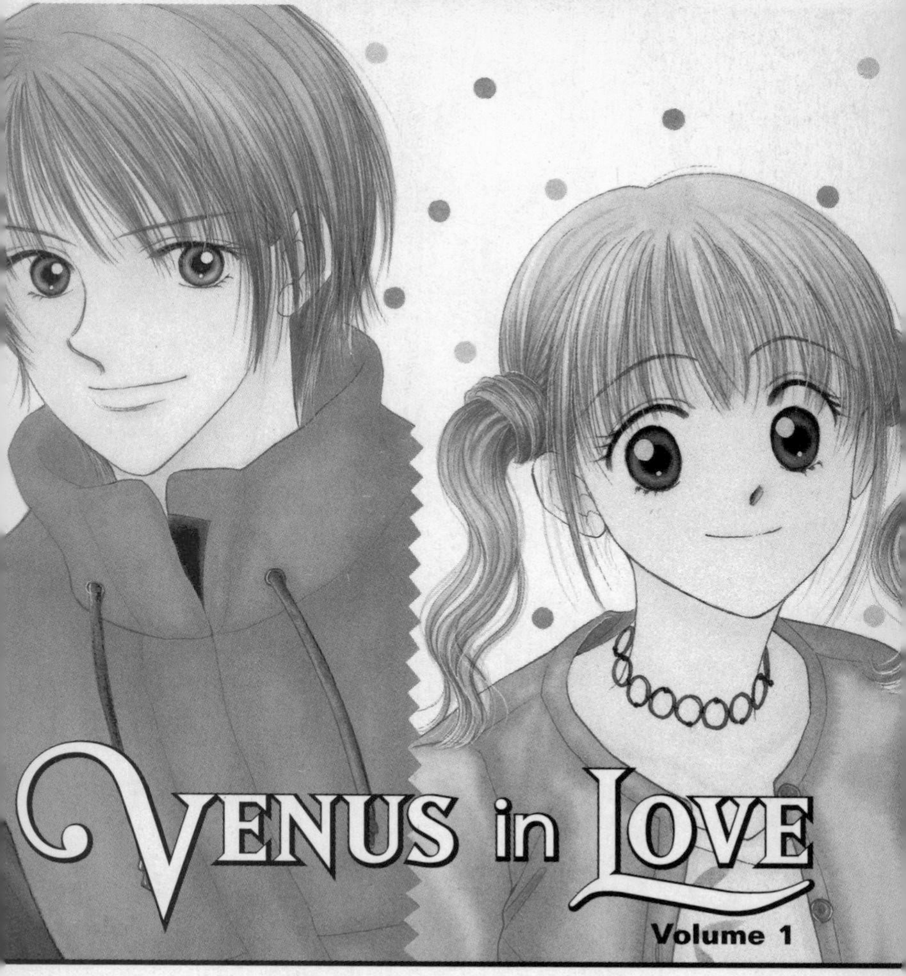
VENUS in LOVE
Volume 1

By Yuki Nakaji. As a college freshman, Suzuna is looking forward to making friends, joining a club and hopefully getting a boyfriend! She develops a crush on Fukumi—charismatic tennis player and friend of her neighbor, Eichi. But her other new friend—the beautiful Hinako—has some interesting information regarding Eichi that's going to force Suzuna to take a second look at the whole situation. She's about to discover that love can come with some unexpected competition.

CMX